DARWINIAN Myths

DARWINIAN

Myths

The Legends and Misuses of a Theory

EDWARD
CAUDILL

THE UNIVERSITY OF TENNESSEE PRESS/KNOXVILLE

An earlier version of chapter 1 appeared as "The Bishop Eaters: The Publicity
Campaign for Darwin and *On the Origin of Species,*" in *Journal of the History of Ideas*
55, no. 3 (July 1994): 441–60. Used by permission of the Johns Hopkins
University Press, Baltimore, Maryland.

Caricature of Charles Darwin from *Vanity Fair,* 1871, part of the magazine's "Men
of the Day" series. In addition to Darwin, other scientists in the series were Richard Owen, Darwin's primary antagonist, and Thomas Huxley, Darwin's "bulldog."

LIBRARY OF CONGRESS CATALOGING-IN-PUBLICATION DATA

Caudill, Edward.
Darwinian Myths: The Legends and Misuses of a Theory /
Edward Caudill.—1st ed.
p. cm.
Includes bibliographical references and index.
ISBN 0-87049-984-X (cloth : alk. paper)
1. Evolution (Biology)—Philosophy. 2. Social Darwinism. 3. Darwin, Charles,
1809–1882—Legends. I. Title.
QH360.5.C38 1997
576.8'2—dc21   97-4691

For Larissa, Daniel, and Robert

Contents

Acknowledgments

Thanks first and foremost to Paul Ashdown, friend and colleague at the University of Tennessee. He has criticized thoughtfully, listened patiently, and encouraged endlessly. Two others who provided valuable, insightful criticisms of the manuscript are Bruce Evensen of DePaul University and Bruce Lewenstein of Cornell University.

Individuals of particular help at archives include: A. J. Perkins and his staff, especially Godfrey Waller, Cambridge University Library; Cheryl Piggot, archivist, Library and Archives of the Royal Botanic Gardens at Kew; Anne Barrett, College Archivist, Imperial College of Science, Technology and Medicine, London; and Beth Carroll-Horrocks, archivist, American Philosophical Society Library, Philadelphia.

Some years ago, Donald Shaw of the University of North Carolina at Chapel Hill encouraged and directed my interest in interdisciplinary studies. His insight and interest continue to inspire.

A note of thanks also is due Carol Zeugner, research assistant and doctoral student in the College of Communications, University of Tennessee, Knoxville.

The research for chapters 1 and 6 was supported by grants from the University of Tennessee, Knoxville. For these I am grateful.

Introduction

Myths and Misuses, Science and Society

> History has many cunning passages, contrived corridors and issues, deceives
> with whispering ambitions, guides us by vanities.
> —T. S. ELIOT, "GERONTION"

The breadth of Darwin's impact and the ability of his ideas to inspire legends is illustrated by a few clippings from English newspapers of the 1890s. After a Darwin memorial was proposed in Shrewsbury, a storm toppled the spire of Saint Mary's Church. One paper reported, "Some people believe that the spire collapsed before the extraordinary strength of the gale, but [the vicar] says it was the breath of an avenging deity." The vicar said God disapproved of the memorial and shattered the spire as a warning to proceed no further. Furthermore, it was noted, all this happened on February 11, the day before the anniversary of Darwin's birthday. One newspaper asked why the spire had not fallen at another nearby church, where the vicar actually supported the Darwin memorial. Or why didn't it fall during a calm, windless day? That would have been a clearer signal.[1] Like other mythmakers, the vicar of Saint Mary's actually was revealing his own feelings, not God's, and flouting his own importance, not Darwin's.

Darwin's natural selection, the most important scientific idea of the nineteenth century, was more than a mere theory of speciation. It stood at the center of an often heated scientific debate over the purpose of science and the nature of evidence and generalization. Darwin changed evolution from an idea to a theory. In so doing, he made it more powerful, more convincing, and more appealing. However, in seizing upon the new scientific evolution—the theory of natural selection—many have disregarded the limitations of scientific theory and dragged it into areas where little empirical support was available. Darwinism was unshackled from the constraints of data and transformed into a social-political philosophy. Darwin's theory has spawned ideas and movements that range from the bizarre and murderous, such as Nazi Aryanism, to the simply aphoristic, as in advertising and sports references to "survival of the fittest." Darwin and evolution also have generated several compelling myths, including the unlikely but entertaining story of his recantation of evolution on his deathbed in 1882. In that story, the evangelist Lady Elizabeth Hope claimed to have sat at Darwin's side as he praised scripture and lamented the fact that his ideas had been taken seriously. Another myth is more believable: that of Thomas Huxley's intellectual and moral triumph over theological conservatism, as represented by Bishop Samuel Wilberforce.

In examining the variations and myths concerning Darwin and his ideas, I have divided the book into two parts. The first part is devoted to myth. The very word is problematical, because that which is "mythic" may or may not literally be true. Here, *myth* means that which has become somewhat more fecund than reality. The famous debate between Huxley and Wilberforce on a hot summer day in 1860 in Oxford, England, is such an example. The debate really occurred, of course, but many histories have transformed it into an important symbol for the way in which science boldly seeks truth despite adversity. The sources documenting what really happened usually are sketchy or biased or both. But the event now stands in the history of science as a resounding repudiation of meddling theologians, or, as Huxley would have put it, a scientific smiting of the Amalekites. An event, person, place, or idea that has become in this sense *mythic* may have a foundation in fact, as the debate does, but the constraints of historical evidence have been broken by the significance of the symbol. In the case of the debate, the existence of facts or the lack thereof has done little to prevent its metamorphosis into a myth that confirms the intellectual and moral superiority of modern science over those who would challenge it.

Part II of this book, which focuses on social Darwinism in popular culture, examines the "twists" or misapplications of Darwinism. These are points at which historians have dealt peculiarly with Darwinism by imposing it where it either did not exist or existed only tangentially, or where people consciously have appropriated the name of Darwin for political or social programs. The eugenics movement—basically a better-breeding program—in America and Nazi Germany is an example. Here a scientific concept was misappropriated for political purposes, based on the ideas that individuals were more and less fit and that the species could be improved by winnowing out the less fit, with the assistance of government. In Nazi Germany, the same ideas were incorporated into a wholly racist philosophy, with ghastly consequences.

An important question arises from American society's *flirtation* with social Darwinism, and Germany's more lustful embrace of the concept in the 1930s: Why were the ideas so appealing to so many people? The first answer has nothing to do with people and everything to do with the idea itself. Like most revolutionary ideas, social Darwinism was a highly malleable concept; it was easily interpreted to support very different values, and that is exactly what occurred. Second, social Darwinism was *empirical*—an attribute that gave it credibility, especially in America and Germany, two cultures which were quite taken with science and technology. Third, social Darwinism easily appealed to the educated middle and upper classes, whose social and economic superiority it explained in terms of scientific law. Finally, the idea ostensibly was fairly straightforward and without moral complexities and burdens. Social Darwinism had these attributes while retaining the imprimatur of scientific truth. This last point also explains why different groups have adopted one or two of the three myths discussed in this book. "Truth" was the common thread in all three of the very distinctive myths—the myth of Darwin's purely intellectual triumph, of his recantation, and of Huxley's defeat of Wilberforce. In Darwin's triumph in the 1860s, the essence of the struggle was the nature of scientific truth. Was it to continue as a subsidiary of theological truth, or was science to become an independent intellectual realm?

The Consolation of Myths

In its popular meaning, a myth is a tale that lacks truth or refers to nonexistent people, things, or events. But, as the term is used here, *myth* exists at two levels. First, a myth is a story, which may or may not be fictitious. It often teaches a lesson, and this function leads to the second level: myth as a vehicle of a greater truth, a truth that transcends the immediate events and details of the story. For example, the myth of Darwin's deathbed recantation of his theory is a good story. The engaging piece of fiction is set in the splendor of an English autumn, with the protagonist aglow in his newfound faith, nobly regretting his earlier deviations from the Word. But Darwin's words are secondary to a more important purpose of the myth—to portray the grandeur of God. This tale is still a story about Truth, but one about great and profound Truth, an eternal and religious truth that transcends the mere earthly phenomena of empirical science. The story has Darwin giving up the lesser truth for the greater one. So the word *truth,* too, has dual meanings in myth. Truth may be the literal facts of the story, or it may be the values and ideals that are conveyed by the story. In the recantation myth, *truth* signifies values, not real events.

The Huxley-Wilberforce myth, however, reveals both levels of truth. At the first level, it is a wonderful story, and many versions have the young, idealistic scientist intellectually trouncing the arrogant, closed-minded bishop. It is a good story, with drama, conflict between good and evil, an underdog, winners and losers. Some el-

ements of that version of the story, such as Huxley's brashness in taking on an Anglican bishop, are true. Other parts are questionable, such as whether or not Huxley
actually won a debate with Wilberforce. This is a myth, then, because the story that
has come down over the past century or so goes beyond evidence that its events
literally occurred. However, the tale is mythic because a greater truth is at stake.
By solemnly renouncing the bishop's levity about serious scientific issues and the
search for knowledge, Huxley, ironically, made himself more devout than the bishop
with regard to truth, a virtue held in very high esteem by Victorians. The issue is
not just who won a debate about evolution in 1860. At stake, rather, are the boundaries for seekers of knowledge. Who will decide the limits of science? Are there
limits? This myth is about the triumph of light over darkness, the former represented
by Huxley, the latter by Wilberforce. As is evident in its outcome, the values enshrined in the story include individualism, represented by Huxley, and the moral
superiority of genuine truth seekers. The idea of "truth" may reside in the story, in
its moral, or in both. However one creates, conveys, or receives a myth, though,
it is a way of coordinating reality and values.

Myths provide assurance. With the help of the recantation myth, those threatened by evolution could dismiss the concept and any threats it posed to religious
ideas. The idea that Darwinism's rapid triumph was solely scientific, without regard to his and others' courting of public opinion, is a historical myth that assures
us of the power of science and its victory on the merits of evidence, regardless of
ideology, religion, or social mores. It is the same with the myth of Huxley's triumph over Wilberforce. The culture of science and science historians have created
a myth which fits very well a history that depicts the intellectual, even moral, superiority of science. The pursuit of truth is a moral endeavor, which means that it
promotes the welfare of the human condition. In this respect, Huxley prevailed.
When Wilberforce asked Huxley a demeaning question about his simian ancestry,
the bishop abandoned the theologian's proper pursuit of knowledge and truth. He
gave that pursuit to Huxley, who took it—for science. The bishop's question had
nothing to do with science, religion, or truth. It was derision, a rhetorical smoke
screen, and Huxley recognized it as such. The evidence is mixed as to who won
the debate that day. But history, if not historical evidence, has given the laurels to
Huxley.

Myths are ways of dispensing with problematical issues, such as the thorny theological implications of science—the concern in both the Huxley-Wilberforce and
recantation myths. Today, the Huxley-Wilberforce myth properly may be understood as simply an inversion of the recantation myth. In the debate myth, the champion is the young scientist, who rises to conquer the formidable obstacle of conservative theology, represented by Wilberforce. In the recantation myth, the hero
is Lady Elizabeth Hope, an unknown evangelist, at the bedside of the world's most
famous agnostic; through her, religion triumphs. The debate myth is more widely
known and accepted, because science has prevailed in the fight to exclude theol-

ogy from science. In the Huxley-Wilberforce debate, the myth of victory perfectly fits the outcome, the triumph of Darwinism. The story begins with Huxley, the underdog, having doubts about being able to face such a formidable opponent in debate, and builds to that moment when, through courage, righteousness, and truth, the bishop-dragon is slain. The story ends, not literally but symbolically, with the scientists living "happily ever after."

In the same way that myths simplify the issues, they also obscure the anomalies of a world view.[2] From the creationist perspective, it is difficult to dispose of the evidence for evolution. As the evidence continues to accumulate, several alternatives arise, some of which would be very radical for creationists. First, creationism could be abandoned, a course that would entail an extreme change in perspective. Second, the evidence can be reinterpreted. This occurs, for example, when creation-scientists "discover" that dinosaurs and human beings coexisted.[3] Thus they challenge the idea that the earth is very old and has had series of extinctions and so render the account in Genesis more plausible. Third, it is possible simply to deny the evidence, which gets more difficult with each new fossil. Fourth, the premises upon which science is built, its logical foundation, can be attacked. The Lady Hope myth gilds this final alternative. The myth does not challenge natural selection directly. Instead, it is an indirect attack, undermining the whole intellectual structure by having its progenitor change his mind. If not even Darwin believed it, why should anyone else? Lady Hope's tale ultimately is an effort to bring science back under the authority of religion or at least to reassert the primacy of religion in people's lives.

Beyond Scientific Theory

The theory of natural selection was an elegant scientific concept for which people found applications far beyond Darwin's primary concern with the origin of species. The theory itself was properly abstract, which is necessary if a theory is to have explanatory power. But a high level of abstraction also made the theory pliant. When political leaders, social philosophers, and social scientists adopted natural selection, they often focused on the grimmer components of both Darwinism and social policy. For Darwinism, that meant exaggerated attention to competition and strife in the selection process, and ignoring the equally important role of cooperation in his theory. As for social policy, energy was directed at correcting real or imagined ills, especially poverty, as well as immigration and supposedly "abnormal" people. Rarely was it focused on illuminating problems associated with such institutions as oil or railroad monopolies. Darwinism's latent implications for social science often became tooth-and-claw guidelines for those who wanted to direct social policy.

While natural selection has shown itself a worthy scientific concept, its bastard cousin, social Darwinism, has kept some dubious company and traveled some shadowy paths. Social Darwinism, as it originated with Herbert Spencer, arose in a period in which reform was beginning to develop. The issues and solutions posed by Spencer, a professional philosopher who distanced himself from social realities, often were little more than abstractions. And Darwin himself, for whom the Spencerian philosophy was misnamed, also was physically and socially detached from the social ills to which social Darwinism would be applied. In the 1860s and 1870s, social Darwinism (or, more correctly, social Spencerianism), as long as it remained a grand theory of social progress and not a social program, was rather benign. The intentions ostensibly were moral—to improve humanity.

The use of social Darwinism to explain "inferiority" in other people highlights both the persistence of, and the insecurity masked by, some social attitudes. (It is always "others" who are inferior.) The idea that people are inferior or superior is as old as recorded human history. By adopting social Darwinism, people were grasping at the latest rationale for old prejudices. Human attitudes didn't change, but ideas did—in this case with the rise of science and scientism in the nineteenth century. Social Darwinism helped to legitimize attitudes by providing a new name and a new explanation. Because the theory evolution, at least as Spencer interpreted it, *seemed* to explain everything, it inevitably was used to do just that.

A Philosophy for the Masses

Part of the problem with understanding the meaning of nineteenth-century social Darwinism was the fact that the philosophy was nurtured in numerous articles in the popular press in the late nineteenth century, especially in *Popular Science Monthly*. For natural selection, one had the words of the theory's originator in a single, coherent volume, *On the Origin of Species*. But as Herbert Spencer became both author and subject of dozens of articles about social Darwinism, the cogency of the philosophy was dissipated. Social Darwinism became a public issue through magazines and newspapers, as the ideas subsumed under this rubric were being shaped by those same publications. I rely heavily upon the popular press in dealing with social Darwinism, because a substantial amount of public debate took place in publications for *general* audiences. The popular press is one of the very few resources available to historians studying the relationship between ideas and public opinion. In this respect, I have presumed a relationship between the ideas expressed in a publication and the members of the public who purchased it. The congruence of opinion between publication and audience can only be guessed very generally. Obviously readers find fault with magazines and newspapers they purchase. But newspapers and magazines are more likely than not to coincide with views of their audiences, or the audiences would not buy them.

The idea that a relationship exists between the press and public opinion is based upon a number of phenomena, beginning in the nineteenth century. From 1860 to the end of the decade, a tremendous expansion of the press occurred in Britain and the United States. The expansion was the result of a number of factors, including urbanization, the development of railways (which delivered the newspapers and magazines to larger audiences, and which enforced a form of idleness that encouraged reading), decreased price, even improvements in household lighting. In Britain, the development of an affordable newspaper was aided by the abolition in 1855 of the compulsory newspaper stamp duty. By the 1890s, even the poorest people were reading newspapers; in America, Pulitzer and Hearst, in their press war that would result in a truly "mass" press, had begun aggressive marketing to working classes in New York. In Britain, the second half of the nineteenth century saw the newspaper become an "established as part of the normal furniture of life for all classes." Newspapers became central to public life as they became cheaper, more interesting, and more widely available in 1860s and 1870s.[4]

By the time of the Spanish-American War, social Darwinism had become a nice complement to laissez-faire economics. The historical evidence that social Darwinism drove a policy of aggression is thin. But a few people, Theodore Roosevelt among them, found congenial the philosophy's potential as an engine of policy[5]— in this case foreign, not domestic, policy. Social Darwinism was a set of ideas pervasive in American culture, as Hofstadter has shown; but it was not necessarily a catalyst for imperialism. By 1900, the ideas had become coherent and had found wide acceptance. Because social Darwinism was so adaptable to diverse ideologies and sentiments and because it was so widely known in the 1890s, historians often have assumed its connection to the war against Spain. However, the economic issues were enough to drive the conflict; social Darwinism was an incidental rationale. While convenient, useful, and appealing to an intellectual elite, it was not a primary force in justifying American action in Cuba and the Philippines. Social Darwinism remained largely an abstraction, not a prescription for dealing with foreign people or nations. In the nineteenth century, the theory's edge was dulled by a growing economy, American confidence, and the absence of the sort of external threats that arose in the next century. Henry Adams, as he characterized the years 1870–96, described the security of familiarity and predictability: "No period so thoroughly ordinary had been known in American politics since Christopher Columbus first disturbed the balance of American society."[6]

The expansionism of the 1890s, the first decade to find any substantial amount of Darwinian thought in foreign policy, was not the first *opportunity* to bend Darwinism to such ends. As early as 1870, the Grant administration, perhaps inspired partly by the European powers' examples in Africa and Asia, attempted to annex Santo Domingo.[7] In that earlier time, however, there was no hint of the Darwinian or Spencerian rationale, even though each was more current in the 1870s than in the 1890s. The first effort at restrictive immigration policy, the Immigration Act of 1875, failed to slow the immigration of Chinese, and that act was prompted by economic concerns, primarily the effect of Chinese laborers on wages. The Chinese Exclusion Act of 1882 actually suspended the immigration of Chinese laborers for ten years, but it allowed merchants and students to immigrate. Clearly, economics and not social Darwinism was the primary impetus for such action. Additional legislation to restrict the Chinese was passed in 1893, 1894, 1898, 1902, and 1904; and organized labor, including the American Federation of Labor, was a major pressure group stimulating the actions. Even after the turn of the century, following the so-called "vogue" for social Darwinism[8] and the Spanish-American War, restrictive immigration legislation still was motivated largely by economic considerations. The Immigration Act of 1903 was aimed specifically at radicals, especially anarchists. Its restriction was based upon beliefs and associations, not economics or "fitness."

It was not until 1907 that eugenics began to be promoted as a factor in immigration legislation. Theodore Roosevelt signed into law the Immigration Act of 1907, which established a commission to investigate the problem of immigration. The Immigration Restriction League began to stress the eugenic issues of immigration, arguing that the health of the nation necessitated excluding those of "inferior" blood. The league had failed in its agenda during the Spanish-American War and with the McKinley administration, which it had felt would be friendly to its goals. What should have been a grand opportunity for the xenophobes, if the war years really were a high point of social Darwinism, instead proved a defeat. The league said that the defeat came because the foreign war distracted Congress from domestic issues.[9] This argument in no way does justice to the complex history of immigration, but it does serve to point out that fear of depressed wages or lost jobs, or the need to find scapegoats for depression, such as the Jewish bankers in the depression of 1873–77, have been good motivators for restriction, even at a time when social Darwinism was presumed to be at its pinnacle.

Nineteenth-century social Darwinism may have been more benign than its twentieth-century descendant because it was closer to both its founder, Spencer, and its namesake, Darwin. As a result, in the former period the emphasis was more on the implications for the group, which was society, paralleling Darwin's unit of analysis, which was the species and not the individual organism. The unit of analysis, then, was collective and not individual, and the implications for the group were poorly defined. But by the twentieth century, this was changing. The founder of eugenics, Francis Galton, analyzed the distribution of human characteristics in a statistical fashion, and his successor was biologist-statistician Karl Pearson. With the advent of statistics, it was easier to establish group norms and to study individuals in relation to those norms.

As the focus on individual deviation from group norms intensified, so did the viciousness of the applications of pseudo-Darwinian ideas. The most radical, and irrational, enforcement of group standards also marked the height of social-Darwinian brutality. From the nineteenth to the twentieth century, as these ideas moved farther from those of Darwin and Spencer, the movement accelerated, fueled by new sciences, especially genetics, eugenics, statistics, and the development of empirically grounded social sciences. Eugenics reached its zenith in Germany, a nation embittered and economically crippled by the Treaty of Versailles. In both America and Germany, eugenics thrived during crisis—the Great Depression in America, both economic depression and political upheaval in Germany. During the 1920s and 1930s, eugenicists focused upon the promise of their endeavors, which ultimately would be an "improved" human race. At the same time, eugenicists tended to dismiss or ignore ethical issues. By 1941, nearly thirty-six thousand Americans had been sterilized under eugenics laws in some two dozen states that permitted vasectomies and tubal ligations for inmates of prisons and other institutions. The most common justifications were epilepsy, insanity, and feeblemindedness. Most of the eugenicists' research on heredity eventually proved worthless, as did the behavioral categories based simply upon class and racial prejudices.[10]

Eugenics declined after World War II, evolving into sociobiology, which generally avoided political and policy issues. But science followed the undulations of social security and insecurity. For example, in the 1980s and 1990s, the politics of differences, of group distinctions, thrived. In these decades, groups stressed their social and demographic distinctions, rather than cultural commonalities. The political and social climate was conducive to scrutinizing ever more closely the ways in which people differ and the degrees of variability.[11]

In this environment, and with advances in research on the human genome, eugenics revived. In the effort to search out this "Holy Grail of biology," the Human Genome Project became an uneasily cooperative project of the U.S. Department of Energy, the National Institutes of Health, and a number of private and publicly funded U.S. laboratories. The goal was to forge, among often competing and sometimes contentious scientific groups, approval for a multi-billion-dollar program over several decades to map the DNA sequence for the twenty-four human chromosomes. Over time, the aim became more modest—understanding human disease. But that modification of the goal did not diminish the ethical issues involving the potential for genetic engineering. Genes for a number of debilitating diseases were identified, including some cancers, cystic fibrosis, Huntingdon's disease, and Ducheme muscular dystrophy. And the list continues to grow.

The ethical issues, which bear striking similarities to ethical blind spots of eugenicists in the 1920s and 1930s, remain. Who defines "defectiveness" in gene makeup? When does a disease become a defect? How much defectiveness is tolerable? Does one simply abort so-called defective children until one with the desired genetic profile comes along? Will too much information about one's susceptibility to genetic disease diminish the quality of life? And, outside the immediate human issues, what impact will engineered organisms have on the environment? Perhaps the Human Genome Project is the engine of a new eugenics, based upon principles according to which genetic flaws can be identified and possibly fixed. As in earlier eugenics movements, identification of deviance is a first step in controlling it. The genome project, like eugenics programs, requires government cooperation. It also has provoked questions about a variety of issues, ranging from selective breeding to immigration policy. Will people be dissuaded from having children if they have defective genes? Will immigration of those with genetic disorders be curtailed? The genome project developed as a massive identification program. The unit of analysis has shrunken to the deviant gene, rather than the deviant individual, and the scientific tools are more powerful than ever. Ethical and social issues became a footnote, worth only 3 percent of the more than $60 million that the federal government budgeted for the massive project.[12]

The reason social Darwinism survives in these newer guises can be seen in the history of these ideas. First, cultures, as well as individuals, are egocentric and inevitably see themselves as the mainstream, the standard against which all others are judged. This was critical to the eugenics movement in the United States and to Nazism in Germany. Second, ideas have lives of their owns. Individuals and societies adopt, alter, and propel ideas to such an extent that the new concepts may resemble the original only faintly. Third, modern Western societies tend to be rational and logical, so they look for rational explanations for irrational prejudices. For example, Nazis wore the scientific robe of rationalism while behaving demoniacally.

Science Culture

The problems that arose with Darwinism were in the application of Darwin's ideas to society. Darwin himself suspected that Spencer might be remembered as a great philosopher, but Darwin had little use for him as a scientist.[13] Darwin even said, "With the exception of special points I did not even understand H. Spencer's general doctrine."[14] The moral loss was exacerbated as social Darwinism moved from general to specific and as it moved farther from Darwin and Spencer, both in time and conceptually, especially as the idea of social cooperation was abandoned in favor of competition. At the idea's most extreme reach, group identities were highly specific: Jews were the problem; "Aryans" were the saviors. There is nothing innately moral or immoral about science, but scientific ideas inevitably are extended to humans, an extension that does involve morality. Darwin's science was without morality, just as Newton's mechanistic universe also was amoral. But Newton was not talking about people. He was talking about objects, mere physical matter. When Darwin's inductive science was applied to humans, morality became an issue.

For both Huxley and Darwin, science was a world apart, one seeking a truth removed from ecclesiastical dictates and social qualms. Both men struggled with the impact of their ideas on society, but their first allegiance was to science. The dilemma they faced is illustrated by Huxley's invention of the word *agnostic,* which Darwin adopted. It had the virtue of clarifying a view and setting them apart in a clearly defined way. Perhaps the word was a dodge, inasmuch as Darwin and Huxley then were able to ignore the theological issues raised by science; but its creation and use helped to detach scientific method from religious oversight by labeling and defining a perspective for doing so. Events in the 1930s, however, showed that the relationship of science to other social institutions, both political and religious, was an important one. The consequences were disastrous when science lost the moral rudder of religion in Nazi Germany and became a servant of the politicians. Thus, the myths and misapplications surrounding Darwinism provide insights into the cultures that generate them, not into evolution and natural selection.

Part 1

MYTHS OF DARWINISM

Chapters 1 through 3 are studies of three myths. These myths are drawn from the history of science and ideas (chapters 1 and 2) and religious anti-Darwinism (chapter 3), variously termed *creationism or fundamentalism.* The tensions and issues involved in those myths are not limited to the subcultures from which they are drawn, but rather reflect concerns and enduring values of the broader cultures in the United States and Great Britain. Chapter 1 concerns the nature of Darwin's "victory," the first myth, which, I argue, was not due solely to its scientific merit. Darwin actually had quite a publicity machine at work, and the rapid triumph of his conception of the origin of species over the idea of special creation is indebted substantially to the avalanche of reviews and popular lectures loosed upon the public. When a small group of young scientists agreed in 1860 to help publish the *Natural History Review,* their purpose was to enlist scientists in the Darwinian cause and to assail the opposition.[1] The publication died after a only a few years, but a clique committed to Darwinism coalesced around it. Its members understood public opinion and how to manipulate it.

Chapter 2 is devoted to the Huxley-Wilberforce debate, which has become mythic by virtue of becoming a symbol of the triumph of modern science, despite the fact that the evidence for Huxley's victory is very thin. According to the myth, Huxley was a fiery young pro-Darwinian who courageously took on the forces of conservatism and darkness, represented by the Bishop Samuel Wilberforce, and, in an 1860 debate, conquered them. Histories have found high drama in the conflict, as well as a decisive victory and a conclusive resolution in the debate. Most histories have endorsed the mythic view, which relegates the facts, as they are knowable, to a secondary role, and elevates the event as a symbol of learning's triumph over ignorance. So the debate endures as a case study in intellectual justice.

Chapter 3 is about a third myth, Darwin's supposed recantation of evolution on his deathbed. The evidence for such an event is almost nonexistent, but the tale persists even to this day. As the chapter notes, sources claim—falsely—that Darwin made an astounding confession: "I was a young man with unformed ideas. I threw out queries, suggestions, wondering all the time over everything; and to my astonishment the ideas took like wildfire." Darwin then praised scripture and asked that hymns be sung. The myth had its origin in an evangelical publication in Boston, Massachusetts, in the early part of this century. It survives in the literature of those who reject evolution, and it does so despite fact and logic.

To separate the myths of science and the myths of culture is to draw an artificial distinction. Because science lives and grows in a cultural context, it is susceptible to that culture's beliefs and prejudices. A culture, in order to sustain itself, must adapt to change and simultaneously create new myths. Science, sometimes consciously and willingly, has been a wellspring of cultural myths both good and evil. Perhaps the problem with linking the history of ideas and cultural history is akin to the pure Baconian's nineteenth-century objection to natural selection: If you cannot see new species evolve, then you do not have scientific proof. Of course, no one saw the evolution of new species. Ideas and culture, too, are invisible, but powerful.

Chapter *1*

The Bishop Eaters: The Campaign for Darwin and On the Origin of Species

> Of course as a scientific review the thing is worth nothing,
> but I earnestly hope it may have made some of the educated mob
> who derive their ideas from the 'Times,' reflect. And whatever
> they do, they *shall* respect Darwin and be d——d [*sic*] to them.
> —Thomas Huxley to Joseph Hooker, discussing a review of
> Darwin's *On the Origin of Species*, published in the *London Times*

In January 1861, Thomas Huxley launched the first issue of the *Natural History Review*. It was aimed at enlisting young scientists in the Darwinian cause, and at least one of the founders of the journal intended to use it to skewer the scientist-theologian adversaries of Darwin and his book *On the Origin of Species* (1859). Huxley, soon nicknamed "Darwin's Bulldog," was the *Review's* chief architect. In what may stand out in Huxley's career as one of the few things he ever proposed to do in moderation, he promised a journal that would be "mildly episcopophagus." In fact, he proved anything but mild in bishop eating. The journal died after a little more than four years of publication, but it became a microcosm of the crucial aspects of Darwinism's rapid triumph—the existence of a cohesive group committed to an idea, individuals who understood public opinion and how to manipulate it, and scientists with the breadth of intellect to address both experts and laymen. As Huxley later explained, "The English nation will not take science from above, so it must get it from below. We, the doctors, who know what is good for it, if we cannot get it to take pills, must administer our remedies par derriere."[1]

The publicity campaign was conducted largely by Darwin and his two foremost champions:[2] Huxley, the man he called his best "general agent"; and Joseph Dalton Hooker, a rising young star in botany and a confidante of both Darwin and Huxley. Huxley and Hooker stood at the heart of a campaign on behalf of evolution and natural selection, sharing strategies and advice. Both intentionally and accidentally complemented the other's efforts in the public arena. Because science partakes of the society in which it exists, three important scientists, promoting what became the most important scientific idea of the century, were influenced by public debate and also attempted to guide discourse on the theory of natural selection. Scientists and the public alike rather rapidly accepted Darwin's theory, which "won" in little more than a decade. This conversion of so many people to what initially seemed a radical idea was not achieved solely as a result of the scientific merits of natural selection. One catalyst for change was a concerted campaign to institute that change.

Ultimately, natural selection did prevail due to its scientific virtue, but the *speed* with which the Darwinian paradigm was accepted must be considered, too, in light of the considerable effort that several people put into making sure that other scientists and the general public gave Darwin at least a fair hearing, and preferably a favorable one. Second, this examination of Darwinism's publicity is undertaken in order to shift the emphasis away from scientific history and toward a history of Darwinism in a broader social context. Darwinism was, and remains, not just a biological concept, but a set of ideas that have found their way into economics, communications, politics, psychology, sociology, and other social-scientific realms. Darwin's ideas, like those of all scientists, form part of culture, politics, and society—and are not separate from them.

The initial campaign was mounted in the first few years after publication of *On the Origin of Species* in 1859. The transitional years were, approximately, the middle of the decade. By this time the shock of Darwin's book had worn off, and proponents and opponents had identified themselves and defined the primary issues fairly well. The victory years, which were the end of the decade and the first two years of the next, saw the general acceptance of natural selection in the scientific community. This period is roughly bracketed by two more books by Darwin, *The Variation of Animals and Plants Under Domestication* (1868) and *The Descent of Man, and Selection in Relation to Sex* (1871). With publication of *Descent*, Darwin had faced the most urgent issue raised by *The Origin*, but it was indicative of the rapid acceptance of his ideas that there was far less clamor in 1871 over a book linking man and apes than there had been twelve years earlier over a book which basically skirted that question. The two most important works of Darwin's career provide the boundaries of this chapter, *On the Origin of Species* (1859) and *Descent of Man* (1871). By the time

Descent was published, natural selection had been accepted by most of the scientific community.

Darwin and His Allies

The clamor over *On the Origin of Species* centered upon its implications for humanity and God. In *The Origin*, Darwin said very little about the development of humanity, and he did not address the impact of natural selection on human beings. Worse yet, he did not pull God into his scheme of speciation. Natural selection was materialistic, eschewing the scientific orthodoxy that was committed to revealing God's design and purpose in the organization of nature. Before Darwin, the standard world view was one in which God created a grand order for the physical world, imposed it on reality, and left it in place for eternity. It was the role of natural scientists to reveal that order, to show the hand of God at work. The *a priori* assumption also was the conclusion: the order of the world reflected the role of God in its creation. By ignoring both the assumption and the conclusion, Darwin became the center of a scientific firestorm. In effect, he ignited an intellectual conflagration and then hid from the public heat.

Darwin was the son of a doctor, and his inherited wealth meant that he never held a university job or a salaried position, being instead left free all his life to pursue his scientific interests. The Darwin family had a name in science. Not only was Darwin's father a physician, but Charles's grandfather, Erasmus Darwin, had been a well-known scientist whose *Zoonomia* (two volumes, 1794–96) dwelled extensively on the transformation of life and thus on evolution.

Charles Darwin's early education was primarily in classics and mathematics, and his study of medicine at Edinburgh was shortened by his disgust with surgical operations. Darwin earned a degree at Christ's College, Cambridge, but abandoned his plan to enter the clergy after graduation. Instead, he took a post as naturalist aboard the *H.M.S. Beagle,* which was to survey the South American coast (1831–36).[3] When Darwin returned to England in 1836, he found that the collections and letters he had sent back to England had brought some attention to his abilities as a naturalist. He joined the Royal Geological Society and the Zoological Society, and any possibility of joining the clergy was further diminished by an illness apparently contracted in Chile in 1834, during the voyage. His physician father declared Charles unfit for regular worldly duties. Whether psychosomatic or physical, the ailment rendered him unfit for strenuous work and activity, as he suffered for the rest of his life from dizziness, headaches, indigestion, and insomnia.

There has been a good deal of speculation about what ailed Darwin. Darwin undoubtedly was afflicted, whether physically or mentally. Nevertheless, skeptics note that Darwin's illness served him extremely well, excusing him from having a professional career, from undertaking public duties or attending public functions, and even from thinking about God and metaphysics, which he claimed caused him physical discomfort as a result of all the concentration required.[4] Ultimately, this was a convenient sickness that allowed him to pursue his science single-mindedly and at the same time to skirt the very debates that he fueled. In 1839, he married his cousin, Emma Wedgwood. They resided in London for three years and moved to Down House outside the village of Downe in 1842, where he resided until his death in 1882. Darwin only occasionally journeyed from the village of Downe during his life, often for quack medical treatments such as "water cures" for his ailments. Because he and his family lived very comfortably on inheritance and investments, he never was forced to find his way with the public in the same fashion as many of his scientific colleagues, who typically held university or governmental positions or both. The reclusiveness of the most important scientist of the century is striking; but the degree to which he avoided social life outside the village of Downe seems incredible when considered in the context of the scientific network he built and the public activity he generated and directed.[5]

Hooker, like Darwin and unlike Huxley, was born to the upper echelons of British science. His father, William Jackson Hooker, was one of Britain's leading botanists and director of the botanical gardens at Kew. After returning to England in 1843 after a four-year voyage to Australia and the Antarctic aboard the *H.M.S. Erebus,* the younger Hooker set to analyzing and publishing the results of his botanical collecting. By 1855, when he was named assistant to his father at Kew, his scientific achievements were well known and his credentials established. Hooker was named director of Kew in 1865 upon the death of his father, who had held the post for twenty-five years. In addition to the paternal imprimatur, he came to the inner circle of Victorian science by marriage to the daughter of John Stevens Henslow. Henslow, a professor of botany at Cambridge who also befriended the Cambridge student Charles Darwin, was not a great scientist but was an important figure in science. His major accomplishment was to bring botany back to life at the university. He conducted a very successful series of lectures and planned and financed the resurrection of a herbarium that had fallen into disrepair.[6] The correspondence between Darwin and Hooker reveals a strong personal and professional relationship. They first met in Trafalgar Square in 1839, only four months after Hooker returned from his Erebus voyage. By 1844, Darwin had confided to Hooker his belief that all animals were descended from common stock.[7] Hooker supplied Darwin with specimens, answered questions of anatomy, and provided critiques of Darwin's and other scientists' ideas. Unlike Huxley, Hooker contributed substantially to the theory of natural selection, especially with respect to geographical distribution of plants. Hooker's *Himalayan Journals,* published five years before *The Origin,* was dedicated to Darwin.

Hooker was instrumental in arranging a joint paper presentation for Darwin and Alfred Russel Wallace to the Linnean Society in 1858. Darwin had received from Wallace a letter that basically outlined the ideas on which Darwin had been working for years,[8] sending Darwin into despair over the threat of being preempted. Wallace had not fully developed the idea of natural selection, but the paper he supplied to Darwin was sufficient to spur Darwin to finish his manuscript on the subject and to try to solve the dilemma of priority without appearing ungentlemanly. Hooker, ever politic, helped find the solution. Compared with Huxley, Hooker was much more tactful in dealing with anti-Darwinians. The fact that he was the first Darwinian to be elected president of the British Association for the Advancement of Science is a testament not only to his stature but also to his personal style. By the time he attained the post in 1868, most scientists had been won over to natural selection, but there remained numerous doubters and many questions to be answered. Hooker's presidential address garnered attention for its damnation of natural theology, which basically saw nature as the progressive unfolding of a divine plan of creation, and variations in life as simply parts of God's plan.

Hooker was an extremely hardworking and thorough individual, and a loyal friend. His careful, methodical style is reflected in his reading of *The Origin,* which took months.[9] Huxley, on the other hand, published a review of *The Origin* within a matter of weeks after its publication. Hooker was powerful in his ideas and logic, but he did not pursue a rhetorical scorched-earth policy, as did his friend and colleague Huxley.

In temperament and public presence, Huxley was Darwin's antithesis. His nickname, "Darwin's Bulldog," was appropriate. Huxley, whose expertise was in anatomy and paleontology, early in his career became convinced that science must be independent of theology. In fact, it was Huxley who provided the enduring metaphor of a war between science and religion.[10] He was dissatisfied with creationism but found it difficult to support evolutionary ideas because there existed no good explanation of how evolution worked. When natural selection solved that problem for him, he became a lifelong proponent of Darwinism. In public lectures and reviews, Huxley thrived in the glare of publicity that would have withered Darwin.

There was another dimension to Huxley's dogmatism: he was anticlerical, and Darwin's work became Huxley's pulpit for pounding theologians. Advocating science as a profession meant rejecting the idea that people who were amateurs, or even entirely ignorant of the field, might be arbitrators of the new scientific knowledge. If scientists were professionals—and Huxley believed they were—then clerical criticisms and meddling not only were irrelevant but also were ironically immoral, because they hindered the search for truth. His animosity toward the clergy grew out of a number of factors, including his own humble origins and hard-won economic well-being, an ingrained skepticism that struck sparks against comfortable tradition in both science and religion, a sincere search for truth, and a love of debate and intellectual battle.

Huxley's invention of the term *agnostic* reveals his acumen in dealing with not only the clergy but also the public. He invented the word to describe his religious views, and Darwin adopted the label. Huxley came up with it when a group of liberal churchmen was trying in 1869 to find a religious consensus among British intellectuals. Huxley irritated their "Metaphysical Society" when he published, in the

Fortnightly Review, an article on "The Physical Basis of Life." For his materialistic views, the churchmen condemned him as an atheist. But before the group could label Huxley, he labeled himself. *Agnostic* meant absolutely secular, neither believing nor disbelieving the existence of God, which Huxley saw as endlessly debatable and empirically unknowable. Despite his hostility toward religion, he freely used biblical allusions, perhaps angering his opponents even more by doing so. He stated, for example, that "it is as respectable to be a modified monkey as modified dirt."[11] However, Huxley's antagonism toward religion was not a necessary correlate of defending natural selection. The fight was something Huxley enjoyed, which was illustrated in a letter he wrote to Darwin shortly after reading *On the Origin.* Huxley warned Darwin of the abuse that would come, and stated, "I am sharpening up my claws and beak in readiness."[12]

Huxley probably was Victorian England's foremost public advocate of science. He was born above a butcher shop in 1825 in Ealing, Middlesex, a village about six miles outside London. His father was an assistant schoolmaster and later a bank clerk, and suffered from mental illness. Huxley wrote in his autobiography that he drew from his father a hot temper and a tenacity that some would deem obstinacy. The son was tortured by indigestion, fits of depression, chronic headaches, and, later in life, liver and heart ailments.

Unlike Darwin, who was educated at Cambridge, Huxley was largely self-educated. As a youth, he read widely but largely without direction. His studies included mathematics, history, geology, philosophy, physics, and physiology. He admitted in his autobiography that he was an undisciplined student. He was a notable success as a medical student at Charing Cross Hospital, where he supported himself on scholarships. A sea voyage was in order at this point in his career, and Huxley spent 1846–50 aboard the *H.M.S. Rattlesnake* in the South Seas. Huxley's *Rattlesnake* voyage, like Darwin's *Beagle* trip, was a steppingstone to a life in science, and Huxley later said that it gave him direction and disciplined habits.[13] His work aboard the ship brought him recognition as a comparative anatomist, but, unlike Darwin, he remained hard-pressed financially. His monetary insecurity and very modest means early in life probably contributed to his willingness to lash out at the established men of science, who tended to be very secure both financially and philosophically.

In 1854, Huxley finally attained the role of lecturer at the Royal School of Mines and was appointed naturalist for the Geological Society in 1855. From that point on, his story was one of success, as his professional and public stature grew. Though brilliant and a formidable debater, Huxley's style was not always so admirable. His public addresses and private letters were steeped in very personal attacks, as he impugned the character and intelligence of opponents. He typically turned any scientific dispute into a personal one. He also tended not to be content with making and winning a point, but instead wanted to grind his opponent to nothingness, a trait recognized by both Darwin and Hooker and one discussed in more detail below. Like Darwin, Huxley commonly viewed the scientific world as "us versus them," with an individual cast as either an ally or an enemy. In spite of Huxley's fierce defense and advocacy of Darwinism, his own research never relied much on natural selection, and he never contributed significantly to the idea. In fact, Huxley felt that natural selection was not completely proven,[14] but obviously he felt that it was the best explanation of speciation.

Darwin's theory also was a useful tool for Huxley and other young scientists who were attempting to climb the ladder of status within Victorian science. Early in his career, Huxley was angered by the fact that one had to begin as a person of means in order to succeed in science.[15] Huxley stayed angry, and a substantial amount of his rage was directed at Richard Owen, whose name was synonymous with scientific prestige in the pre-*Origin* era. Huxley quipped that Owen's scheme of classification adorned his lectures "like a Corinthian portico of cow-dung."[16]

Owen (1804–1892), one of Great Britain's leading comparative anatomists, was the center of anti-Darwinism in the 1860s. Owen's illustrious career included the Hunterian Professorship at the Royal College of Surgeons (1836–56), the post of physiology lecturer at the Royal Institution, and service as superintendent of the natural history department at the British Museum. His connections included the friendship of Prince Albert and other members of the royal family, political leaders, and major figures in the Anglican Church.[17] Idealism permeated his scientific thinking. Owen believed in an underlying unity of all living forms and sought to identify the "archetype" upon which all forms of life were based. The archetype that he envisioned was an idealized form of the simplest living structure, stripped of all the specialized organs of real life forms. Owen described this simplest structure in 1848 in his *Archetype and Homologies of the Vertebrate Skeleton*. He emphasized a unity of type, existing at a level deeper than the physical world, and felt that the archetype, the common plan, was the one upon which all vertebrate animals were simply thematic variations. This idealism, however, did not mean that Owen was opposed to the whole idea of evolution. In fact, he was willing to accept the idea that animals adapted and changed. But he believed that change was a matter of adding organs to the archetypal form. So Owen could accept transmutation if it were supernaturally guided. Owen even conceded that his work on specialization supported the notion of natural selection.[18]

In spite of his status and prestige, Owen seems to have been somewhat insecure and fearful of being upstaged scientifically. He was, for example, not nearly as adept at public speaking as his nemesis, Huxley, whose working-class audiences adored him, asking for autographs. One audience, thinking that Huxley was doing the lecture for free, even took up a collection. Cab drivers refused fares from Huxley. In contrast, Owen's 1865 attempt at lectures for the working classes ended abysmally. Charles Dickens, one of the London elite who endorsed the effort, wrote to Owen that "the time is not ripe for the proposed lectures," although he did note that Owen's opponents got the working men together for lectures.[19] On one occasion, Owen lectured before radical Quakers in industrial Newcastle. He was late and offered the excuse that he had been "detained at Ravensworth Castle." Lord Ravensworth was a strong conservative, and Owen's audience of workers was not impressed.[20]

This difference between the two antagonists became increasingly important as the public battle intensified. Owen was not graceful in contending with opposition, so the young Huxley, brash and bright, must have surprised and angered Owen. But he was a complex man, for his later battles with Darwin and Huxley contrast with his earlier dealings with the two. Early in their careers, both Darwin and Huxley benefited from his solicitousness. When Darwin returned from his voyage aboard the *H.M.S. Beagle*, Owen reviewed manuscript proofs of Darwin's *Journal of Researches into the Geology and Natural History of the Various Countries Visited by H.M.S. "Beagle"* (1839) and even identified a Toxodon skull Darwin sent him. Owen also helped Huxley win government support for studies aboard the *H.M.S. Rattlesnake*.[21]

Owen's opposition to Darwinism was a matter both of scientific thinking and of personality. Huxley's research in comparative anatomy countered Owen's archetypal theory, but Huxley also hounded the older scientist. For example, Huxley in 1855 lambasted Owen's classification system as "one of the most thoroughly retrograde steps ever taken since zoology has been a science." It appears that gauntlets already had been thrown down in the Huxley-Owen feud even before publication of *The Origin* in 1859. Owen had begun calling himself a "professor" at the School of Mines, where he was a visiting lecturer and where Huxley was employed. Huxley interpreted this as an insult to his own status and afterward publicly contended that the word *archetype* was "fundamentally opposed to the spirit of modern science." Owen had little choice but to be offended and said that those who denied life's design exhibited "some, perhaps congenital, defect of mind."[22]

This public division may have meant that whatever Huxley supported, Owen opposed. So Owen may have pushed himself, by virtue of being an obstinate prima donna, into an opposition that was far more severe than what he really felt. In fact, before Huxley took up the Darwinian cause, Owen's first public response to Darwinism had been reserved but not unsympathetic.[23] One scholar has stated that, after 1859, Owen's insecurity and anger were manifested in personal hatred of Huxley and in philosophical dislike of Darwinism. This in turn made Owen's fight with Huxley ideal for the Darwinians' purposes, because it became opposition based upon feelings rather than science.[24] Owen's opposition thereafter became a matter not of showing alternative explanations for variations and speciation, but rather simply of declaring the improbability of natural selection and charging that Darwin had not presented enough evidence. A combination of personality, philosophy, and professional jealousy, then, drove Owen to his rabid opposition.[25] Darwin, Huxley, and Hooker recognized Owen's status and understood his importance as a leader of anti-Darwinism.

The Initial Battle

The residences of Darwin, Huxley, and Hooker suggest their respective roles in the first few years of the fight over natural selection. Darwin, who of the three lived farthest from London, also was physically the most remote from the daily battle and the personal confrontations that marked so much of this period. Darwin was engaged, as he urged others to action and alerted them to intellectual offenses published by others, but he never participated in the actual debates. Hooker resided on the outskirts of London at Kew, a location much more easily accessible to the city than was the village of Downe, but one still removed from the grittier environs of everyday London. Hooker played an important role in the debates and in defining other scientific issues, especially as they related to the botanical gardens he supervised. He spent a substantial amount of time in London and was a regular participant in scientific meetings and informal gatherings of the intellectual elite. He was the middle ground between Darwin and Huxley. Like Darwin, Hooker was dedicated to science, which was his first priority. Unlike Darwin, Hooker had public and administrative obligations that had to be met, and in this respect his career was more like that of Huxley. Huxley, however, unlike Hooker, was a street brawler when it came to the scientific debates. He resided in London, the heart of Victorian intellectual life, and spent his life in public debates centered on science and education.

These residential dissimilarities did not impair the strong personal and professional relationships among the three men. In the first few years after *The Origin* was published, Darwin promoted a sense of mission among the triumvirate, and much of their correspondence reflects a long-term view of the challenges involved in creating converts to natural selection. As soon as *The Origin* was published, Darwin was telling Hooker, "We shall soon be a good body of working-men and shall have, I am convinced, all young and rising naturalists on our side."[26] Darwin often referred to "our side" or "our cause" when writing to Huxley and Hooker, but he was actually talking about "my cause." It was not entirely presumptuous to address the issue to Hooker in this way so early in the fight, because Hooker had been privy to the idea for some time. However, it does show Darwin's willingness to manipulate others for his own purposes. He wrote to Hooker on another occasion about the "old fogies in Cambridge" and their attacks on "our work." Actually, only Darwin's work was attacked, but he exhorted, "Our work is worth doing." He even went so far as to say that it made him "resolve to buck on my armour," which he did, but never in public and only well behind front lines and friends.[27] At times, Darwin bordered on intentional falsehood. He wrote to Hooker, "You have worked me up to that extent & that I now feel I can face a score of savage Reviewers."[28] Darwin never in his life seriously entertained personally taking on critics. It was always done by proxy. He wrote a more honest letter to Huxley shortly after the famous clash with the Bishop Samuel Wilberforce at Oxford over the validity of Darwin's ideas: "I honour your pluck; I would as soon have died as tried to answer The Bishop in such an assembly."[29]

A letter from Darwin to Huxley shortly after the latter's review of *The Origin* appeared in the *Times of London* was indicative of the relationship between the two. Darwin for the rest of his life heaped praise on Huxley, telling him what a service his efforts were to the cause of science.

> Who can the author be? . . . The author is a literary man. . . . He has read my book very attentively; but what is *very* remarkable, it seems that he is a profound naturalist. He knows my Barnacles book & appreciates it too highly. . . . Who can it be? Certainly, I should have said that there was only one man in England who could have written this essay & that *you* were the man. But I suppose I am wrong, & that there is some hidden genius of great calibre. . . . [emphasis in original]
>
> Well, whoever the man is, he has done great service to the cause. . . . The grand way he soars above common religious prejudices and the admission of such views into the Times, I look at as of the highest importance, quite independently of the *mere question of species* [my emphasis].[30]

Darwin said the cause was not just "mere" speciation, making his own interests those of science generally, not just his peculiar niche. This gave Huxley and Hooker a wider philosophical swath to march through, while arming them with Darwin's special case. In his usual self-deprecating fashion, though, Darwin immediately denied the significance of the work by saying that the reviewer thought too much of the monograph. Darwin's self-interested behavior was highlighted by the fact that his criterion for profundity appeared to be familiarity with his own monograph. Beginning in 1846, Darwin had spent eight years studying barnacles, publishing two technical monographs on the subject in 1851 and 1854. The volumes received high praise, and the Royal Society awarded him the Royal Medal for the work. It made him the world authority on barnacles and established Darwin as a zoological specialist. The work ran to more than a thousand pages, covering both living and fossil barnacles. In addition, it supported his ideas about variation. Earlier he had believed variation to be the exception in species, but the barnacle research convinced him that stability in species was illusory because the various species of barnacles were so widely variable that it was difficult to tell when varieties ended and species began.[31]

A few months after the *Times* review, Darwin praised Huxley as "the best of general agents" and commended his "capital service" in "stemming prejudice."[32] As with his references to serving science in general, this also cast Huxley's favors for Darwin as more than merely promoting a narrow interest, and gave Huxley the greater mission of fighting prejudice. But Darwin's longer view of the campaign was made clear when he told Huxley that the only way for the theory to be generally adopted was by "young men growing up & replacing the old workers."[33] Huxley was acutely aware of the possibilities of his role and believed that he and Hooker very well could become the leaders of their scientific disciplines. Several weeks before Huxley's review was published in the *Times,* he wrote to Hooker:

It is of no use having any false modesty about the matter. You and I, if we last ten years longer . . . will be the representatives of our respective lines in the country. In that capacity we shall have certain duties to perform to ourselves, to the outside world and to Science. We shall have to swallow praise which is no great pleasure and to stand multitudinous bastings and irritations, which will involve a good deal of unquestionable pain. Don't flatter yourself that there is any moral chloroform by which either you or I can render ourselves insensible or acquire the habit of doing things coolly.[34]

Darwin recognized the uniqueness of these two allies and directed them toward offending publications as well as friendly ones. Very early in the controversy over *The Origin,* Darwin had identified this trio; from his remote outpost, he kept Huxley and Hooker alerted to the writings of allies and enemies.[35] Now that *The Origin* was out, Darwin was a publicity orchestrator, bringing issues, publications, and individuals to the attention of his allies. He skillfully matched the talents of his friends to the obstacles his theory faced, calling on Huxley when a frontal assault was in order and on Hooker when the situation needed more finesse or closer ties to the inner circle of science. It was a pattern that would be maintained throughout the decade.

Educated Mobs and a One-Man Public

Darwin called Hooker "my public."[36] Huxley called his larger audience the "educated mob."[37] These distinctive, but hardly opposed, characterizations neatly encapsulate the two different levels at which the trio operated in the campaign for natural selection. Darwin and Hooker tended to work with a narrower conception of the public, while Huxley attacked and defended on all fronts. This did not mean that Darwin was abandoning a larger public, but more likely that he was being realistic in his assessment of who would accept the theory. In early 1860, Darwin warned Hooker of being unrealistic about changing opinion:

I think you expect too much in regard to change of opinion on the subject of species. One large class of men, more especially I suspect of naturalists, never will care about *any* [emphasis in original] general question . . . ; and secondly nearly all men past a moderate age, either in actual years or in mind, are, I am fully convinced, physically incapable of looking at facts under a new point of view. Seriously, I am astonished and rejoiced at progress which [the] subject has made; look at [the] enclosed memorandum. Owen says my book will be forgotten in 10 years; perhaps so, but with such a list I feel convinced the subject will not. The outsiders, as you say, are strong.[38]

As Darwin analyzed opinion among different groups, he had at this very early stage of the campaign adopted the perspective of "outsiders versus insiders" and had even drawn up a roster of enemies. Owen's status was sufficient to make Darwin worry about even an offhand comment on *The Origin.* Darwin's concern was well founded;

although Owen could not speak as a representative of all of science, he spoke with the authority of one who had been contacted from as far away as Africa, by Stanley Livingston, who protested about *The Origin*, and by such prominent government officials as the Duke of Argyll, who was postmaster general. As such, Owen's assessment was that of an important statesman of science.[39]

Both Hooker and Darwin were sensitive to the various groups with which they had to contend. Hooker showed good political sense in his handling of a request to teach the young royal family at Buckingham Palace about zoology. He reported to Darwin that he had a "narrow escape" and was "saving my credit by offering to teach the children a little practical Botany." He hoped that the individual he enlisted to do the job would "not repudiate Owen in lecturing there on zoology."[40] Hooker was extremely busy, and he probably did have little time to spend on any new assignment. Still, the royal family had to be handled tenderly. In addition, Hooker was wisely concerned that the powerful Owen not be challenged in this particular forum. This did not mean that Hooker was getting soft on Owen. Hooker told Darwin that he knew an article was Owen's by its logic, "so are the long winded phrases & so is the immutable rubbish of the doctrine."

Hooker disliked having opponents among the influential or well known, even when they were not naturalists. When informed that Thomas Carlyle was "a violent anti-Darwinian," Hooker said that it was of no consequence, "but I should not have expected it."[41] He did not say why he did not expect it, but it may have been because the essayist in 1850 had written in *Latter-Day Pamphlets* that the new prisons were coddling the most useless parts of the population. In addition, Carlyle was contemptuous of common people and faulted Christianity for its deference to the weak. Carlyle dismissed most of orthodox Christianity and found God in a mystical, almost pantheistic, identification with nature. For him, the universe was "one vast symbol of God," in which Carlyle saw evidence of the constancy of nature's laws, not miracles.[42] Hooker may have been surprised that a man who had adopted Malthusian ideas found fault with Darwin, but Hooker probably found the opposition of little consequence because Carlyle was not a scientist. However, he was of the intellectual elite and a very popular writer, which made him worth reporting to Darwin, who believed Carlyle to be antiscience, narrow-minded, and often contemptuous of ideas that were not his own. Darwin admitted that Carlyle "has been all-powerful in impressing some grand moral truths on the minds of men."[43]

This sensitivity on the part of Hooker and Darwin extended to their concerns about the audiences for reviews and articles. Hooker was sad to see the *Saturday Review* run an article from a hostile reviewer but admitted, "It is *perfect* [emphasis in original] & if S.R. [*Saturday Review*] always wrote like that instead of out-corresponding the Times correspondent in indulging in flatulent & pompous language I would take it in."[44]

The circumstances surrounding Huxley's *Times* review of *The Origin* provide a glimpse into his opportunistic nature. When Huxley had the chance to review *The Origin* for the *Times,* his son Leonard later wrote, "Never was windfall more eagerly accepted." A journalist at the *Times,* characterized by Huxley as "an excellent journalist . . . innocent to any knowledge of science," asked Huxley to get him out of the difficulty of reviewing *The Origin.* However, the journalist said he would have to take credit for anything Huxley wrote by prefacing two or three paragraphs of his own: "I was too anxious to seize upon the opportunity thus offered of giving the book a fair chance with the multitudinous readers of the Times, to make any difficulty about conditions."[45] Though not given credit for the presumably anonymous review, Huxley said that many people suspected him immediately of being the author, and the secret leaked out in time. But Huxley was aiming for a large audience—"multitudinous"—and he suffered no illusions about what he was doing in the *Times* review. He told Hooker: "Of course as a scientific review the thing is worth nothing, but I earnestly hope it may have made some of the educated mob who derive their ideas from the 'Times,' reflect. And whatever they do, they *shall* [emphasis in original] respect Darwin and be d——d [*sic*] to them."[46] The letter showed Huxley at his best—or worst, depending on one's sympathies. He was the hard-headed realist, skewering a whole class of people, bombastically declaring that they would be converted, and finally flinging a curse at them. Huxley's review in the *Times* has been made large by history, but by 1859 his power as a communicator already was well established.

Vitriol and Stealth

In 1861, Darwin commended his "general agent" Huxley for a notice in the *Athenaeum* but said it was "almost too civil," something for which Huxley seldom was criticized.[47] Darwin apparently wanted Huxley to put the sharpened beak and claws to good use. Huxley, however, was not involved only for the joy of the fight. He had a great vision of what he and a few others were to accomplish. He wrote to Hooker: "I look forward to a great revolution being effected. . . . I firmly believe in the advent of an English Epock in science and art. . . . I shall return after the British Association. The interesting question arises, Shall I have a row with the great O. [Owen] there?"[48] Huxley's meanness, his colorful and quotable insults, his habit of overstatement, and his ambition all shine through in the letter.

Like Darwin, Huxley considered tactics and took note of the consequences. His *Times* review was not the only example of Huxley's foregoing a bit of notoriety for the sake of getting something published. In December 1859, when the *Times* printed its review, he also provided notes to the *Quarterly Review* for an article to be written by someone else. "I confess I look upon this as a great step gained and we must take measures at once to utilize our advantages in possessing so powerful an organ. . . . I am thoroughly roused now, and by ——— [*sic,* for "damn"] we will have our way."[49] In addition to pursuing publications in the *Natural History Review* and the *Quarterly Review,* he told Hooker that he had sent "draft notes" to eighteen other people.

Huxley wrote that note a little over a year before the first number of his *Natural History Review* was published on January 1, 1861. Originally an anti-Darwin publication, the *Review* was purchased by Huxley after he drew others into the venture. He resigned as editor in 1863 because of the heavy workload, complaining that he had failed to appeal to the masses. The audience, which was not the "masses," did tend to be educated upper- and middle-class people with an interest in science.[50] In contrast to the *Natural History Review,* the *Quarterly Review* concentrated on politics, literature, and philosophy, but it also tended to have a more upper-class audience.

More than a year before his *Times* review, Huxley outlined to Hooker a plan for "one or two of us" writing scientific articles for *Saturday Review,* another high-quality periodical, also with an educated middle- to upper-class audience.[51] He planned to involve several scientists. He and Hooker would do articles on biology, and they would find people to do articles on chemistry, mineralogy, ecology, mathematics, and physics.[52] At times Huxley sounded as if he were planning a career in politics, not science. In 1860, he told Hooker, "I hope your ear is better. Take care of yourself. . . . I can't do without you these twenty years. We have a devil of a lot to do in the way of smiting the Amelkites [*sic*]."[53] In labeling the opposition Amalekites, he again used biblical imagery to identify the Darwinians as the righteous—this time in the guise of the Israelites—and with great irony cast the anti-Darwinians as those fighting God's chosen people.

Huxley was not the only one capable of meanness. Darwin, too, had a dark side, which sometimes gave a peculiar tone to his correspondence. He would criticize someone, such as Owen, then belittle himself, then proceed to outline a strategy for winning the minds of the English to his theory. In 1860, he lamented to Hooker about a "coarsely abusive article" in the *Dublin Magazine of Natural History*:

> It outdoes even N. British [Review] and Edinburgh [Review] in misapprehension and misrepresentation. I never knew anything so unfair as in discussing cells of Bees. . . . I am inclined to give up attempts as hopeless. Those who do not understand, it seems, cannot be made to understand. . . . I should be very glad to know where this beautiful contrivance is described. A Rev. Mr. Dunn wrote N. British Review as I hear from Lyell, who heard from Chambers. Hopkins of Cambridge has Article in Fraser's just published. He speaks of me in kindest manner personally, but evidently thinks me an illogical and rash blunderer.[54]

Darwin whined about being misunderstood and then went to third-hand gossip before coming back to what pained him. His mood picked up a little a month later, after he heard that Huxley and Hooker had taken on Bishop Wilberforce at Oxford:

> How I should have liked to have wandered about Oxford with you, if I had been well enough;

and how still more I should have liked to have heard you triumphing over the Bishop. I am astounded at your success and audacity. It is something unintelligible to me how anyone can argue in public like orators do. I had no idea you had this power. I have read lately so many hostile views that I was beginning to think that perhaps I was wholly wrong and that Owen was right when he said [the] whole subject would be forgotten in ten years; but now that I hear that you and Huxley will fight publicly (which I am sure I never could do) I fully believe that our cause will in the long run prevail. I am glad I was not in Oxford, for I should have been overwhelmed with my stomach.[55]

Darwin, as usual, was not well enough to attend a meeting at which there was a great probability that his theory would be a major issue. It was a lifelong pattern: Darwin always had an excuse, usually his health, for not attending the debates that he generated. He also reminded Hooker that it was a long-term battle, especially in light of the hostile reviews that were troubling him. For good measure, he threw in Owen to stoke the fire for "our" cause. Owen was a good one to bring out some meanness in Darwin, who wrote to Hooker:

> I am become quite demoniacal about Owen, worse than Huxley, and I told Huxley that I should put myself under his care to be rendered milder. But I mean to try and get more angelic in my feelings; yet I never shall forget his cordial shake of the hand when he was writing as spitefully as he possibly could against me. But I have always thought you have more cause than I to be demoniacally inclined towards him. Bell tells me that Owen says that the Editor mutilated his article in Edinburgh R., and Bell seemed to think it was rendered more spiteful by Editor; perhaps the opposite view is a probable. Oh dear this doesn't look like becoming more angelic in my temper.[56]

Owen also provoked Darwin's fears of conspiracy. He told Hooker that an article in the *Quarterly Review* was "uncommonly clever" in skillfully pointing out the difficulties in Darwin's theory, adding darkly, "I can plainly see, here and there, Owen's hand. . . . I can see there has been some queer tampering with the Review for a page has been cut out and reprinted."[57]

Darwin's initiative, beyond his correspondence, was to pay for publicity. In 1860, he asked Huxley's advice about reprinting a review by Asa Gray, the prominent Harvard botanist who was something of an American Huxley for Darwin. After having Gray's articles republished as a pamphlet, Darwin sent copies to the *Natural History Review* and paid for advertisements. He had earlier justified sending reprints of Gray's review of *The Origin* to a publication because the editor had published reviews from two Englishmen, and Darwin thought that running the American's review should be done in the spirit of "fair play." He was even willing to pay four pence to the magazine.[58] Darwin also paid for advertising the pamphlet in the *Gardener's Chronicle*. Not only did Darwin ask Hooker to persuade the editor to run a short notice of the publication, but also he asked if there were any other botanical journals into which Hooker could place a notice of the pamphlet. Darwin claimed that he would like for Gray's sake to get some of the pamphlets sold but admitted that it would help him, too.[59]

Hooker usually was much stealthier as a Darwinian agent than Huxley. In fact, Hooker could be so understated that Darwin at times fretted about his commitment to the cause, telling Hooker:

> It delights me that you are interested in watching progress of opinion on change of species; I feared that you were weary of subject. . . . As for progress of opinion I clearly see it will be excessively slow, almost as slow as change of species. In fact, it will, I believe, be insensible. I am getting wearied at the storm of hostile Reviews; and hardly any useful. Did you see in Literary Gazette that Prof. Clarke of Cambridge says the chief characteristic of such books as mine is "their consummate impudence"—mild and gentleman-like language![60]

Darwin's fretting about opinion and Hooker's loyalty probably was to be expected, given his tendency to worry. That he really was ill-suited to fight his own public battles was shown in the last sentence, in which he took offense at ungentlemanly language, the very thing for which he praised Huxley.

Hooker's reticence was not just with anonymous reviews. On one occasion, when he was having difficulty getting the editor of *Gardener's Chronicle* to run a notice of Darwin's *On the Various Contrivances by Which British and Foreign Orchids Are Fertilised by Insects,* he simply wrote it himself—and attempted to mimic the style of the editor, John Lindley: "I worried Lindley over & over again to notice your orchid book in Chronicle, by the very broadest hints man could give at last he said, 'really I cannot. You must do it for me,' & so I did. . . . Lindley felt that he ought to have [indecipherable] it himself, & my main effort was to write it 'a la Lindley' & in this alone I have succeeded—that people think it is exactly Lindley's style!!! Which diverts me vastly. The fact is between ourselves."[61] Still, Hooker, ever the gentleman, criticized the ally Lindley for an article that was "sneering contempt" of his enemies, as too violent in its attacks. The whole tone was wrong, Hooker said.[62]

Transitional Years: A Foothold Established

After the debates about *The Origin* had subsided by mid-decade, some doubts about Huxley emerged. Darwin and Hooker valued and respected him highly, but Darwin agreed with Hooker that Huxley was a poor judge of the importance of science to the public: "It is very true what you say about Huxley having no idea how little science is generally regarded."[63] Relating news of a public meeting in 1866, Hooker told Darwin: "Huxley had sounded the charge . . . In short I was a stink-pot which he was to pitch into the evening. . . . Huxley made a capital presentation . . . & was being conciliatory, prudent & amusing too."[64] Hooker was pleased not only that Huxley was in his usual role of sounding the charge, but that he even was able to take the edge off his remarks. But Huxley was not tamed. Hooker reported to Darwin:

Have you read Huxley's . . . slashing leader in today's Reader? It is uncommonly able & but as usual with him he goes like a desert whirlwind over the ground . . . blasting & suffocating the opposing objects, & leaving nothing but dry leaves on the ground. The vegetation he withers was one of vile weeds to be sure, but vile weeds are green & all is *black* after him [emphasis in original].

The Reader seems to me rather dull & aimless—the articles too learned & boring for men who work hard during the week & want some entertainment to read science on Tuesday. Huxley has taken the scientific editorship I am told; but he never stuck to anything of the kind long & I have no hopes of it succeeding under him—he is far too good for such work, & has no aptitude for it—no man can write such good articles upon science as he can. But he is no caterer for the public, . . . he wants breadth of sympathy.[65]

Hooker probably was right in being dubious about the prospect of Huxley's hitching himself to the *Reader,* an upscale literary organ with a liberal political outlook, appealing to highly educated people.[66] Hooker's criticism of the *Reader's* lack of appeal may have reflected doubts about Huxley's strategy, if it could be called one. Huxley had been lecturing to working men, and with the *Reader* he turned his attention to the other end of the social spectrum—a very different audience.

Huxley still loved the fight. He wrote to Darwin that a "Society for the Propagation of Common Honesty in parts of the world" was established at Cambridge. Owen came to attack, according to Huxley, but was beaten, and there was the implication that if one wasn't a member, as Owen was not, then one must be not be in favor of common honesty: "We all praised you. . . . All the people present who could judge saw that Owen was lying & shuffling. The other half saw he was getting the worst of it but regarded him I think, rather as an innocent sheep, being worried by . . . active young wolves."[67] Huxley relished his role as predator.

A Wider Public

By the middle of the decade, it was clear that Darwin had a broader view of his public than that represented by Hooker. Darwin was charting the inroads he was making in foreign countries, indicating—if he could afford to worry about his ideas' progress in France and Germany—a sense of having "won" in England. Charting foreign progress, too, was a way for Darwin to bolster himself, much like keeping a list of allies and enemies so that one could keep score of victories.[68] Darwin's appreciation of the campaign work had grown, and, given Darwin's earlier warnings not to lose sight of doing "original research" for the sake of the *Natural History Review,* he sounded a bit hypocritical as he urged Huxley to do even more popular writing. Darwin went so far as to put such work on a plane equal with what he called "critical work": "It is an absolute marvel to me how much you do.—I know there was very little chance of you having time to write a popular treatise on Biology; but you are about the one man that could do it. All the time I feel it would be almost a sin for you to do it, as it would of course destroy some critical work. On the other hand,

I sometimes think general & popular Treatises are almost as important for the progress of science as critical work."[69] The remarks highlight very well the different roles that had evolved for Hooker and Huxley in the public battle: Huxley was the one who wrote reviews and debated clergy; Hooker was the politician who operated in the circles of power, less publicly than Huxley but well connected. Darwin even went so far as to urge Huxley to write a popular book on zoology because of the lack of such books for beginners. By now Darwin could justify such work because it also would be useful to naturalists. Of course it would have benefited Darwin immensely to have had an introductory text in zoology written by one of his most zealous proponents.[70]

Along with a general softening of the rhetoric, unity among allies became more important to Darwin and Hooker, who had discovered that even the "vile weeds" in the scientific landscape might have some value and need not be blackened by Huxley.[71] Apprehension concerning divisiveness was illustrated in a spat between Hugh Falconer, a young paleontologist sympathetic to natural selection, and Charles Lyell, a geologist and mentor to Darwin, who had taken Lyell's *Principles of Geology* on his *Beagle* voyage. The younger scientist was upset over not getting proper credit for scientific insight. The dispute became public in the *Athenaeum,* and Huxley privately wondered if Falconer could be assuaged: "But what the deuce impelled him [Falconer] to wash so much scientific dirty linen coram publis in the Athenaeum? . . . But to go and kick up all this dust about a priority question or a share-of-credit question when Lyell had offered to make amends for any oversight or understatement, is what I cannot understand. . . . the breeding of bitterness between Lyell and himself can but do harm to everybody."[72] A few weeks earlier, Darwin had said that he would do anything he could to bring peace and that he hoped Hooker would do the same in order to keep from "widening the gap." Darwin regretted that Falconer was going to publish a formal reclamation of his claims. The squabbling, Darwin feared, would "sink scientific men."[73] In searching for a solution to the problem, Darwin finally relied upon a historical image: "Do see Falconer and see whether you can at all influence him by saying what in appearance reclamations always have, and that the future historians of science alone ought to settle such points. It is wretched to see men fighting so for a little fame."[74] The incident so pained Darwin that he actually wrote a letter to the *Athenaeum* ("the first and last time I shall take such a step"). He said he would include a word in his own defense (though it was never clear that he was attacked) and provided a publicist's dictum: "On the principle if one puffs oneself, one had better puff handsomely."[75]

Darwin always regretted direct involvement. When he ventured to write to the *Athenaeum* in response to letters urging publishers to sell their books "cut," Darwin called himself an ass for doing so.[76] It was also noteworthy that he could get worked up enough to write a public letter about something as trivial as trimming the edges of pages, but he did no such thing concerning the profound implications of his theory for humanity. On another occasion, he claimed to be "gnashing my teeth at my own folly" for writing in a newspaper. And part of the reason for his chagrin was the airing of scientific dirty linen in public; he added, "It shows well that a scientific man had better be trampled in dirt than squabble."[77]

Darwinism Triumphant

By the end of the 1860s, the Darwinians had won. Among the educated classes, the evolutionary view prevailed, but a large part of the general public probably remained ignorant of Darwin's theory. The "missing links" argument had been popular among the uneducated majority, which had focused on the religious and ideological implications of natural selection. More specifically, it was the contradiction of the biblical creation story that attracted most attention when religion was the issue. The broad public may not even have understood why there was so much fuss about Darwin—other than the implications of man's relationship to apes rather than angels. But the response in the higher classes, including scientists and clergy, showed the rest of society that the issues *must* be important.[78]

The triumph of Darwinism was working in conjunction with social and political factors, not just scientific ones. The professionalization of science helped to sharpen the debate concerning the role of the church in British higher education, a role that weakened during the mid-nineteenth century. Ultimately, one could be a professional scientist without being indebted to the Church of England. *The Origin* was a useful lever for Huxley and other young scientists who wanted to widen the gap between science and theology. Darwinism also was both cause and effect in the way power was shifting—from being vested exclusively in an elite class to being shared with a growing middle class. Huxley's lectures to the working class were constructed artfully to take advantage of the political ferment. Evolution, he told his audiences, was a weapon against traditional prejudices and a tool for improvement. Evolution showed how far man could come from lowly origins, and science became a window revealing the potential of those not born to aristocracy.[79]

As early as 1859, Huxley's lectures were a success by any standard, as artisans from all over London packed the talks. Three decades of dissent against a state-supported church came to a head during the period. The bishops' monopoly on knowledge, government, and education was being eroded. Huxley was not attacking religion so much as he was "Theology [and] Parsondom . . . both of which are in my mind the natural & irreconcilable enemies of Science." Huxley's devotion to the rebellion against aristocracy and "parsondom" later took the form of creating his own Working Men's College, teaming up with the Christian Socialists to do so.[80]

Hooker became president of the British Association for the Advancement of Science in 1868, followed by Huxley's ascendancy to the same office in 1870. Hooker had begun to tire of combat. Even Owen was having a hard time provoking Hooker, who wrote to Huxley: "I have answered Owen, & wish to God that Lockyer [Norman Lockyer, science editor of the *Reader*] would close the correspondence with my answer. This work will do no end of evil to Science. I say again I do not care for Owen's attacks, as I hope the chastity of my answers will show. . . . Ever yours in truth."[81] The letter was written by a man certain of his knowledge, to which the closing attested. Hooker still loathed the personal aspects of controversy and was especially irritated at being dragged against his will into a debate with Owen.

By the end of the decade, the Darwinians' hard push to open science to new ideas was less urgent, as they had won their professional goals and they themselves had become the high priests of scientific truth. Hooker criticized a scientist's work with a microscope, and then, sounding rather like those old-guard scientists whom Owen epitomized and whom Huxley and Hooker had fought so fiercely, facetiously proposed what amounted to indoctrination: "I proposed a tax on microscopes some years ago, exempting Professors only—Recommend to him a mild course of study—to be followed by a reperusal of your lecture, after which you may tell him safely that he may write again."[82] Science again was the province of an elect—who now were Darwinians.

Hooker had not lost his sensitivity to what would influence the public. In discussing heredity with Darwin, Hooker told him that Darwin's hypothesis of pangenesis— how traits were passed from one generation to another—was hazy. After alluding to articles in the *Athenaeum* and *Gardener's Chronicle,* Hooker noted that Darwin did not explain himself "sufficiently for the common reader's understanding." He did not have an answer for Darwin because neither he nor Darwin understood heredity, but he did advise that Darwin consider using Huxley's concept of *potentiality* in explaining heredity, rather than the term *gemmules.* Hooker's reasoning was simple: "Potentiality" was a useful image, much as the atom was useful for chemists, and "'throwing off gemmules' is hard to hold in head as a real vital process." Huxley's image of "differences in influence," on the other hand, was deemed intelligible.[83]

A major problem for Darwin was explaining how traits were passed from one generation to the next. Though Gregor Mendel had published his work on heredity in mid-decade, it remained "undiscovered" until the turn of the century. Darwin's theory of "pangenesis" simply hypothesized the existence of "gemmules" in body fluids, and those gemmules were manufactured by each part of the body, which in turn was replicated in offspring. In the process of fertilization, the gemmules from each parent were blended in the offspring. Darwin believed that characteristics of offspring were the result of blended traits of parents, an idea that stands in contrast to the Mendelian "all-or-nothing" existence of a trait in offspring. But in the letter quoted above, Hooker was concerned only about the image conveyed by Darwin's words, not about the substantive scientific issue.

Darwin and his allies did not relax, though. Hooker wanted to know how many languages *The Origin* had appeared in, how many American and English editions, and "any other data as to its reception abroad," in order "to disprove the statement that the theory is 'Just fading away.'" Darwin was glad to hear that Hooker was taking the offensive and reported that there was almost "universal" belief in evolution.

Despite this universal belief, Darwin went on carefully to provide data: four English editions, one or two American, two French, two German, one Dutch, one Italian, and "several (as I was told) Russian editions." Darwin added that *Variations Under Domestication* had appeared, or would soon appear, in two English editions, one American, one German, one French, and one Italian. For good measure, he reported that Haeckel recently had written him that interest in *The Origin* continued very strong in Germany.[84]

Darwin concerned himself with a wide range of publications, reflecting diverse audiences and perspectives. This fact suggests that he did not consider the debate a narrow scientific one and did grasp its significance beyond questions of biology. The periodicals included the *Pall Mall Gazette,* which one might call an establishment paper, and the radical *Leader.* The *Pall Mall Gazette* was a conservative organ and was one of a few papers that every member of Parliament would read. Its circulation was only about eight thousand by the early 1870s, its readers typically having educational levels from fair to high and belonging to the middle and upper classes. In contrast, the *Leader* was a radical-socialist-positivist journal and appealed to a small circle of middle-class, educated radicals. Its circulation in 1860 has been estimated at only about five hundred, and its content was divided between politics and cultural matters.

Another publication followed by Darwin, the *Athenaeum,* endorsed Darwin in the 1860s. A weekly with in-depth coverage of events in the learned world, it was regarded highly by literary and scientific people. The *Quarterly Review*, noted for its coverage of economics, parliamentary reform, and church and state, had the largest circulation among quarterlies of the period. It appealed to an educated, upper- and upper-middle-class audience, especially people with Tory views. The *Spectator* was another noteworthy periodical of limited circulation, having only about five thousand readers by the early 1870s, but it, too, had good coverage of scientific and religious issues, with readers in the middle to upper-middle classes. A politically liberal publication, in the 1860s it was among the most influential monthlies concentrating on political commentary.[85] These few publications suggest the breadth of Darwin, Huxley, and Hooker's concern—radical to conservative politics, circulations ranging from small to substantial, audiences running the gamut from working-class readers to members of Parliament, and content including cultural issues, religion, science, and politics.

Darwin, still a behind-the-lines officer, was not going to let the troops relax. He brought to Hooker's attention a "monstrous" article in the *Pall Mall Gazette* and an article in the *North British Quarterly* that apparently had criticized both Hooker and Huxley. Darwin also asked Hooker to let him know the author of a *Quarterly Review* article on design.[86]

Despite being convinced of the almost universal belief in evolution, Darwin still was obsessed with winning public approval. He complimented an address by Hooker and had seen reports in the *Times, Telegraph, Spectator,* and *Athenaeum,* had heard of reports in other newspapers, and had ordered a bundle. He said that the *Times* had reported "miserably," that he "was very glad" with *Leader,* and that the *Spectator* had pitched into Hooker a little over theology. After a little more praise for the address, Darwin said that he was especially proud of what Hooker said about him: "What is far more important than anything . . . is the conviction which I feel that you will have immensely advanced the belief in the evolution of species. This will follow from the publicity of the occasion. . . . It will make a great step in public opinion."[87] For good measure, Darwin said he hoped that Owen would find the snubbing by Hooker to be "bitter." Sounding like Huxley, Darwin was going to be satisfied with nothing less than annihilation of his opposition, wanting Owen to suffer a bit more in the wake of defeat. Obviously, Owen still irritated Darwin, who was angered by the suggestion that he would take any ideas from Owen, "there being nothing to take"; "I do not care a d—— [*sic*] for Owen." Darwin had little magnanimity in victory.[88]

Triumph did not temper Huxley's rhetoric. Even though the Darwinians had prevailed, Huxley remained on the offensive, blunt to a fault. He queried a colleague about a *Pall Mall Gazette* reviewer who had "made a donkey of himself." "Do you care to skewer him? If so I will write you a note which you can if you like send on to the Pall Mall."[89] A well-meaning minister asked Huxley where one could find answers to questions about Darwin's theory. Huxley sarcastically replied that he would find "fair answers" by "five or six years serious & practical study of physical & biological science, accompanied by due discipline in the principles of Newton's inductive logic," followed by a return to *The Origin.*[90] Huxley, probably provoked by the mere fact that the man was a cleric, still had little charity toward men of the church. Earlier, Hooker related to Darwin that Huxley had delivered a splendid lecture to working men but had offended "the clergy totally without cause or warrant."[91] Huxley's life-long fight with the clergy was related partly to philosophy and partly to life circumstances. Philosophically, he attacked the clergy for shackling science in theological chains. But ecclesiastical privilege goaded him, too, seeing the Cambridge clergy draw a thousand pounds a year while he toiled and scrimped to support his family. By the time of *The Origin,* he was spoiling for a fight with the clergy,[92] and the book served him doubly well by giving him both an excuse and solid scientific material.

Hooker still found Owen offensive but kept his dislike to himself. Hooker told Darwin that Owen was "an awful ass," telling lies in every paragraph of an article, but he did not bother to go public with the damnation.[93] He remained the gentleman, and it was becoming more good fun, now that the war had been won. But still he worried about the image of science:

> What a bother the papers link up about any mild theology! . . . one calls me an atheist & all that is bad; to me, who do not intend to answer their abuse, misquotations . . . & blunders it is all really very good fun. There were gentle disapproving allusions at Kew church today I am told! I am beginning to feel quite a great man! . . .
>   . . . Several got drunk as usual at the Red Lion. I do wish I could persuade Lubbock to drop

that very silly club. He is now the head & front of it; & it really is a scandal to science, & how-ever it might have once been good . . . 25 years ago is now completely out of place, out of date, & out of keeping with the age & standing of the member.[94]

John Lubbock, a banker and distinguished amateur scientist, had taken revelry too far for Hooker's sense of decorum. The Red Lion Club would not have suited Hooker, anyway, despite being a group of progressive scientists. The club was in-clined toward very boisterous, often juvenile socializing, which included growling at the waiters who served them, rather than saying "thank you," and wagging pos-teriors instead of applauding after club speeches. The club crest was a red lion holding a tankard of ale in one paw and a churchwarden pipe in the other.[95]

The confidence of the Darwinians was reflected in Darwin's advising Hooker not to bother addressing an issue—specifically, pangenesis, which Darwin said had too few friends, even though he still had faith that it was the best hypothesis of inherit-ance. Darwin probably stretched things a bit when he said that he did "not now care how much I may be pitched into." A few months later, he told Hooker to take no notice of an attack in the *Athenaeum,* although it was written by Owen and was "trans-parently false" in stating that Darwin's theory was grounded in pigeons.[96] The war was over, and by the end of the decade, the victors were engaging the enemy less frequently and more selectively. When they did engage in a fight, it was more a matter of habit than necessity.

A New Age for Science

During the 1860s, the Darwinian triad built a coalition that was systematically and simultaneously both scientific and public-minded. Darwin cheered for "our cause," verbally caressed Hooker as "my public," and goaded Huxley's efforts before "edu-cated mobs." The sense of the public was limited generally to scientists and the edu-cated elite, as Darwin, Huxley, and Hooker incrementally won opinion over to their side with carefully placed reviews and vigorous public debates. Over the course of the decade, the concept of the public broadened, and the lust for rhetorical blood-letting declined. Darwin and Hooker criticized Huxley's verbal brawling, and Huxley too regretted incidents that might bring science into disrepute. Although Darwin could present his English and foreign editions of *The Origin* as empirical evidence of his success, he remained irritated by Owen and continued to direct Huxley and Hooker toward offending publications. However, Darwin was able to tell Hooker and Huxley to ignore some articles.

The three ushered in a new era in science, not just in terms of Darwin's momentous scientific achievement but also in the way in which the three consistently and deliber-ately responded to the public and planned for presentation to the public. It was the be-ginning of the new period of science, in which a trained class of specialists was devoted to science as a profession, in contrast to an earlier generation of natural scientists who often had a theological agenda. Huxley, the provocateur, seized upon the opportunities to separate the two types, and in so doing, he promoted the growth of science as a profession.

From a purely scientific perspective, the vigorous cultivation of public opinion was unnecessary, but it was important if one hoped to influence the direction and force of opinion in a democratic society. Perhaps the significance of publicity concerning natural selection can best be argued by analogy to another important idea born in the 1860s, and that is Mendelian genetics. Darwin used similar logic when he extrapolated from domestic pigeons to wild animals. In *The Origin,* he pointed out that pigeon breeders selected traits in order to breed fancier animals; in doing so, they were acting as a mechanism for controlling the attributes of offspring. Natural selection was like the pigeon breeder—traits that benefited survival were selected over those that did not, and the favorable traits were passed on to subsequent generations. In the course of a single decade, the scientific community largely was won over to a Darwinian view.

In the middle of the decade, a Moravian monk, Gregor Mendel, presented a paper on the heredity of characteristics in peas. He was answering one of the great questions—how traits were passed from one generation to another—that still puzzled Darwin.[97] Mendel bred some thirty thousand peas at the Augustinian monastery at Brunn, as he studied the distribution of paired characteristics, such as short and tall, wrinkled or smooth texture of seeds, from one generation of plants to the next. He revealed his results in 1865, in a paper delivered to the Natural Sciences Society of Brunn, and published it in the 1866 proceedings of the society. His work on dominant and recessive "elements," as he called them, was distributed to more than a hundred scientific institutions across Europe, and Mendel sent reprints to scientists.[98] Although Mendel had contact with the scientific community, he did not have the kind of publicity network that Darwin nurtured. Some scientists had access to Mendel's work, but probably they were not ready to look at the problem of heredity through the Mendelian lens. They were still focused on issues raised in the Darwinian perspective of evolution. Nevertheless, the circulation of Mendel's ideas was limited, compared to that of Darwin's, and it was not until 1900 that Mendel was "discovered." However, alternative outcomes do not exist in history, and it is not possible to know which factor—prevailing scientific ideas or publicity—put Mendelian genetics aside for a third of a century. Without the public debate, there is little way of knowing if Mendel was too early or was simply unknown. Darwin and his allies, on the other hand, proclaimed his ideas to the public and explained them time and again. The publicity helped his ideas emerge from the tangled bank in which theology, science, and public apprehension were entwined.

Chapter *2*

Huxley and Wilberforce: The Day That Made "Darwin's Bulldog"

> The standard account is a wholly one-sided effusion from the winning side,
> put together long after the event, uncritically copied from book to book, and
> shaped by the hagiographic conventions of Victorian life and letters.
> —STEPHEN J. GOULD, "KNIGHT TAKES BISHOP?"

In the study of history, sometimes it is necessary to remind ourselves that we may have a very different perspective on historical events than the actors who took part in them—namely, that we know what happened next. Through a century-old lens, Darwinism's march through history appears bold and inevitable, due to the historical habit of presuming the correctness of consequences.

This distortion of the Darwinian triumph is encapsulated in the now-mythic debate in 1860 between Huxley and Bishop Samuel Wilberforce. The confrontation has become a symbol of the conflict between Darwinism and conservatism, the latter in both science and theology. The debate involved figures who were central to the controversy—most notably Huxley and Hooker for the defense, Owen and Wilberforce for the prosecution. It also was the public-science event of the year, not because a few people argued about *The Origin,* but because it took place under the auspices of the British Association for the Advancement of Science and so involved prominent names and ideas in science.

The Darwinians' publicity tactics and scientific ideas had prevailed over the course of the 1860s, but the opposition had not been quiet. The debate shows the extension of the publicity-building activities of the 1860s into the process of writing history and creating history. Huxley has come to personify progressivism and enlightenment, as he took on and conquered in debate the forces of conservatism and darkness, represented by Wilberforce. At an 1860 meeting of the British Association in Oxford, Wilberforce, defending orthodoxy and assailing Darwin's recently published theory of speciation, asked Huxley from which side of his family, his grandmother's or his grandfather's, he claimed descent from an ape. When Huxley's turn came, he intellectually dissected Wilberforce's weak arguments and then verbally leveled him for turning the pursuit of truth into trite mockery. The audience loved Huxley, the winner. Or at least the myth says so.

Gould maintains that the debate was the "key event" in the history of science and calls the story "archetypal," with Huxley and Wilberforce as symbols of science and religion, light and darkness.[1] In the 1860s, Darwin, Huxley, and Hooker were fighting for the more immediate purpose of winning support for natural selection, but the construction of the myth of Huxley's victory occurred over nearly four decades and across two generations of scientists. The myth was created with a clear vision of the symbolic significance of the event for scientists in the late nineteenth century and in the future. The details of the standard histories vary slightly, but there is general agreement about the importance of the debate as a symbol of the triumph of scientific method. The event has become mythic, in that it has transcended time and place to become a symbol of truth triumphing over falsehood, learning over ignorance. This myth has been accepted as fact in most histories of the event, although in recent decades several revisionists have criticized the validity of such an inflated depiction.

The symbolic and mythic potential of the event is enhanced by Wilberforce's being such an ideal historical foil to Huxley. The young scientist is set against the older theologian, the former clawing his way up the professional ladder while the latter basks in the glow of an Oxford education and the material blessings of church affiliation. Huxley the agnostic treats the controversy with great gravity and studiousness, while Wilberforce does not, instead relying impetuously upon wit, charm, and the knowledge of others, especially Richard Owen, to carry him through the public squabbles about evolution. These contrasts make Wilberforce an ideal candidate for the role of villainous theologian, a personification of intellectual conservatism and church meddling. Even the bishop's nickname, "Soapy Sam," which he earned for being slippery in debate, supports the myth by implying he was merely sly, not intelligent. However, Wilberforce represented only one strand of thought within the Anglican church, albeit a significant one. In his day he was viewed as one of the "old-style Tories," who the liberal *London Telegraph* felt hampered the strong progressive leadership needed by the Church of England. In fact, he was unpopular among church liberals, whom he criticized for not taking miracles seriously enough.[2] Wilberforce's skill as an orator was undeniable, but his reputation rested largely upon his style, his ability to communicate with a large audience, and a sense of humor that put people at ease. These assets probably contributed to his reputation as a fund-raiser and organizer. He was less comfortable with a university crowd, perhaps due to the fact that his talent was not in his intellect or reasoning power. For example, Wilberforce enjoyed nature, but it was attractive to him as evidence of God's power and mystery, not as a logical puzzle to be solved by mere mortals. The idea that he lost the debate seems more gratifying in light of certain less-than-admirable personality traits, especially his tendency toward impulsivity, which may account for his ill-advised, offhand remark about Huxley's ancestry, and his belief that speculative freedom had boundaries. Wilberforce believed that Darwin had exceeded these limits in *The Origin*.[3]

Most writers and readers of history must derive a certain satisfaction in seeing honesty and bravery win over treachery and deceit. Personal characteristics of both Huxley and Wilberforce can be offered selectively to create exactly that image. Thus, Huxley pursues truth at any cost as he toils mightily without family or institutional favors. And Wilberforce, a bishop with a Cambridge-educated father, could appear to dismiss an issue as important as evolution with flippant, even rude, remarks.

Almost immediately after the debate concluded, facts incongruous to the mythic version of the debate appeared. The bishop was not sufficiently shamed to end his comedy about evolution. In an undated poem, apparently written sometime after the debate, he joked and punned:

> Oft had I heard, but deemed the tale untrue,
> That man was cousin to Kangaroo;
> That before whose face all nature quailed,
> Was but the monkey's heir, though unentailed;
> . . .
> From self-degrading science keep me free,
> And from the pride that apes humility![4]

In the year following their clash, Huxley and Wilberforce actually served together as vice presidents of the Zoological Society. Although this cooperation apparently drew little public attention, they worked with one another on five occasions as they dealt with society finances and acquisitions. Wilberforce wrote to Huxley in 1871 to thank him for an article, unspecified in the letter; this action hints that the breech and animosity were not so complete as legend might suggest.[5] It is not surprising that historians have given very little attention to these bits of joint effort on the two men's parts, because the actions do not fit very well with the common depiction of victor and vanquished or supposed spite and strife. They are incongruent with the image of a clergy-damning Huxley or a reactionary, snide Wilberforce.

The Debate

The absence of a verbatim record of what either man said, minutes of the meeting, or even a very complete account from any single contemporary news story means that the debate must be reconstructed from a patchwork of sources. The outline of events presented here is a composite of common elements presented in several major works on Darwinism and the nineteenth century, including quotations and details from Leonard Huxley's *Life and Letters of Thomas Henry Huxley.*[6]

The British Association for the Advancement of Science held its thirtieth annual meeting in Oxford from June 27 to July 4, 1860. According to *Jackson's Oxford Journal,* about seventeen hundred people attended the meeting.[7] Issues raised by Darwin, whose *On the Origin of Species* had been published in Britain the previous year, had caused some controversy for several months. Some saw the meetings in Oxford as an opportunity for confronting Darwinism, and as a chance for Darwinians to present a defense.[8] At a mid-week meeting, Richard Owen restated his anti-evolution opinions about the differences between man and other animals. Huxley, then a young professor of paleontology, rose and gave "direct and unqualified contradiction" to Owen and promised to provide the denial in print. Huxley was on the association's Saturday program with Wilberforce, whose reputation as an orator gave the young scientist second thoughts about taking part in the program. By Friday, rumors were flying about the inevitable clash of Darwinians and anti-Darwinians. Owen primed Wilberforce on the weaknesses of Darwin's theory.

There was some excitement in the air about the coming meeting, and the session even had to be moved to a larger room to accommodate the unexpectedly large audience. Huxley and Wilberforce were only two of about a dozen speakers. A major attraction may have been Professor John William Draper, of New York, a well-known historian of science who was scheduled to present a paper about Darwin. Draper's sixty- to ninety-minute presentation, which followed six shorter reports, apparently prompted some lively discussion and provoked some anti-Darwin remarks. Then Wilberforce spoke, provoking some hearty shouts of approval from clergy in the audience. He was carrying the audience of scientists along with him by virtue of his wit and confidence, although Huxley could see that the bishop knew little of evolution. According to Leonard Huxley, the speech had small scientific value, and it was obvious that the bishop had been "'crammed up to the throat,' and knew nothing first hand." The bishop spoke for a full hour, with "inimitable spirit, emptiness and unfairness."[9] Then, apparently taken by the force of his own rhetoric, the bishop turned to Huxley and asked him if it was through his grandmother or grandfather that he claimed descent from a monkey. At that point, Huxley turned to the man seated next to him and whispered, "The Lord hath delivered him into mine hands."

Huxley wrote years later that the bishop had justified the severest response, "and I made up my mind to let him have it."[10] The bishop seated himself, the audience roaring approval and applauding thunderously. The young professor, his solemn demeanor contrasting sharply with his opponent's jovial, sarcastic needling, prepared to speak. He said that he had heard nothing in terms of science to rebut evolution and briefly explained Darwin's ideas. Then, gravely, quietly, Huxley said he would rather have an ape for a grandfather than a man possessed of great means and influence who employed those faculties merely to introduce ridicule into serious scientific discussion. The audience applauded and cheered Huxley, and some accounts say that a woman even fainted amid such intellectual crisis.

Two or three anti-Darwinians followed Huxley, then came pro-Darwinian presentations by John Lubbock and Joseph Dalton Hooker, who probably made the most substantive statement in support of evolution. At the time, the forty-three-year-old Hooker, assistant director of the Royal Botanic Gardens at Kew, was a respected botanist. Several historians have cited Hooker, not Huxley, as offering the more important *scientific* response to Wilberforce.[11]

Variations on the story claim that Huxley said he would rather have an ape than a bishop for a grandfather, while others stress the bad manners of the bishop rather than his ignorance of science. Leonard Huxley says that the debate could not be represented as an immediate victory for Darwinism. Even though he presents a version of the story portraying his father as every bit the hero, Leonard Huxley hedges it slightly by stating that the importance of the event is in the "open resistance . . . to authority. . . . Instead of being crushed under ridicule, the new theories secured a hearing."[12]

Although the stories differ, this is not to say that the modern mythic version of the debate is factually wrong. General agreement exists as to the broad outline of the event, with differences usually focusing on specific quotations or audience responses.[13] But the debate has become more important as a symbol than as an intrinsically significant event. In fact, at least three revisionists have offered strong arguments that the debate was rather inconsequential and in fact went unnoticed in the nineteenth century.[14] The historical problem is the lack of authoritative or complete records of the debate. Those that exist are very biased, such as letters by participants and witnesses, or accounts written long afterward, such as those contained in biographies and reminiscences published in periodicals. Thus, the first task is to assess the traditional, or mythic, views of the debate and see how these compare to the record that does exist—in letters, biographies, and the press.

Historians and the Debate

A reading of more than twenty accounts of the Huxley-Wilberforce debate shows that most historians declared Huxley the winner. A few challenged the conventional wisdom about the meeting, but most accounts depicted the encounter as dramatic, sensational, and symbolic. Only a handful noted that the actual facts of the debate might be at issue.[15] The typical portrayal gave Huxley a decisive victory, and saw the dramatic moment as a symbol of truth over ignorance. The revisionists, taking a contrary view, questioned Huxley's victory, the drama, and the impact of the session. The problem, the revisionists also noted, is the lack of a good record of the event.

The debate myth shows how history is built, at times, more upon foundations of belief and hindsight than upon historical evidence. This is not to deny the evidence for a Huxley victory; in fact, there is substantial evidence for such an outcome. But letters and articles that support a contrary conclusion, a Wilberforce victory, or that call into doubt that anyone actually won the debate, often have been ignored. In addition, material supporting a Huxley triumph has been treated rather uncritically. For example, the source most commonly cited for Huxley's victory is a letter by Huxley himself. The letter, written a few months after the meeting, clearly is biased,[16] and rarely has it been balanced with a self-interested report by Wilberforce, whose correspondence shows that he was quite unaware of his defeat. He even believed himself the victor, writing a few days afterward of "thoroughly" beating Huxley. Wilberforce's son Reginald, in *Life of the Right Reverend Samuel Wilberforce, D.D.,* wrote that the bishop "made a long and eloquent speech condemning Dr. Darwin's theory. . . . which made a great impression."[17] Reginald originally reported that "a certain learned professor" retorted, "I would rather be descended from an ape than a bishop." But after a protest by Huxley, the remark was changed in the Errata page of the volume to "If I had to choose between being descended from an ape or from a man who would use his great powers of rhetoric to crush an argument, I should prefer the former." Wilberforce's son, unlike Huxley's, did not build a history favorable to his father. The Huxley letter also gets far more attention than another important source—Darwin himself, who in a July 1860 letter referred to Hooker's victory, not Huxley's.[18] So Darwin either was under the impression that Hooker had carried the day, or Darwin just wanted to make Hooker feel good. As we have seen, Darwin had a habit of heaping praise on his allies.

In the letters, reminiscences, and biographies that have been cited by more than one historian, the problems of bias and—particularly in sources written or published many years later—selective recall persisted. Among sources cited frequently, several stand out. In *Letters of John Richard Green,* the author refers to Huxley's "smashing" of Wilberforce. Green, who became a historian of note, was an undergraduate at Oxford at the time, and the letter was written on July 3, 1860, which makes it a timely source. However, according to the editor of Green's letters, the undergraduate had a strong personal dislike of Wilberforce.[19]

Two other letters written shortly after the debate also are commonly cited: a letter from Hooker to Charles Darwin on July 2, 1860; and a Darwin letter to Huxley on July 3, 1860.[20] The problem of tendentiousness in the sources is apparent. Two other accounts showed up some years later. In *Reminiscences of Oxford* (1907), the Rev. W. Tuckwell provides a colorful and dramatic rendition—almost a half-century after the event. There is nothing to suggest that Tuckwell had any strong prejudices concerning the participants. But with such an expanse of time, Tuckwell's recollections could have been influenced greatly by subsequent stories, told by historians and participants, that had grown up around the debate.[21] In *Macmillan's* magazine in 1898, an article by Isabella Sidgwick, who was in the audience, briefly characterizes Huxley's victory. As with the Tuckwell account, the time lapse is cause for concern about the accuracy of the recollection.[22] Perhaps the "best" accounts are those in the *Athenaeum* newspaper, July 7 and July 14, 1860; these are the contemporary versions that might be the most objective, as no prejudice is apparent. The newspaper does not mention a winner.[23] The *Athenaeum* had a modest circulation of about fifteen thousand, was unaligned either politically or religiously, and aimed at an upscale audience. The *Athenaeum* led other weeklies in the nineteenth century, as it covered a wide range of subjects, including literature, music, theater, art, and news of learned societies. It argued for the acceptance of Darwinism in the 1860s but changed course in 1871, when the magazine changed editors.[24]

Janet Browne, commenting on the Darwin-Hooker correspondence, points out that information published in works belonging to the nineteenth-century "lives and letters" genre "was often presented so that the subject was moulded to fit the ideals and conventions of his memorialist, and so that myth and dogma were perpetuated." Huxley, she says, was an example of a great man who created his own biography. In the case of the 1860 debate, historians continue to use the *Lives and Letters* of Darwin, Huxley, and Hooker, all of whom put forward the same "official" version, which is a composite story written almost twenty-five years later by Hooker. Francis Darwin and Leonard Huxley, with the help of Hooker and Thomas Huxley, "forged a legend that remains in the same conventional format today."[25]

This compilation of commonly cited sources reveals a historical record that is slanted and limited. Of course, all historical records are biased to some extent, so often having survived by fiat rather than by design, and never according to principles of random sampling. Here the revisionists have taken the initiative, with their very different interpretations of essentially the same record. However, the *Athenaeum* reports reveal that it has not been necessary to rely so heavily upon such self-interested sources as letters. In fact, Lucy Brown, in her book on the Victorian press, concludes that the period's newspapers were more dominated by "news" than modern newspapers, which devote proportionately more space to features, analysis, and even fiction. Newspapers of the era, she says, tended to provide readers with factual reports rather than opinions and assessment.[26]

The Revisionists

Jensen, who cites newspaper reviews and stories, says that the lack of press coverage may have been the result of poor handling of the press by the British Association.[27] This apparently resulted in part from poor planning by the British Association, but the press was not devoting extensive coverage to the annual meeting. In addition, the press tended to give an inordinate amount of attention to the papers and addresses with Darwinian themes. Of the hundreds of papers presented each year, only a few dealt with Darwin, but those few usually were selected for press attention.[28] Like Jensen, Altholz says that it is difficult to assess specific actions at the meeting, but he maintains that the debate was of symbolic and historical significance. Gould is the one revisionist who gives adequate attention to the press coverage, which, he notes, was limited, and he quotes the *Athenaeum* extensively. Gould differs from the conventional histories not on the issue of whether Huxley or Wilberforce won, but in arguing that it was Hooker who actually made the better argument.[29]

These revisionists agree that good eyewitness accounts of the debate are lacking, and all three, while skeptical of the details of the event, acknowledge its symbolic value. The last point is difficult to assail because symbols are cultural, and as such they may be questioned but will thrive, so long as members of the culture acknowledge the symbol's meaning. The intellectual culture of science history has no doubt about the vitality of the Huxley-Wilberforce symbol. However, given the lack of good primary evidence—including the lamentable absence of specifics and of eyewitness accounts—historians have compensated by relying on later letters and reminiscences. There is a press record, one that merits reconsideration not only for its content but also because it is a fairly extensive source. Press reports constitute a problematical record, because what appears in print is filtered not only by the observer, but also possibly by several editors, and the content must conform to style and space constraints. That is in the best case. It also was a common practice, found once in the reports of the 1860 British Association meetings, simply to reprint stories from other newspapers. Before rummaging about in the newspaper reports, the historian must reconsider traditional sources of information—the letters of people recalling the event—not only for content but for the circumstances under which they were collected. Of particular interest are the efforts of Leonard Huxley and Francis Darwin to reconstruct the event and the impact their solicitations may have had on people's memories.

The Historical Foundation of the Myth

Huxley did not provide an immediate account of the clash, and Leonard Huxley said that "the same cause which prevented his writing home the story of the day's work nearly led to his absence from the scene."[30] Huxley had planned to leave Oxford before the debate in order to join his wife, a plan that he postponed when a colleague in science chanced to meet Huxley and pleaded with him not to abandon them. So Huxley stayed and the next morning after the debate left to join his wife, perhaps sacrificing an immediate opportunity to write his story. However, he provided some detail a little over two months later in a letter to Dr. Frederick Dyster, who had been a friend since the mid-1850s as a result of Dyster's interest in marine zoology.[31] Huxley's version fits easily with the heroic account that has evolved:

I had listened with great attention to the Lord Bishop's speech but had been unable to discover either a new fact or a new argument in it—small indeed the question raised as to my
personal predilections in the matter of ancestry. That it would not have occurred to me to bring
forward such a topic as that for discussion myself, but that I was quite ready to meet the Right
Rev. prelate even on that ground—I then said the question is put to me would I rather have a
miserable ape for a grandfather or a man highly endowed by nature and honoured by great means
and influence, and who employs these faculties and that influence for the mere purpose of in-
troducing ridicule into a grave scientific discussion—I unhesitatingly affirm my preference for
the ape.

    . . . Lubbock and Hooker spoke after me with great force and among us we shut up the
bishop.[32]

Huxley went on to say that there were several hundred people in the room, and "if
he had dealt with the subject fairly and modestly I would not have treated him in
this way. . . . I believe I was the most popular man in Oxford for full four and twenty
hours afterwards." But even Huxley's own account divides the glory with two others and does not assign it all to himself, as the legend has it.

Huxley believed that he had prevailed, and the fact that he was energized by the
confrontation was revealed in a letter to Hooker in early August, in which Huxley
said they had "a lot to do in the way of smiting the Amalekites."[33] But Huxley's perception of victory was not created in isolation. Letters to him shortly after the event
may have helped the young professor cultivate a sense of triumph. In three letters
written within a few weeks of the meeting, Darwin, the senior statesman of evolution, praised the younger man's intelligence and daring. In the first letter, Darwin
said that he had heard from Hooker, "giving me some account of the awful battle
which has raged about 'species' at Oxford. He tells me you fought nobly with Owen
(but I have heard no particulars) and that you answered the Bishop of Oxford capi-
tally." Darwin asked Huxley for an account of the battle and concluded, "Hooker
says he must have answered the bishop well."[34] Two days later, Darwin wrote again,
playfully asking Huxley how he could dare to attack a "live Bishop. . . . I am quite
ashamed of you. . . . By Jove, you seem to have done it well."[35] A few weeks later,
Darwin referred to a *Quarterly Review* article in which he was criticized by Owen.
Darwin asked Huxley, "By the way, how come it that you were not attacked? Does
Owen begin to find it more prudent to leave you alone? . . . From all that I hear
from several quarters, it seems that Oxford did the subject great good." The letter
did not say that Huxley had won, but Darwin clearly believed that the event had
concluded to his benefit.[36] Professor George Allman, a scientist who had known
Huxley for more than a decade and who later became president of the British Association, wrote a few days after the event that he had heard that Huxley had "pitched
into the Bishop of Oxford in grand style."[37] Darwin, as was his habit, was heaping
flattery upon allies, and a few years later he gave Hooker credit for the victory, saying that Hooker "did the Bishop so well at Oxford," showing Darwin's willingness

to give credit wherever it best served him—depending upon whom he was address-ing.[38] The idea of Huxley's victory was reinforced when George Rolleston, profes-sor of anatomy and physiology at Oxford, wrote Huxley that he, too, intended "to have a slap at the Base Bishop." He went on to chastise the "ignorantly orthodox" and assert how he believed he could "hold [his] own" with them.[39] Huxley appar-ently stoked Rolleston's bravado.

But in maintaining perspective on the event, a very important person in the affair should be kept in view—Hooker, who also gave Huxley credit for "turning the tables." But in the same letter, Hooker said that the audience could not hear Huxley. Hooker believed it was he, not Huxley, who finally "shut up" the bishop. Here, in part, is the important letter from Hooker to Darwin, written a few days after the meeting:

> Huxley and Owen had a furious battle over Darwin's absent body at Section D before my arrival of which more anon. Huxley was triumphant—you and your book forthwith became the topics of the day and I d——d the days and double d——d [sic] the topics too. . . . all the world was there to hear Sam Oxen. Well Sam Oxen got up and shouted for half an hour with inimitable spirit, ugliness and emptiness and unfairness. I saw he was coached by Owen and knew nothing and he said not a syllable, but what was in the Review. He ridiculed you badly and Huxley savagely. Huxley answered admirably and turned the tables, but *he could not throw his voice over so large an assembly nor command the audience and he did not allude to Sam's weak points nor put the matter in a form or way that carried the audience* [my emphasis]. The battle waxed hot. Lady Brewster fainted, the excitement increased as others spoke. My blood boiled. I felt my-self a dastard; now I saw my advantage. I swore to myself I would smite that Amalekite Sam hip and thigh if my heart jumped out of my mouth and I handed my name up to the President (Henslow) as ready to throw down the gauntlet. . . . I hit him in the wind at the first shot in 10 words taken from his own ugly mouth—and then proceeded to demonstrate in as few more: (1) that he could never have read your book; and (2) that he was absolutely ignorant of the rudiments of Botanical Science. . . . Sam was shut up—had not one word to say in reply, and the meeting was dissolved forthwith, leaving you master of the field after 4 hours battle. Huxley, who had borne all the previous brunt . . . told me it was splendid, and that he did not know before what stuff I was made of. I have been congratulated and thanked by the blackest coats and whitest stocks in Oxford.[40]

His comment about Huxley not being heard or understood by the audience is espe-cially noteworthy because Hooker had no reason to diminish the impact of Huxley. If anything, his motives would cause him to exaggerate the impact. But the com-ment also contradicts the many accounts that have a hush falling over a very atten-tive audience. Hooker believed, though, that it was not until after he spoke that Darwin "mastered the field."

When the Darwin and Huxley progeny began assembling materials for the *Lives and Letters* volumes of their fathers, the creation of the myth had started in earnest. Both Francis Darwin and Leonard Huxley presumed Huxley the conqueror, and they collected accounts and wrote books reflecting that view. They colluded in affirming details of the debate, as shown in a letter from Francis Darwin to Leonard Huxley:

> Dear Huxley,
>
> The eyewitness was Hooker. I suppose he told me not to publish his name, tho' I can't imagine why. I am pretty certain it was written for the "Life" in the '80s. It is most curious how different accounts vary.
>
> You will see your father's account of "the Lord has delivered" etc in the one volume version of the life "Charles Darwin, his life told etc" 1892[,] p. 240. There also is Freemantle's acct of the scene which I had not got when I was doing the Life. Your father's letter to me is by a misprint dated 1861 instead 1891. I have perfectly unfounded prejudice against Canon Farrar which would extend itself to his notes and you seem a little doubtful about them.[41]

Farrar, who is discussed below, emphasized in his account the impact of bad manners rather than science, a view that may not have suited Francis Darwin's purposes. A few years earlier, Francis Darwin had written to Thomas Huxley, "I wish I had some account of the celebrated Oxford meeting. . . . I should be glad of any account of it even if slightly tiflebornian [disarranged]."[42] Among the letters collected by Francis Darwin was one of 1895 from G. Johnstone Storey, in which Storey said, "The critical words were few, striking and easily remembered." He said that the audience was "unpleasantly partisan, a majority on the Bishop's side" and that Wilberforce introduced the subject of the descent of man, rousing the audience in the process: "When he sat down amid vociferous and excited applause, Huxley rose very slowly; and the first words of his rejoinder were '*I* had rather be the offspring of *two* [emphasis in original] apes, than be a man and afraid to face the truth'—an announcement which was followed by the counter-cheers of his minority. He then proceeded . . . , in contrast to the Bishop's passionate appeal, to correct the Bishop of Oxford's statements where erroneous and to reply to the parts of his argument which remained."[43]

The author of the letter was certain of the words, although the missive was written thirty-five years after he heard them. The account differs not only in words, but in placing the climactic part of Huxley's retort at the beginning rather than at the end of the speech. Huxley was in a minority, and there was no mention of his winning. Francis Darwin did not use the letter in *The Life and Letters of Charles Darwin*. One can only speculate as to why Leonard Huxley did not use the letter. First, the letter added little, if anything, to the portrait of Thomas Huxley that his son was painting in the *Life and Letters* volumes. However, one easily could interpret the omission of Storey's letter a bit more cynically: It did not fit well with the other versions of the debate that Leonard was collecting, for Storey did not report a victory, and he put the evolutionists in a minority in the audience. Though minor points, they were dissonant with the myth.

Several letters between Francis Darwin and Hooker show the effort involved in recreating the scene and the presumption that Huxley prevailed. Hooker wrote in

1897 that the idea of a "drawn battle" was "incomprehensible."[44] Francis Darwin said that Hooker's assessment was received with "much satisfaction," and that no one had considered Darwinism established after the Oxford debate, "but considered as a preliminary skirmish no one can doubt that it was won by evolutionists."[45] In that cycle of affirming opinions, Hooker wrote Francis Darwin again to state, "I never heard anything more effectively and calmly delivered than that crushing." He said that one of the "most potent prelates in England [was] brought to judgement."[46] Francis Darwin repeated his opinion a few years later, writing, "I do not see that there can be any doubt as to Huxley's having crushed the Bishop." He backed his opinion by pointing out that Huxley had said that the accounts by Green and Freemantle were "pretty correct."[47] So, over the course of about a decade, Francis Darwin had gone from trying to find "any" account to stating that there could not be "any doubt" that Huxley had crushed Wilberforce.

Leonard Huxley's motive in reconstructing the story is clear, but it should be conceded that, in seeking support for the Huxley side, he was finding it. At times he took the more conservative approach to history. For example, two accounts that he received in 1899 agree on Huxley's victory. The Oxford chemist A. G. Vernon Harcourt said that his recollections were very clear, though he could only approximate the words:

> The Bishop had rallied your father as to the descent from a monkey, asking in a sort of joke how recent this had been, whether it was his grandfather or further back. Your father in replying on this point first explained that the suggestion was of descent through thousands of generations from a common ancestor, and then went on to this effect—
>
> "But if this question is treated not as a matter for the calm investigation of science but as a matter of sentiment, and if I am asked whether I would choose to be descended from the poor animal of low intelligence and stooping gait who grins and chatters . . . , or from a man endowed with great ability and a splendid position who should use these gifts" (here, as the point became clear, there was a great outburst of applause which mostly drowned the end of the sentence) "to discredit and crush humble seekers after truth, I hesitate which answer to make."[48]

He went on to say that Huxley's words were better than these. At about the same time, only three days later in 1899, the Rev. F. W. Farrar wrote to Leonard Huxley about the meeting:

> [The bishop] had been talking of the perpetuity of species in Birds and then denying a fortiori the derivation of the species man from apes. He rhetorically invoked the help of feeling, and said (I swear to the sense and the form of the sentence, if not to the words) "if any one were to be willing to trace his descent through an ape as his grandfather would he be willing to trace his descent similarly on the side of his grandmother.["] It was (you see) the arousing of antipathy about degrading women. . . . It was not to the point, but it was to the purpose. It did not sound insolent, but unscientific and unworthy of the zoological argument which he had been sustaining. . . .

. . . and the impression distinctly was, that the Bishop's party, as they left the room, felt shocked; and recognized that the Bishop had forgotten to behave like a gentleman. The victory of your father was not the ironical dexterity showed by him but the fact that he had got a victory in respect to *manners and good breeding*. You must remember that the whole audience was made up of gentlefolk, who were not prepared to endorse anything vulgar. The speech which really left its mark *scientifically* on the meeting was the short one of Hooker, wherein he said that "he considered that Darwin's views were true in the field of Botany; and that . . . students should 'provisionally accept them as a *working hypothesis* in the field of the animal kingdom.' I am confident in the above statements. [Emphasis in original][49]

Farrar ended by saying, "The spiteful narrative which you quote from J. R. Green . . . is hardly worthy of him! I should say that to fair minds, the *intellectual* [emphasis in original] impression left by the discussion was that the Bishop had stated some tough points about the perpetuation of species, but that no one had really contributed any valuable points to the opposite side except Hooker, but that your father had scored a victory over Bishop Wilberforce in the question of good manners." Farrar's emphasis on manners may seem a bit misplaced, given the conventional interpretations of the meeting and of its importance as a symbol of science's opposing religion. However, his theme is not surprising in the context of the day—when the debate was not yet mythologized—and especially given the values of Victorian culture. It was extraordinarily ill-mannered and uncouth of Wilberforce to stoop so low as to bring into the debate the ancestry of a woman, Huxley's grandmother, because women were symbols of purity, which Wilberforce was tarnishing. Farrar's training was not in science, although he had studied the evolution of language, and so his criteria for judging the outcome went beyond the scientific merits of the combatants' remarks. Farrar, a church liberal who was sympathetic to the evolutionist side, also used the word "legend" in the letter, indicating a sense of the process at work.

There is some evidence that, by the 1890s, the myth was established. In an 1897 article in *American Naturalist,* the president of the American Psychological Association stated that the opposition to Darwinism "spoke through the Bishop of Oxford."[50] He made no other reference to Wilberforce, but in the eyes of some, already he had become the symbol of antiscience theology.

The Press Record

Historians' use of newspapers in interpreting the event has focused largely on only one of the numerous press reports of the 1860 British Association meetings. Thus, accounts that fail to support the myth have been given little attention. The *Athenaeum*, the press source most commonly cited concerning the debate, did not extensively cover the event, but it did report more on the meetings in general than other newspapers. Here is the entire coverage of Huxley-Wilberforce from this oft-cited source:

> Yet the main interest of the week has unquestionably centred in the Sections, where the intellectual activities have sometimes breathed over the courtesies of life like a sou'-wester, cresting the waves of conversation with white and brilliant foam. The flash, and play, and collisions in these Sections have been as interesting and amusing to the audiences as the Battle at Farmborough or the Volunteer Review to the general British public. The Bishop of Oxford has been famous in these intellectual contests, but Dr. Whewell, . . . Prof. Sedgwick, Mr. Crawford, and Prof. Huxley have each found foemen worthy of their steel, and made their charges and countercharges very much to their own satisfaction and the delight of their respective friends. The chief cause of contention has been the new theory of the Development of Species by Natural Selection—a theory open . . . to a good deal of personal quizzing, without, however, seriously crippling the usefulness of the physiological investigations on which it rests. The Bishop of Oxford came out strongly against a theory which holds it possible that man may be descended from an ape,—in which protest he is sustained by Prof. Owen, Sir Benjamin Brodie, Dr. Daubney, and the most eminent naturalists assembled at Oxford. But others—conspicuous among these, Prof. Huxley—have expressed their willingness to accept . . . all actual truth, even the last humiliating truth of a pedigree not registered in the Herald's College. The dispute has at least made Oxford uncommonly lively during the week.[51]

The *Athenaeum* stressed the contention and strife, without mention of a victor in any particular debate. Huxley was not alone among the antagonists, and it was not clear that a resounding refutation of Wilberforce took place. The paragraph says only that "friends" of each side were satisfied, indicating that no one had carried the general audience. The weekly cited amusement and not drama, from which one can draw no conclusions and which only raises more questions about the meeting. It would be a bit unusual for the *Athenaeum* to lean toward humor if the event were of recognizable intellectual significance, primarily because it was a publication prestigious among literary and scientific audiences, in its own field holding a stature comparable to that of the *Times*. The paper was dominant among weeklies and, throughout the 1860s, argued for acceptance of Darwin's theories.[52]

A longer *Athenaeum* account of the debate was given the following week, and this was the most detailed contemporary account of the clash. The article outlined the arguments of both Wilberforce and Huxley on the issue, but Hooker's response received a whole column, about three times as much space as Huxley's. There was no mention of the bishop's question about Huxley's ancestry, nor of the latter's response. The article said only that Huxley "defended" Darwin, leaving the impression of an ordinary academic debate, rather than a fiery collision.[53]

The *London Times* devoted its coverage of the association's meeting to the mundane details of business, the treasurer's report, the appreciation expressed by officers, the site of the 1861 meeting, and a list of all who attended the final meeting.[54] There was no hint of acrimony.

The most interesting material from the *Times* came more than twenty-seven years later, when Reginald Wilberforce and Thomas Huxley exchanged sharply worded letters in the newspaper. The younger Wilberforce took issue with Huxley's response to a review of *On the Origin of Species,* written by the bishop. The occasion for Huxley's alleged offense was the publication of *The Life and Letters of Charles Darwin.* Reginald Wilberforce accused Huxley of quoting material out of context and asked, "What . . . is the reason why these dead ashes are fanned again into flame? . . . Did the lash of the Bishop Wilberforce's eloquence sting so sharply that, though 27 years have passed, the recollection of the castigation then received is as fresh as ever?"[55] Huxley responded: "Those who were present at the famous meeting in Oxford, to which Mr. Wilberforce refers, will doubtless agree with him that an effectual castigation was received by somebody. But I have too much respect for filial piety, however indiscreet its manifestations, to trouble you with evidence as to who was the agent and who the patient in that operation."[56]

Macmillan's magazine has been a major historical source for information about the confrontation. The magazine first began publishing in 1859, the same year in which *The Origin* was published, but it gets little attention in the history of Darwin until nearly the close of the century. It was a cautious magazine, consistently devoting itself to a serial, a political article, a literary or philosophical article, items on history or travel, and a short story or poem.[57] Two relevant articles appeared in this publication. However, the most notable one is a recollection published in 1898. The account is tainted by time, selectivity of memory, and prejudice, but often it is used as a source by historians writing about a lady's fainting, which they have attributed to a sense of intellectual crisis. In an 1860 letter to Darwin, Hooker also mentioned her fainting, but he said nothing of the reasons for her swoon. Although a number of historians have reported this "fact," it should be noted that a very plausible alternative explanation of the fainting exists. The events took place in a crowded room in early July in England, and, given the customs of dress of the period, the woman merely may have been overcome by heat. There is as much evidence for the latter speculation as there is the "intellectual crisis" explanation. In the article, Huxley was called "the hero of the day," and the debate was given full dramatic treatment: Wilberforce turned to "his antagonist with a smiling insolence. . . . Mr. Huxley deliberately and slowly rose. . . . very quiet and very grave. . . . [The words'] meaning took away our breath. . . . the effect was tremendous."[58] The account crackled with the drama so common to histories of the event.

An 1860 article in the same magazine also mentioned the debate. In "A Popular Exposition of Mr. Darwin on the Origin of Species," Henry Fawcett discussed the divisions in the scientific world. He attacked the criticism that Darwin's work was not "true Baconian method," a phrase frequently meaningless, he said, that was "repeated ad nauseam at the British Association."[59] And the author referred to Huxley's retort:

It was sad, indeed, to think that the opponents of the theory sought to supply this omission by summoning to their aid a species of oratory which could deem it an argument to ask a professor if he should object to discover that he had been developed out of an ape. The professor aptly replied to the assailant by remarking, that man's remote descent from an ape was not so degrading to his dignity as the employment of oratorical powers to misguide the multitude by throwing ridicule upon a scientific discussion. The retort was so justly deserved, and so inimitable in its manner, that no one who was present can ever forget the impression it made.[60]

But in the article's conclusion, Hooker, not Huxley, was cited for force of argument and eloquence. There was little drama in the account. The significance of the debate, even in the minds of people who were there, was called into question by this very favorable assessment of Huxley's performance. In the twelve-page article, only a few sentences are devoted to the debate, and those occur eight pages into the article—hardly a position to suggest that the event was a catalyst for, or an inspiration to, the writer.

Chamber's Journal regularly presented articles of a scientific nature, as its subtitle, "of Popular Literature, Science and Arts," suggests. Darwin's "speculations," the magazine said in a paragraph devoted to the association's meeting, were prominent in the zoology and geography sections: "On the former subject [the antiquity of man], the Bishop of Oxford made an oratorical display, which led to the smart and somewhat silencing reply from Professor Huxley. Some objections from Professor Owen, too, underwent a sharp rebuke from the same hand. The audiences seemed much divided on both subjects."[61] Again, the Huxley response was treated as prominent but not of singular significance. The reference to "audiences" suggests that no single occasion encompassed the whole debate; moreover, the audiences were divided. The reply was not completely silencing, only somewhat.

The *Manchester Guardian,* a daily newspaper, gave limited attention to the British Association's meeting, but the high point of the conference for this newspaper was the announcement that Manchester would be the site of the next year's meeting.[62] The action leading up to the site selection was given in great detail, with all names and motions dutifully recorded and commended in the paper. The *Guardian,* a leading publication among political liberals, in the 1860s had a readership ranging from lower-middle to upper classes and approaching thirty thousand in the northern cities.[63] However, in the few days when the *Guardian* was giving the association some coverage, one brief item did note the debate. The paragraph referred to a "very animated discussion" between Huxley and Wilberforce. The latter, it said, "denounced the theory as unphilosophical . . . based upon mere fancy instead of facts, and . . . degrading to the dignity of human nature." Huxley reportedly replied that Wilberforce was an "unscientific authority." Huxley "then proceeded to defend the Darwinian theory in an argumentative speech, which was loudly applauded."[64] Hooker was mentioned as being among the panelists, but nothing was said of his response.

John Bull, a High Church weekly published in London, devoted about a column to the meetings, giving most of its space to a demonstration of electric light and to papers in the chemistry section. A short paragraph mentioned the debate:

> The Darwinian theory of the origin of species was fully and ably discussed in the section of Zoology. Here Professors Huxley and (to some extent) Hooker were opposed by a powerful phalanx, led by the Bishop of Oxford, and composed of Sir B. Brodie, Professors Owen and [indecipherable], Mr. Gresswell, and Admiral Fitzroy. The impression left on the minds of those most competent to judge was that this celebrated theory had been built on very slight foundations, and that a series of plausible hypotheses had been skillfully manipulated into solid facts, while a vast array of real facts on the opposite side had been completely ignored.[65]

The debate was not offered as the capstone event of the meetings, judging by the lesser coverage given it in relation to other subjects, particularly chemistry and electricity, and the limited space devoted to it. The brief report leaves the impression that the contest featured not Huxley versus Wilberforce, but Huxley and Hooker versus an array of formidable opponents, the latter getting the best of things.

The Press of London devoted one long paragraph to the general debate over Darwin's theory, and only briefly cited the Huxley-Wilberforce exchange. After the conclusion of the conference, nearly a full tabloid page was devoted to the British Association's meetings. According to the article, Huxley had started the argument by stating, earlier in the week, that there was "nothing to fear even should it be shown that apes were [mankind's] ancestors." But after reporting the essence of each man's remarks, *The Press* said: "[It] has been pleasant to mark, for the most part, a spirit of wide and wise toleration . . . to mark how well it is possible for the Christian, the classic, and the scientific to co-operate in the one grand end,—the advancement of man and the glory of God."[66] The praise for toleration, in the same paragraph as the Huxley-Wilberforce material, may have been intended as sarcasm. Still, it does not offer a clear resolution of the event.

The *Guardian,* a weekly High Church newspaper, noted the distinct lack of press coverage of the meetings, placing the blame in part on the association's poor provision of accommodations for reporters. The paper reported on an anti-Darwin paper, which the newspaper said was produced by a person of substantial scientific authority. An unspecified Oxford newspaper was quoted briefly on the Huxley-Wilberforce debate, and the *Guardian* concluded, "The result of these discussions . . . seems to be that this celebrated theory of Darwin's . . . is utterly unable to bear the slightest breath of adverse criticism." In addition, the newspaper predicted a "more formal refutation" of Darwin's theory.[67] Another article in the *Guardian* mentioned the debate in passing: "Occasionally even upon the platform itself scenes present themselves in which the ludicrous has considerable share. When Professors lose their tempers and solemnly avow they would rather be descended from apes than Bishops; and when pretentious sciolists seriously enunciate follies and platitudes of the most wonderful absurdity and draw upon their heads crushing refutations from the truly learned, there is mingled with our more serious feelings a sensation of amusement."[68] Neither Huxley nor Wilberforce was given great distinction, and the article left open the possibility that Hooker provided the "truly learned" presentation.

Jackson's Oxford Journal ran a full report of what it deemed the meeting's "more interesting" papers, which apparently did not include Huxley and Wilberforce. Another one-paragraph item began with the fact that Draper read a paper and created "great interest" in a "crowded" room.

> A long discussion took place on the soundness or unsoundness of the Darwinian theory, in which the Bishop of Oxford took a prominent part. He condemned the Darwinian theory as unphilosophical; as founded, not upon philosophical principles, but upon fancy, and he denied that one instance had been produced by Mr. Darwin on the alleged change from one species to another had ever taken place [sic]. He alluded to the weight of authority that had been brought to bear against it—men of eminence, like Sir. B. Brodie and Professor Owen, being opposed to it, and concluded, amid much cheering, by denouncing it as degrading to man, and as a theory founded upon fancy, instead of upon facts.—Professor Huxley, in a calm, dispassionate, and argumentative speech, replied to his Lordship, and was followed by Admiral Fitzroy, Dr. Beale, Mr. Lubbock, and Dr. Hooper [sic].[69]

"Dr. Hooper" was a typographical error, which was supposed to have been "Dr. Hooker," who did follow Huxley and Wilberforce on the program. The *Evening Star* report was similar to that of *Jackson's*. In fact, the two were so similar that they probably came from the same source, with the *Star* correcting the spelling of "Hooper" to "Hooker" but otherwise using the same words.[70] Neither supports the myth.

Sound and Fury and Significance

Who won? There are two answers. The first is that we cannot know, based on the historical record. Each of the principal protagonists—Huxley, Hooker, and Wilberforce—believed that he prevailed. In the next generation, sons of Huxley and Wilberforce each believed that his father prevailed. The letters of eyewitnesses and participants are problematical for two reasons. First, they are biased, with most of the surviving letters coming from people who either were associated with Huxley, such as Darwin and Hooker, or who disliked Wilberforce, such as J. R. Green. Second, many of the accounts in letters are tainted by the passage of time. The writers may not only be providing their recollections, but also may be repeating the stories that arose over the years and became mingled with memory.

A second group of sources is no better in answering the question of who won the debate. Press accounts are inconclusive. They refer to conflict and argument, but not to a smashing of the bishop. Looking at the newspaper stories, two things are apparent: there was an exchange, and the event was not preeminent for reporters and editors. In this case, the popular press's virtue as a historical record is due to at least two factors. First, reporters and editors had less personal investment in the outcome of the debate than so many of the other commonly cited sources. Second, the press accounts generally were laymen's interpretations written for other laymen—the broader culture. Finally, a number of histories have stated that the press record is very limited. This is simply not true. In fact, there is a considerable press record of the event. Even more significant, the record is a substantive one, though obviously not "complete." The press record of the debate suggests that the revisionists are more correct than the traditional histories. The record is incomplete and biased, to be sure, but no more so than the various "life and letters" publications that contain the rest of the record. The debate between the two men did not end with a decisive winner, according to this public record. Although Darwin's theory was noted as being of interest, it was not the subject that garnered all, or even most, of the attention. Huxley's retort attracted attention as much for its brashness and impetuosity as it did for its substance. Ironically, even if one accepts the myth as fact, this great moment in the ascendancy of Darwinism culminated in a retort, by Huxley, that said nothing about natural selection, but only castigated a bishop for being rude.

Who won? A second answer is: Huxley did. His was a victory by history, a victory nurtured at first by Francis Darwin and Leonard Huxley, both of whom labored to confirm their prejudices, knowing that there was no definitive answer. Subsequently, historians accepted as fact the story of Huxley the hero, vanquishing the arrogant and ignorant bishop. Now the debate stands as a symbol. Its transformation from mere argument to such lofty status was not apparent even in those newspapers that gave the edge to Huxley. In other words, the symbolic significance has evolved, a fact whose metaphoric value even Huxley would have appreciated. This second answer also addresses the creation of the myth and why it survives. It survives because, since the late-nineteenth century, science has prevailed as a world view. But the creation of the myth may be largely a result of the efforts of Francis Darwin and Leonard Huxley, who put a lot more effort than Reginald Wilberforce into recreating the events surrounding the debate.[71] By default, then, Wilberforce's son left the writing of history to the sons of his father's opponent. And those who write history get to pick the heroes.

Chapter 3

Darwin's Recantation of Evolution: Birth and Life of a Myth

> What a book a Devil's Chaplain might write on the clumsy, wasteful,
> blundering low & horridly cruel works of nature.
> —CHARLES DARWIN TO JOSEPH DALTON HOOKER, JULY 13, 1856

"I was a young man with unformed ideas. I threw out queries, suggestions, wondering all the time over everything; and to my astonishment the ideas took like wildfire." The dying sage of evolutionary theory, Charles Darwin, goes on to praise the beauty of scripture and to ask that hymns be sung, all the time aglow with his rediscovered Christianity.

The myth persists to this day. It was born in the popular press shortly after the turn of the century, and it survives largely in the literature of those who reject evolution. It persists despite being contrary to historical fact. The myth has just enough fact to give it credibility, a dose of hope to give it purpose, and drama sufficient to make it interesting. This dissection of that myth focuses on two questions: How do we know it is untrue? Why does it survive?

The "Recantation"

The first publication of a full narrative of Darwin's denial of evolution can be traced back to 1915, and it has been reprinted in publications well into the 1980s. The story is based on a talk by a Lady Elizabeth Hope, who addressed an audience in Northfield, Mass., on August 15, 1915. Her account of visiting Darwin on his deathbed first appeared in the *Boston Watchman-Examiner* and was reprinted in the *Bombay Guardian* the following spring.[1] It has spread from there.

The tale has varied little, with only an occasional change in wording. Here is the story as it originally appeared in the *Watchman-Examiner*:

> It was on one of those glorious Autumn afternoons, that we sometimes enjoy in England, when I was asked to go in and sit with the well known professor, Charles Darwin. He was almost bedridden for some months before he died. I used to feel when I saw him that his fine presence would make a grand picture for our Royal Academy; but never did I think so more strongly than on this particular occasion.
>
> He was sitting up in bed, wearing a soft embroidered dressing gown, of rather a rich purple shade.
>
> Propped up by pillows, he was gazing out on a far-stretching scene of woods and cornfields, which glowed in the light of one of those marvelous sunsets which are the beauty of Kent and Surrey. His noble forehead and fine features seem to be lit up with pleasure as I entered the room.
>
> He waved his hand toward the window as he pointed out the scene beyond, while in the other hand he held an open Bible, which he was always studying.
>
> "What are you reading now?" I asked, as I seated myself by his bedside.
>
> "Hebrews!" he answered—"still Hebrews. 'The Royal Book,' I call it. Isn't it grand?"
>
> Then, placing his fingers on certain passages, he commented upon them.
>
> I made some allusion to the strong opinions expressed by many persons on the history of the Creation, its grandeur, and then their treatment of the earlier chapters of the book of Genesis.
>
> He seemed greatly distressed, his fingers twitched nervously, and a look of agony come over his face as he said:
>
> "I was a young man with unformed ideas. I threw out queries, suggestions, wondering all the time over everything; and to my astonishment the ideas took like wildfire. People made a religion of them."
>
> Then he paused, and after a few more sentences on "the holiness of God" and "the grandeur of this Book," looking at the Bible which he was holding tenderly all the time, he suddenly said:
>
> "I have a summer house in the garden, which holds about thirty people. It is over there," pointing through the open window. "I want you very much to speak there. I know you read the Bible in the villages. To-morrow afternoon I should like the servants on the place, some tenants and a few neighbors to gather there. Will you speak to them?"
>
> "What shall I speak about?" I asked.
>
> "CHRIST JESUS!" he replied in a clear, emphatic voice, adding in a lower tone, "and his salvation. Is not that the best theme? And then I want you to sing some hymns with them. You lead on your small instrument, do you not?"

The wonderful look of brightness and animation on his face as he said this I shall never forget, for he added, "If you take the meeting at three o'clock this window will be open, and you
will know that I am joining with the singing."

How I wish that I could have made a picture of the fine old man and his beautiful surroundings on that memorable day![2]

This was not the first time that a member of Charles Darwin's family was reportedly involved in a deathbed change of heart. His grandfather, Erasmus, who was
committed to the idea of evolution and the kinship of all creatures, was known for
his unorthodox religious views. Erasmus believed in the existence of a Deity, but it
was a remote one, and he was attacked posthumously for doubting the Bible. Rumors persisted that Erasmus, on his deathbed, called for Jesus.[3] The story of Charles
Darwin's conversion first surfaced only a few years after his death. An exchange of
letters among Thomas Huxley, Francis Darwin, and the editor of the *Toronto Mail*
revealed the tale in 1887. In January of that year, the editor wrote Huxley that a
Presbyterian minister in Toronto, "preaching on the inspiration of the Bible, denounced modern science and said Mr. Darwin, when on his death-bed, abjectly
whined for a minister and renouncing evolution, sought safety in the blood of the
Saviour. Is there any truth in this?" Huxley forwarded the story to Francis Darwin,
who replied that the statement was "false and without any kind of foundation."
Huxley conveyed the same words to the editor.[4]

One scholar, Ian Taylor, believes that Darwin's wife, Emma, may have been the
source of the recantation story.[5] Emma might make a good suspect, because religion was a sensitive issue between her and Charles. She was a Unitarian, and her
Bible-based faith did not fit well with her husband's views. They simply did not agree
on the issue of eternal life, even though her faith helped him through times of stress,
especially when family members died. She understood that he believed nothing until
it was proven empirically. However, this had been an issue even before they were
married, when his doubts about hell and the existence of a soul already were formed.

The Persistence of the Myth

William Butler Yeats said that science is the critique of myth and that, without the
book of Genesis, there would have been no Darwin.[6] Conversely, without Darwin,
there would be no creationism. The recantation myth has its greatest following,
predictably, in a distinct strand of creationist-fundamentalist literature that has as
its purpose the promotion of a literal reading of the Genesis account of creation,
the refutation of evolution, or both.

Ronald Numbers, in *The Creationists,* has written the most thorough history of
creationism, from Darwin's day to present. Numbers defines creation-science as
essentially the biblical account of creation, stripped of explicit references to God,
Noah, and Adam. Most of the fossil record is attributed to the brief period of the

biblical Flood; earth's history is compressed into less than ten thousand years; and plants and animals represented in fossil strata are believed actually to have lived together at one time in an antediluvian world. Numbers also documents the reemergence of creationism as "creation-science" in the 1960s, with the founding of the Creation Research Society in 1963, its entry into politics in the 1970s, and its spread overseas in the 1980s.[7]

An excellent source of information on the creationist battle against evolution is a book by Tom McIver, *Anti-Evolution: An Annotated Bibliography*.[8] McIver lists a number of publications that are not readily available. Among the works he names, only a small fraction mention the Lady Hope story. But, a review of publications both inside and outside McIver's research suggests that sympathetic recountings of her tale tend to have several traits in common. First, they are written by creationists, who usually are defined by their opposition to evolution. Second, the source given for the story is one of the two newspaper accounts mentioned earlier, or no source at all is given. That is to say, the story is accepted uncritically, without checking its source. Third, these accounts tend to place science and religion in opposition, as posing an either-or choice in which the reader could not choose both. For example, in *The Rise of Evolution Fraud (An Exposure of Its Roots)*, by M. Bowden, the author reprints the story and cites the original version in the *Boston Watchman-Examiner* and the *Bombay Guardian*.[9] *Evolution: Is it Philosophical, Scientific or Scriptural?*, by Rev. Alexander Hardie, cites the *Watchman-Examiner* and reprints the story.[10] *Why I Accept the Genesis Record; Am I Rational?* alludes to Darwin's "repudiation" but gives no source.[11]

Who Was Lady Hope?

Lady Elizabeth Hope is a very minor historical figure whose fame, or notoriety, rests upon a lie. She was a member of the upper classes of Great Britain, being the daughter of a general and the cousin of a field marshal. She was born Elizabeth Cotton Reid on December 9, 1842, in Tasmania. She first married, in 1877, the admiral of the fleet, Sir James Hope, who died in 1881. In 1893, she married again, this time the philanthropist T. Anthony Denny, who died in 1909. She wrote under the name of Lady Elizabeth Hope; the British Library Catalogue lists some thirty titles under that name. She emigrated to America in 1913 and eventually settled in California. She sailed for England in March 1922 but died en route; she is buried outside Sidney, Australia.

In the 1850s, Elizabeth's family lived for a time in Beckenham, in Kent, only a few miles from the village of Downe. She turned eighteen in 1860, the year after *The Origin* was published. She would have been of an age important for her intellectual formation as Darwin's book was causing an uproar. After her father retired, she served as his assistant in evangelical activities. About 1870, the family settled permanently in Dorking, not far from the Darwins' Wedgewood relatives. She and her father immediately began to evangelize the area, targeting working-class families. She gained fame as an evangelist and founder of coffee houses, where men would drink coffee rather than spirits and renounce such bad habits as card playing and cursing. She also was close to American evangelist Dwight L. Moody and his family by July 1875, when his first mission to England was ending. The villages in which she evangelized were within a few miles of Downe. Dorking, which was only fifteen miles away, was visited yearly by Darwin between 1873 and 1880. Elizabeth's husband died in Scotland in June 1881, and Dorking then became her home. She left an account of tent evangelism among the Kent hop pickers and of setting up a coffee-tent for them. In the summer of 1881, James Fegan, whom she had met through Moody, was to have evangelized at Downe when twenty-five hundred laborers were to descend on the area to pick hops. Elizabeth may have been a backup evangelist for Fegan. She also reported meeting Darwin in the autumn of 1881. In her recantation story, which reports his being near death in the autumn, she perhaps was remembering the season correctly, if not the events that occurred during it. After her second husband died in 1909, she fell on hard times financially, went to New York in the summer of 1913, and began preaching in Chinatown and the Bowery. She intended to set up clubs for inebriates, as she had done in England.

James Moore has researched the tale of the recantation thoroughly and has come to the conclusion that an actual meeting took place between Elizabeth Hope and Darwin. His research on her evangelical wanderings puts her in the village of Downe in Darwin's later years. Moore also points out that Darwin's family, after his death, manufactured its own legend about his religious beliefs by tempering sections of his *Life and Letters* to depict his unbelief as a moderate and respectful agnosticism. This characterization stands in contrast with the reality that he renounced faith long before *The Origin* was published and that his religious backsliding began even before his father's death in 1848, after which event he actually broke with Christianity.[12]

There are elements of authenticity in her story. There were unsubstantiated rumors, one author reports, that Darwin encouraged his household help to attend nearby services at which a J. W. C. Fegan was preaching. Darwin may have assented to Fegan's use of the village reading room for services, and even may have heard and praised hymns sung by a boys' choir, organized by Fegan, that performed in front of Darwin's house. Elizabeth's opportunity to visit Darwin most likely would come about as a result of her being Fegan's helper. She was correct about the existence of a summer house on the grounds of Darwin's residence.[13] She alluded to the house as the place where Darwin asked her to lead the services. However, the house was in a far corner on the property and would not have been well located for hearing, let alone watching, services from a bedroom window. The summer house was about four hundred yards from the main house.

The story about Darwin's confession first was told on August 15, 1915, long after Darwin's death in 1882. In Northfield, Massachusetts, Lady Hope recounted the story to an audience at the Northfield Schools, which had been founded in the 1880s by Moody, a leading figure in the nineteenth-century revivalist movement in the United States. It was a good setting for launching such a myth. Northfield was the Mecca of the evangelical movement, a place where the figure of Moody, along with his theological conservatism, still loomed large. He had believed that the Bible should be taken "as it stands" and that the principal tasks before him and his fellow Christians were to preach the gospel and seek converts. Lady Hope was part of an annual summer event, the Northfield Conference, that was held on the Northfield Schools campus and was open to evangelicals of all denominations. By 1915, the conference had become a standard bearer for religious conservatism, and many of its supporters were outspoken proponents of fundamentalism. Ironically, Moody himself, the founder of the institution where the myth was born, knew little of Darwin, for he ignored such intellectual currents in favor of doing the practical work of the Lord.[14]

Lady Hope's story in the *Watchman-Examiner* followed a four-page report on that summer's conference. According to an editor's note attached to her revelation, she told the story at a morning prayer service. The editor leaped at the potential publicity windfall: "At our request Lady Hope wrote the story out for the *Watchman-Examiner*. It will give the world a new view of Charles Darwin. We should like the story to have the widest publicity." He asked that the *Watchman-Examiner* be given proper credit in any reprints.[15]

Another fact that gives Lady Hope's story a hint of credibility is that Darwin really did support Christian missionaries such as Fegan and Hope. However, Pat Sloan has pointed out that such support should not necessarily be construed to mean Darwin was supporting Christian doctrine. Instead, Darwin was supporting the practical work of the missionaries, such as combating drunkenness. In this respect, Darwin's support of the Reading Room mission in Downe was done as an aid to a local charity, not in the spirit of promoting doctrine. He commended their work, but he remained a committed agnostic who wished to promote the welfare of human beings and subscribed to practical deeds, even if they were carried out in the name of religion. As early as 1833, when Darwin was only twenty-four years old and on his *Beagle* voyage, he wrote in his diary about the good work being done by missionaries in reducing licentiousness, intemperance, and dishonesty among the natives.[16] Darwin's support for the missionaries can be attributed to other factors as well. First, as a gentleman of Victorian England, he had a social obligation to support such activity. Second, such actions might ease the tension that existed between Darwin and his wife concerning the issue of religion.

Pat Sloan has traced some of the myth's paths through various publications, from evangelical publications in the United States and Great Britain in the earliest years following Lady Hope's initial publication, through the 1950s. He also notes that having Darwin reading Hebrews is an interesting point that gives some credence to the possibility that Lady Hope visited Darwin. Sloan states that this is the one book of the Bible that presents Christianity in an evolutionary light, as a logical development out of Judaism: "Of all the books of the Bible, Darwin might have been discovered reading Hebrews with very great interest, not as a convert, but as an evolutionist."[17]

Lady Hope was a prolific writer for a short time. Allibone's *Dictionary of English Literature* cites twenty-six works by her published in 1860–87, most of them in the first half of the 1880s decade.[18] Curiously, no publications are listed for 1882, the year Darwin died, although Hope has three entries for 1881 and four for each year from 1883 to 1885. This gives anti-evolutionists some hope that Hope was with Fegan and too busy to be writing during 1881–82. This is, of course, negative evidence; it does not demonstrate that she was there, but only shows that she was not publishing much that year. There still is no positive evidence that she was with Darwin. The subjects of numerous publications confirm her evangelical inclinations: *Gathered Clusters from Scripture Pages: A Book for Parents, Teachers, and Children* (1880), *His Handiwork* (1883), and several volumes of "meditations." Reminiscences also were part of her literary repertoire, and the titles of several works suggest that they are vignettes of everyday life.

In *Our Coffee-Room,* Hope recounts in the first person the creation and popularity of a place for working-class men to consume coffee and the Holy Spirit, rather than distilled spirits. The story begins with her meeting some "rough looking men" while she is collecting donations for the poor. She takes a Sunday school of unruly boys and expands it to include women and men; eventually it becomes a regular Sunday evening revival. Drinking is the sin, she proclaims, that keeps working-class people from God. The book concludes with advice on starting a self-supporting coffee room to serve the poor both physically and spiritually. The book is a testament to her evangelical dedication and Christian faith.[19]

For those who do not believe Hope's story about Darwin, the big question remains: Why did she not *immediately* publish such a blockbuster story? The answer is that she did not have the story. Moreover, there were too many of Darwin's friends and relatives who decisively could have disproved her remarks. By the time she published the story, more than thirty years after Darwin's death, she did not have to contend with so many personal and professional associates who would have contradicted her tale. By the time she revealed her secret, the most likely challengers were a few Darwin family members. Then anti-evolutionists could respond that Darwin's children could be expected to deny his conversion. She also released her big story in America, not in Darwin's native country, where the press would have had easier time checking the facts.

In 1923, a reviewer of Lady Hope's *My Lady's Bargain,* a 299-page romantic novel set in Cromwellian England,[20] found fault because "the arbitrary aid of coincidence is too frequently enlisted to keep the story going. The characters that are taken from history do not conform strictly to the picture history has drawn of them." It is the same problem her Darwin fiction has with the facts, with some of the material being close, but much of it simply wrong. The reviewer praised her "easy grace in the narrative," which also is present in her most enduring fiction, the one about Darwin. The novel is about a young man torn between political alliance and love, who finally finds both "honor and happiness." The book's hero is an individual who was traitorous in his early life, much as young Darwin turned away from God; the young hero in the novel struggles with his conscience and finally returns to "glory." The review concludes, "For such graceful touches [in the writing] we forgive many glaring imperfections, and read on happily to the end." Hope created more than one historical narrative with "glaring imperfections."

With so little evidence to support her account of Darwin's recantation, the most interesting question for speculation is: Why did she do it? There are some plausible motives. First, for a devout fundamentalist-creationist, there could have been no greater "victory" than conquering Charles Darwin himself, who was seen by many as the chief culprit rending the seamless fabric of God and science.[21] Second, perhaps she was so taken by being in front of an audience that she was swept up to the point of mistaking her wishes for facts. Certainly, this was an audience that would have had similar wishes. Her reason cannot be known, just as so much of history cannot be known. As to why she told the story, historians can only ask if she could have had a motive. The answer is a cynical "yes"—self-promotion, religious zeal, or both.

The Evidence against the Myth

Several elements of the intriguing story contradict historical facts. Other parts of the story cannot be shown to be contrary to fact, but they are highly improbable, given Darwin's life and beliefs.

First, the contrary facts. Lady Hope alluded to a beautiful autumn day on which she visited the dying Darwin. But he died in the spring, on April 19, 1882. In addition, it was not the case, as Lady Hope claimed, that Darwin was bedridden for several months before his death. Darwin, although growing weaker, visited Cambridge in December 1881. He fell ill about this time but recovered and was fairly well until February 1882, when he again suffered from heart trouble. But even as late as April 1882, Darwin worked when able and refused to be bedridden. His final spell of sickness began on April 15, but he was working in his orchard only two days later. His terminal illness began on the night of April 17 and ended with his death at 3 A.M. on April 19.[22] It is difficult to stretch these facts to accommodate Darwin's being on his deathbed for months.

Lady Hope recounted Darwin's remorse over opinions that caught fire when he was just a "young man." He was fifty years old when *The Origin of Species* was published, and it went through six editions. Furthermore, Darwin was sixty-two when *Descent of Man* appeared. Again, it is hard to imagine even a septuagenarian scientist attributing the ideas of his sixth and seventh decades to youthful recklessness.

Even if Darwin underwent such a radical intellectual and spiritual change, why would only one person—a veritable stranger to him—know of the conversion? Accepting the myth means believing that Darwin's large family and network of friends and colleagues either knew nothing of the conversion or, in an elaborate and highly improbable conspiracy, managed to keep it quiet. Statements by two of Darwin's children are at odds with Lady Hope's story. Henrietta was at her father's deathbed, and she denied that he ever recanted evolution.[23] Francis, who edited and published his father's letters, denied that Lady Hope ever met Darwin. Nearly five years after Charles Darwin died, Francis Darwin and Thomas Huxley exchanged letters, mentioned earlier, concerning the rumor of the recantation.

Another unlikely detail in the story is Darwin's reading of scripture and the implication that he had been pondering it. Darwin himself said he never read metaphysics, and he was averse even to discussing religion or metaphysics. In 1879, in response to a letter from a German student, Darwin said, "Science has nothing to do with Christ, except in so far as the habit of scientific research makes a man cautious in admitting evidence. For myself, I do not believe that there ever has been any revelation. As for future life, every man must judge for himself between conflicting vague probabilities."[24] In 1876, Darwin sketched the history of his religious views, in which he said that disbelief "crept over me at a very slow rate, but was at last complete. The rate was so slow that I felt no distress."[25] He concluded the passage by stating that he was content to remain an agnostic. A few years before his death, Darwin reaffirmed his agnosticism and noted that the label suited him better than "atheist."[26] Therefore, given Darwin's rather strong endorsement of agnosticism late in his life, recantation would have meant that Darwin rather quickly cast off the ideas that he had developed since the days of his *Beagle* voyage, or over a period of about forty years. Darwin was something of a plodder in his research, slowly building his generalizations from a mass of facts. His habit of laboriously accumulating evidence and carefully supporting his generalizations was not the style of the person who quickly would dismiss a lifetime of work in favor of another interpretation. In his *Autobiography,* Darwin described his gradual movement toward agnosticism:

> Another source of conviction in the existence of God, connected with the reason and not with the feelings, impresses me as having much more weight. This follows from the extreme difficulty or rather impossibility of conceiving this immense and wonderful universe, including man . . . , as the result of blind chance or necessity. When thus reflecting, I feel compelled to look to a First Cause having an intelligent mind in some degree analogous to that of man; and I deserve to be called a Theist. This conclusion was strong in my mind about the time, as far as I can remember, when I wrote the *Origin of Species,* and it is since that time that it has very gradually, with many fluctuations, become weaker. But then arises the doubt—can the mind of man, which has, as I fully believe, been developed from a mind as low as that possessed by the lowest animals, be trusted when it draws to such grand conclusions?
>
> I cannot pretend to throw the least light on such abstruse problems. The mystery of the beginning of all things is insoluble to us, and I for one must be content to remain an Agnostic.[27]

Those eager to find Lady Hope's story credible are given meager support by the myth that Darwin's own family created about his religious beliefs. The *Autobiography*, published in 1886, presents a moderate agnostic who, in James Moore's words, "reluctantly gave up Christianity for lack of historical evidence." Darwin's son Francis, editor of the *Autobiography*, tempered his father's religious views in order to appease Emma Darwin, a Unitarian. She and her husband had never agreed on religious matters, and he seldom spoke about the latter. The *Autobiography* minimizes the materialism in Darwin's early notebooks and eradicates the reference to himself as the "Devil's Chaplain" for exposing nature's cruelty and waste. The *Autobiography* was started in 1876 and was intended to be a private narrative for the family. In it, Darwin revealed his feelings about Christianity and his view of eternal punishment as a "damnable doctrine." When Emma read the manuscript, she wrote next to the sensitive section on religion: "It seems to me raw."[28]

The portrait in the *Autobiography* is very much in line with what Darwin's many biographers and many historians of evolution have concluded about Darwin: his reservations about going forward without a full study of a problem; the discipline of dealing with only observable fact; the mind that always entertained doubts. If anything, the portrait is a bit too moderate, having been edited by the family after Darwin's death. Francis Darwin, editor of his father's *Life and Letters,* removed his father's "devil's chaplain" self-reference and built an image of respectable moderation in his father's religious views.[29] Darwin moved gradually from theism to agnosticism, retaining a sense of the world's mystery. But he simply refused to speculate about God. The nature and extent of Darwin's theism have been the subject of some debate. The most complete study of the subject says that his beliefs about God never did reach a point of finality. After 1863, his theism was, at best, unconventional: "At low tide, so to speak, he was essentially an undogmatic atheist; at high tide he was a tentative theist; the rest of the time he was basically agnostic—in sympathy with theism but unable or unwilling to commit himself on such imponderable questions. Overall his thoughts regarding theological matters could best be described as being in what he himself termed a 'muddle.'"[30]

Even a broad interpretation of Darwin's view of theology still leaves little room for a radical conversion on his deathbed. F. Burch Brown, in his monograph on Darwin's religious views, maintains that Darwin's reservations about the relationship of science and religion did not disappear. After confessing bewilderment on the whole issue of religion, Darwin simply turned his back on the confounding questions of theology. Brown speculated that Darwin's divorce from these questions led the great man to view the universe in a more mundane manner, still seeing the world as curious but as less mysterious and less grand. This shift, Brown said, would create a mindset that would make it difficult for Darwin's earlier theism to survive.[31]

Darwin's style of investigation also makes the recantation story untenable. Lady Hope said that he "threw out queries, suggestions," etc. However, it took Darwin nearly a decade to write *The Origin*, and then he called it only an abstract, implying that it was not final. He would have withheld publication longer had he not been threatened with being beaten to the idea of natural selection by Alfred Russel Wallace, who in June 1858 prompted Darwin to action by writing Darwin a letter outlining ideas that were very close to Darwin's. Wallace proposed that his ideas be presented to the Linnean Society if Darwin believed the concepts fit. After consulting colleagues, Darwin decided to present a joint paper with Wallace to the Royal Society. Then, Darwin finally got to work on publishing *The Origin*. As further evidence of his careful approach, it took eight years of research on barnacles for Darwin to write a monograph on that subject. Darwin's description of his working and thinking habits is difficult to reconcile with the notion of his having a quick change of mind on any subject: "I had, also, during many years, followed the golden rule, namely that whenever a published fact, a new observation or thought came across me, which was opposed to my general results, to make a memorandum of it without fail and at once: for I had found by experience that such facts and thoughts were far more apt to escape from the memory than favourable ones."[32] Darwin did not, as Lady Hope said, "throw out" speculations.

Darwin carried this habit into other areas, not just biology. Francis Darwin said that, with regard to religion, his father was "influenced by the consciousness that a man ought not to publish on a subject to which he has not given special and continuous thought." That he felt this caution to apply to himself in the matter of religion is shown in an 1871 letter in which he declined to be published in a volume concerning religious ideas. Darwin felt that he had not given the subject enough thought to merit publication: "I think you will agree with me, that anything which is to be given to the public ought to be maturely weighed and cautiously put. . . . I feel in some degree unwilling to express myself publicly on religious subjects, as I do not feel that I have thought deeply enough to justify any publicity."[33]

The Purpose of the Myth

Toynbee stated, "It has . . . been said of the *Iliad* that anyone who starts reading it as history will find that it is full of fiction but, equally, anyone who starts reading it as fiction will find that it is full of history."[34] A similar observation can be made about Darwin's recantation, which blurs fiction and history. The facts of the story are consumed by, or even sacrificed to, a larger purpose. The history contained in the Lady Hope myth is not of Darwin and the idea of evolution, but of the shock it created for some and their search for a way back to the security of a universe purposively guided by God and created for humanity. Such people wanted no part of what one English scientist had described as the "law of higgeldy-piggeldy," expressing his belief in a universe created by design and his disgust for the idea of natural selection, with its attendant randomness and materialism.[35]

The story survives in an American subculture because the tale is more than a good story—it is truly mythic in both structure and purpose. Its archetype is the alienation myth, an especially Christian myth. Adam, in acquiring knowledge, alienated himself from God and became estranged from his inner self. Adam could recover only by seeking God's forgiveness.[36] The recantation myth is given purpose by organizing, for some, the chaos imposed by a system of thought—empirical science—that attempted to reduce the world and knowledge to an amalgamation of data, which resulted in defining reality by enumeration rather than faith. With Darwin's alleged recantation, the world was returned to order, and faith again reigned supreme over mere knowledge. The myth was an attempt to return the old system to preeminence. It was a reassertion of divine, universal unity over cold, fragmentary calculations about the material world. Like other myths, this one was a way to bring order out of chaos and to comfort a culture.[37] There may even be some significance to Lady Hope's selection of "Hebrews" as Darwin's deathbed reading, because it constitutes an elaborate proof of Christianity, and specifically of its superiority over Judaism. The recipients of the letter were about to abandon their Christian faith, and the author of the letter emphasized three points in his exhortation to win them back: the superiority of Christ over the Prophets; the superiority of Christ's priesthood to Levitical priesthood; and the superiority of Christ's sacrifice to the animal sacrifices of Levitical priests.[38] So Darwin's habit of "proving" his theories was turned around by Lady Hope, who put in his hands a proof of Christianity.

The creation of the Lady Hope myth in 1915 coincides with the establishment of modern creationism-fundamentalism. This movement was not merely a response to Darwinism, nor was it representative of the Christian response to twentieth-century Darwinism. It was, rather, a reaction against liberal theology and associated attempts to make Christianity and science compatible.[39] Publication of *The Fundamentals,* a twelve-volume work that appeared in 1910–15, was an early defining event for fundamentalists. By drawing on spokesmen from different denominations, the work broadened its appeal. It made the conservative theological case in a dignified, moderate, and intellectually powerful manner. In effect, it started the fundamentalist movement.[40]

In the late nineteenth century, fundamentalists—believers in a literal reading of Genesis—increasingly had been alarmed by the tendency to view the Bible simply as a historical document, not as the inspired word of God; and by the growing debate over the place of evolutionary thinking in religion. Darwinism was not the sole impetus for the fundamentalist movement, and this was demonstrated in *The Fundamentals'* relative lack of concern about evolution, which was cited but not in the shrill fashion that became characteristic of fundamentalism of the 1920s.[41] Then, much of the public attention to fundamentalism came to focus on the fight to prohibit teaching of evolution in schools; in the 1920s, at least thirty-seven antievolution bills were introduced in state legislatures, and four became law.[42]

After the Scopes Trial in 1925, the movement was in decline until the early 1960s, when two events marked a revival of fundamentalism. These were the publication of *The Genesis Flood* in 1961 and the establishment of the Creation Research Society in San Diego, California. *The Genesis Flood* argued for inerrant Scripture (as did the Research Society) and did so by *looking* scientific.[43]

The treatment of the "facts" of the Lady Hope myth is indicative of the state of the fundamentalist subculture. American myths of the eighteenth and nineteenth centuries reflected an expanding culture,[44] one that was boisterous and bold. In the Daniel Boone and Davy Crockett myths, for example, the facts constituted an opportunity, serving merely as a foundation for a grandiose story. But the facts behind the Darwin myth remain furtive, slinking about the edges of reality, sometimes touching it but usually missing, never abandoning the facts for audacious, symbolic assertions of significance. These are timid facts, begging the reader to skip on toward the moral of the story, suggesting a culture in decline, on the defensive. In addition, the recantation featured a remote place (Darwin's residence), a culprit from another country, and an idea valued only for its negative ability to unite people in condemnation.

Lady Hope differed from other myth makers in several respects. First, she was an unwitting creator of myth, writing for an immediate problem, not attempting to transcend time and place, gluing her story to mundane reality. She even made her protagonist, Darwin, ordinary rather than heroic. Her real hero, Christ, was in the story only as a symbol. Second, other myth makers, from ancient Greece to the American West, have used facts in a manner antithetical to that employed in Lady Hope's story. The Boone and Crockett myths, for example, are based upon real people who became symbols of individual triumph, conquering the wilderness and expanding America. These men lived in myth as ideals of individualism, a characteristic cherished throughout American history. These myths transcended the limits of the frontiers with which the individuals so strongly were identified. The Boone and Crockett myths unchained facts from mere reality and went immediately to the fantastic, writing in order to create an eternity, not to defend one. Because Lady Hope's story is defensive and antiheroic, it has remained in a cultural side stream, out of the main currents of both myth and theology.

Why the Myth Lives

This is not a myth of the general culture, but of a fundamentalist-creationist subculture, and this is an important factor in understanding how such a story has survived. The anecdote is virtually nonexistent in the academic subculture of historians of science. It is difficult to find references to Lady Hope in mainstream scholarly works on Darwin and evolution. The myth survives in the one subculture because it defines what the subculture opposes. It is rather like the situation of a nation at war, in which many factions pull together in opposition to an apparently monolithic enemy, which the nation subsequently may discover was not so unified. No monolithic belief structure exists that is endorsed by all people who believe in evolution, any more than there is a single definition of *creationist*.

Both evolution and creationism are multifaceted ideas, each more easily defined by what it excludes than by what it includes. Any group is bound together more easily and effectively by addressing a common enemy than by exploring factional differences—which, for both creationists and evolutionists, are numerous. Creationism has a wide range of definitions, including people who literally believe the seven-day account of Creation as presented in Genesis, as well as those who find evolution an acceptable but incomplete explanation and commit themselves only to the idea that God had a role in the creation of life, albeit an unknowable and undefined role.[45] Similarly, it is simple and safe to say that an evolutionist does not believe in the spontaneous, supernatural generation of each and every variety of life.

The myth of Darwin's recantation has survived in part because it is a good story. It contains a celebrity, the drama of life and death, higher truth. Darwin, in his return to Christianity, becomes a new incarnation of the Prodigal Son. The story involves conflict at two levels: religion versus science, and Darwin versus his conscience. There is, for the creationist subculture, the satisfying finality of the story's conclusion: the triumph of Christ, the conversion of the man who was a symbol of "godless science," and a reassertion of the power of faith. It has an appealing irony. The real Darwin spent years building a factual foundation for his ideas about evolution, and he devoted little time to thinking about theology. Natural selection, for Darwin, was well grounded in logic and observation; theology, however, was speculative. The Lady Hope story reverses this reality. He claims merely to have been "throwing around" ideas, but he is certain of the truth of Scripture. In real life, the "scripture" upon which Darwin relied was the observable, material world. The fictional Darwin's surprise at the acceptance of his scientific ideas stands in contrast to the real Darwin's resigned acceptance of his inability to tackle metaphysical problems. Like the romantic and aristocratic myths of the American South,[46] this story served a culture in retreat. The South, and the idea of the South, remained vital in America long after the South died as a separate culture. The region retained its distinctiveness and its complexity. Similarly, fundamentalist-creationism, or antiscience, remains vital, complex, and misunderstood—defined in part by myth.

Also strengthening the myth is the fact that there is no way to prove that the story is absolutely wrong. The available evidence merely shows that it is highly improbable, not that it is absolutely impossible. This provides an opening for those who are content to rest their cases on the weaker evidence for the validity of the story.

This historiographical excursion comes to a momentary ending with an unsettling question: Why study a lie? Well, this lie is not important for what it reveals about Darwin and evolution. Instead, its significance resides in what it reveals about the reaction to Darwinism. Ultimately an irreconcilable collision of science and religion occurred, but it was not irreconcilable for all of religion. It was a dilemma only for those Christian denominations that persisted in a literal reading of Genesis. Darwin served as an icon unifying those believers, who persist to this day.

A final reflection on the survival of the myth is this: perhaps the myth is Faustian.

Lady Hope's story is of a redeemed Faust. Darwin traded his faith for knowledge and then discovered that he also had traded his God. He could regain God only by recanting his knowledge. So he did. The myth holds forth that possibility that we mere humans can break our Faustian contract and can return the knowledge after paying for it with faith.

Part 2

Misuses of Darwinism

The "twists" on Darwinism that are the subjects of chapters 4–7 are based on a single, general idea, which we call "social Darwinism." This umbrella idea has thrived as a catch-all explanation—enlisted to explain such things as individuals' wealth or poverty, the rise and decline of nations, the role of regulation in economic policy. Its most notorious application has been to promote racial superiority and inferiority.

Social Darwinism found its way into American culture by way of both the academy and the popular press. The founder of the philosophy, Herbert Spencer, never held a university post, but he found an enthusiastic audience in the American academy. His most ardent and important disciple in the United States was William Graham Sumner of Yale University. Sumner believed that Spencer's philosophy was the death knell for social-reformer fantasies of using legislation to change American culture.

Social Darwinism's existence is entwined with the popular press for two reasons. First, Spencer found invaluable encouragement and financial support in popular publications, and he published extensively in some of these. Second, newspapers and magazines gave a great deal of attention to Spencer, and in the late nineteenth and early twentieth centuries they were by far the most effective and efficient avenue for wide dispersion of an idea. The popular origins of social Darwinism are significant because magazines and newspapers not only conveyed its messages to general readers, but also sustained the flow of information about it across decades and thus helped to create a climate friendly to the movement, as its familiarity made it increasingly acceptable.

Since Part II considers the adoption of Darwinism for cultural and political purposes, it seems appropriate to begin the section, chapter 4, by examining that most problematical and ill-defined of terms, "social Darwinism," and its meanings in popular, not scientific, culture. Even those arguing for "survival of the fittest" in human affairs actually were preaching the gospel of Spencer, but the label "social Darwinism" has remained. Spencer was an English evolutionist-philosopher, and he spent his life developing and explaining his all-encompassing philosophy. Darwin got the credit, even though Spencer had published his ideas about evolution more than a decade before *On the Origin of Species* appeared. Social Darwinism was popular in America and acted as a catalyst for emerging social sciences that were attempting to explain people and their institutions. Many leading thinkers seized upon Spencerianism in opposing labor unions, immigration, and economic regulation.

Chapter 5 reconsiders the supposed Darwinian rationale for the Spanish-American War, which took place in the decade after Spencer reached the zenith of his popularity in America. He was published extensively in magazines, particularly *Popular Science Monthly,* in the 1870s and 1880s, and he became an intellectual darling of leading academics, publishers, and a even a few industrialists and politicians. But were Americans really attempting to justify, in a scientific fashion, their expansionist ambitions? Who said that America should control Cuba and the Philippines in the interest of "survival of the fittest"? There is little evidence of such thinking in magazine and newspaper articles of the day. Like Huxley's heroic victory over Wilberforce, the idea of a Darwinian justification for war needs scrutiny because there is a gap between the historical record and the received history. Like the exploration of the Huxley-Wilberforce myth, this chapter makes extensive use of the popular press, understanding the limits of that source but also raising the issue of the "cultural record," which is more than selected letters and writings of a few prominent men. Thus the chapter constitutes an effort to get closer to the ideas being circulated in the broader culture.

The rise of the eugenics movement in the 1920s and 1930s in the United States, to which chapter 6 is devoted, is an episode in which science served political and ideological purposes. The idea of improving the human race by selective breeding is at least as old as Plato's *Republic*. The American eugenics movement was a crusade to improve humanity via science and was based on the work of Francis Galton, a renowned geneticist who was a cousin of Charles Darwin. Not all eugenicists were racists, but those who were had a profound impact on the movement. During the 1920s, American eugenicists became more active in the movement to restrict immigration, as they provided a scientific rationale for an emotional issue, culminating in the Immigration Restriction Act of 1924. Many leading eugenicists were brilliant publicists, using such gimmicks as sermon contests and "fitter families" contests to generate attention and funding. This chapter studies eugenics as a publicity activity aimed at gaining political and financial support, much as chapter 1 examined Darwin as a publicist.

It was only a short step from being a devout eugenicist to endorsing the philosophy behind Nazi racial politics. Chapter 7 looks at the response in America to the rise of Nazism, especially the Darwinian themes in popular publications. Germans had been leaders in evolutionary research, and in the 1930s they became the foremost practitioners of radical eugenics. They equated race and ideology, so a "non-Aryan" became anyone who was anti–National Socialist. Enactment of the Nuremberg Laws by the Reichstag in 1935 was a major legal and scientific event because the laws wedded the two realms in an evil pact. Each relied upon the other to carry out its visions. This marriage did not come about suddenly in Germany. In the previous century, in his *Philosophy of Right,* Hegel had proclaimed the divinity of the state. Gobineau followed, concluding that Aryans were the highest race and that Germans were the apex of that race. Gobineau was a major prophet of Hitler's Aryanism, in which purity of blood was paramount, a predictor of race quality. Hitler used Aryanism and the divinity of the state as justifications for world war, political terror, and genocide. The myths and the facts of science and politics became blurred. Did Americans distinguish between the myths and facts? Did rejecting Hitler mean rejecting the ideas connected with eugenics and race? If so, that would have seemed a sudden change for a nation that had enacted its own racist legislation only a decade earlier. Were pseudo-science and science separated in reactions to Nazism?

The term "social Darwinism" itself implied something of a myth. First, its connections to Darwin were tenuous. It would be more accurate to label the philosophy "Spencerianism." Second, social Darwinism became a conduit for transferring social values, such as individualism, ethnocentrism, capitalism, and even religion, to science. Spencer's popularity was enhanced by the fact that he embraced social values popular in Victorian England and Gilded-Age America. In other words, the culture shaped Spencer's philosophy, which further was empowered by its connections with Darwin and science. It was a cycle in which a scientific idea grew out of cultural values, thrived and was promoted as a science, and then was used to reinforce the cultural biases that had contributed to its development in the first place.

Chapter 4

Social Darwinism: Adapting Evolution to Society

For a concept that seems so familiar to so many historians, the meaning of the term "social Darwinism" is strangely elusive.[1] Despite the familiarity of the term, it is a misnomer. That social Darwinism could be derived from *On the Origin of Species* is obvious, but it is debatable whether Darwin supported the idea.[2] Although he never endorsed the idea, Darwin did not protest the application of his biological theory to society, and passages from his writings even suggest that Darwin himself made such applications. For example, in his *Descent of Man*, Darwin wrote:

> The wonderful progress of the United States, as well as the character of the people, are [*sic*] the results of natural selection; for the more energetic, restless, and courageous men from all parts of Europe have emigrated . . . and have there succeeded best.[3]
>
> With savages, the weak in body or mind are soon eliminated; and those that survive commonly exhibit a vigorous state of health. We civilized men, on the other hand, do our utmost to check the process of elimination; we build asylums for the imbecile, the maimed, and the sick; we institute poor-laws; and our medical men exert their utmost skill to save the life of everyone to the last moment. . . . Thus, the weak members of civilized societies propagate their kind. No one who has attended to the breeding of domestic animals will doubt that this must be highly injurious to the race of man.[4]

Nevertheless, social Darwinism's relationship to Darwin himself is problematical for several reasons. First, the philosophy was attributed to the wrong person.
Second, it was a *social* philosophy, based on the writings of the English philosopher
Herbert Spencer, rather than a scientific theory. This distinction often was lost in
popular accounts and, in later decades, in the work of eugenicists. Third, the ideas
that eventually grew up around it, particularly in the field of eugenics, went far
beyond even Spencerian ideas about evolution and human society.

Darwin responded to Spencer with a lack of enthusiasm, his remarks about the
philosopher ranging from snide to befuddled. Darwin wrote to Hooker that he was
sorry pangenesis, Darwin's theory of heredity, perplexed Hooker, confessing "that
it is abominably wildly horridly speculative (worthy even of Herbert Spencer)."[5] On
another occasion, Darwin admitted that he enjoyed his talk with Spencer, "though
he does use awesomely long words."[6] Darwin, with his habits of observation and
inductive reasoning, confessed his exasperation in reading Spencer: "I am quite de-
lighted with what you [Hooker] say about Herbert Spencer's book; when I finish each
number I say to myself what an awfully clever fellow he is, but when I ask myself
what I have learnt, it is just nothing."[7]

Social Darwinism was not merely the adaptation of Darwinism to economics.
Originally it was a social philosophy that applied evolution to human society. In this
respect, the philosophy coincided with Darwin's insistence on seeking material and
not supernatural explanations of phenomena. Social Darwinism gained its "tooth-
and-claw" reputation because, too often, people explained competition in Darwinian
terms but forgot about the role of cooperation in his theory of natural selection. In
its popular origins, social Darwinism was not a rationale for eliminating the weak.
For example, many social Darwinists noted the inevitability of suffering in society.
This was not, however, a proclamation of the necessity of suffering; it was an empirical observation about the state of society. Social Darwinism also pushed evolution far beyond the evidence presented by Darwin, who worked largely in natural
science rather than in the emerging social sciences. For the two individuals who are
the focus of this reassessment of social Darwinism, improving society was the goal,
not eradicating unfit people. Those two were the most prominent social Darwinists of America in the late nineteenth and early twentieth centuries: Spencer, the
philosopher of evolution, and William Graham Sumner, a Yale professor of sociology. Spencer enjoyed greater fame and notoriety in America than in his native
England, and his concept of survival of the fittest in society was the primary inspiration for Sumner's social philosophy.[8] These two were the leading intellectual powers behind that idea and were great popularizers, writing extensively for the popular press as well as lecturing and voicing opinions on such public issues as
immigration and tariffs. A gap exists in the history of ideas because Spencer and
Sumner have been studied widely as intellectuals, philosophers, and sociologists.[9]
But their polemical writings in the press have not been examined.

The role of social Darwinism in American history cannot be understood fully without going to the newspapers and magazines, particularly *Popular Science Monthly*, in which much of social Darwinist thought was elaborated. Richard Hofstadter, in his seminal *Social Darwinism in American Thought,* cited many popular journals but did not recognize the popular nature of the movement.[10] Spencer was a gentleman scholar, not supported by a university position. It is ironic that Spencer, the intellectual fountainhead of social Darwinism, while writing coarsely textured, hard-to-read volumes on evolutionary philosophy, nonetheless derived great support from a popular magazine, *Popular Science Monthly,* which recognized the mass appeal of ideas surrounding Darwin, Spencer, and evolution.

Spencer himself was a journalist of sorts, having written, early in his career (1842), a series of articles for the *Nonconformist,* a weekly newspaper, on "The Proper Sphere of Government." In 1848–50, during one of the short periods in his life when he actually worked for a living, Spencer was a "sub-editor" of the *Economist.*[11] In the 1850s, he wrote a number of articles for such publications as the *Westminster Review,* the *Leader,* the *North British Review, Fraser's Review,* and the *British Quarterly Review.*[12] *Popular Science Monthly's* editor saw in Spencer a popularizer, and the magazine pointed out that he had "always taken a vital interest in leading public questions, making them the subjects of frequent communications to the press."[13]

Social Darwinism and the Problem of Definition

Social Darwinism seems a very straightforward proposition: applying natural selection, Darwin's explanation of how evolution works, to human society. However, defining the idea has been difficult. It has been used to defend both socialism and capitalism, to explain the need for cooperation and for competition, and to justify both social harmony and conflict. The rise of eugenics in the early twentieth century added another layer of meaning to the term, incorporating Mendel's theories of heredity and Francis Galton's genetics. The ultimate consequence of eugenics—Nazi Germany's attempt to purify the "Aryan" race in the 1930s—gave social Darwinism an especially evil cast and destroyed whatever intellectual integrity it may have had.[14]

Social Darwinism has encompassed concepts that are broadly evolutionary, as well as those that apply to society only the narrower theory of natural selection. A number of scholars in the twentieth century have written about the subject, with Hofstadter remaining the one cited most frequently. However, Hofstadter's very broad definition of the term blurs distinctions among important thinkers, especially between Darwin and Spencer, and is so expansive that just about anyone can be classified as a social Darwinist, merely by accepting the idea that life has evolved. Barzun, in *Darwin, Marx, Wagner,* notes the confusion surrounding the idea. Darwin's *Descent of Man,* Barzun says, "wobbled between keeping man under the regime of natural selection and putting him under the modified regime of co-operation, reason, and love."[15] That work also wobbled between asserting the primacy of the individual and reserving primacy for the group. Was the fittest individual to survive, or the fittest group?

In addition, there has been debate over the extent of the influence of the movement. Hofstadter, Curti, and others assign it great power, while Wyllie and Russett believe that it was appropriated by the few, not the many.[16] LaVergata points out that social Darwinism has been used to defend capitalism, socialism, and even anarchism. Interpretation, he says, ranges from seeing the idea as a merely reactionary phenomenon to seeing it as part of a larger movement of "biologism."[17] Bannister, studying the "myth" of social Darwinism, does an excellent job of exploring this definitional morass, stating that social Darwinism "consistently derived its sting from the implication that the struggle and selection of the animal realm were also agents of change (and progress) in human society—the governing assumption being that men shared natural laws with the rest of Creation."[18] So social Darwinism has been many things, including contradictory.

Spencer and Sumner: The Heart of Social Darwinism

Spencer, not Darwin, was the original and foremost social Darwinist. And in America, Sumner was the most eminent, visible, and vocal disciple of Spencer. Part of the strength of the idea of social Darwinism lay in its "scientific" foundation, which was extremely important to both Spencer and Sumner and greatly affected the meaning they attached to the concept. Spencer was a self-taught Englishman with an ambition to explain everything in the universe. Over the course of a dozen volumes of philosophy, he argued for an evolutionary philosophy of the universe, encompassing the inorganic and organic worlds, including human society.[19]

Spencer was a social determinist who believed that society gradually would move toward its potential in a uniform manner. The progress of society would be accelerated by favorable conditions or slowed by neglecting or impeding those conditions, although social evolution could not be diverted from its general direction. He was a defender of free enterprise and was extremely critical of government intervention in the economy. Free competition, he argued, was a natural law of economics and the best guarantor of a community's well-being. Governmental interference with the natural law of competition would hinder social progress and ultimately would result in economic misfortune. From the end of the Civil War through the 1880s, Spencer influenced thinkers in virtually all intellectual fields and had a particularly strong impact upon the founders of American sociology. One of those founders was Sumner.[20]

Sumner, who was most prominent in the 1880s and 1890s, always was oriented toward the practical consequences of his work. He taught the first sociology course in the United States (perhaps in the world) and offered the first methodology course in the subject.[21] Sumner believed that state interference in any economic matter betrayed the individualism that was so highly valued in the nation and so firmly fixed in the laws of nature. For Sumner, competition was as much a natural law as gravity, and regulation of competition ultimately was as futile as attempting to regulate gravity.[22] Sumner used Spencer's social determinism to battle reformers, who he believed were operating under the illusions that there were no natural laws of society and that society could be remade with legislation. Sumner attacked socialists, sentimentalists, and metaphysicians as well, as he advocated free trade and laissez-faire economic policies.[23] He believed that Spencer's science would explode socialist and reformer fantasies.

Spencer: High Priest and Popularizer

For Spencer, who first published an article on evolution in 1850, nearly ten years before Darwin's *Origin of Species* appeared, Darwin was more a solidifying force than a creative one. As early as 1852, Spencer used the famous phrase "survival of the fittest," which Darwin later adopted.[24] In 1855, Spencer published *Principles of Psychology,* in which he applied the theory of evolution to man's mental as well as physical being. Darwin's and Spencer's intellectual roots were similar, in that both were influenced early in their careers by Thomas Malthus (1766–1834) and Charles Lyell (1797–1875). Malthus's *Essay on a Principle of Population* (1798) concluded that humanity must always be subject to famine, disease, poverty, and war, unless populations could gain control over their resources. Malthus was responding, in part, to a proposed restructuring of England's "poor laws," which were being debated in the late eighteenth century. He argued that providing relief to the poor would only aggravate the problem of poverty by encouraging the poor to breed and consequently would drag all of society down.[25] Malthus's contribution to the development of social science was making humanity subject to the same laws as the rest of the animal kingdom.[26] To Spencer's and Darwin's educations Lyell contributed the idea of "uniformitarianism," which held that geological changes might be the result of gradual alteration over a very long period of time. His approach required that scientists seek out evidence for change in the fossil record, rather than dismissing change as the result of catastrophic events of unknown origin and magnitude. The latter account of change, known as "catastrophism," was popular in the early nineteenth century; it attributed geological and biological change to sudden, cataclysmic events, such as the Flood in Genesis, that were unlike any phenomena known in modern times.[27] By contrast, uniformitarianism assumed that nature and physical laws remained constant throughout time.[28] Spencer adopted Lyell's concept of large-scale, gradual change, while Malthus gave him the idea of applying natural law to humanity.

Throughout the 1870s and 1880s, *Popular Science Monthly* was the primary conduit to the American public for Spencer's writings and ideas. Spencer even wrote the first article of the first issue in 1872.[29] The popular nature of both Spencer's work and social Darwinism more generally is clearly evident in *Popular Science Monthly*, in which columns and articles about Spencer and his writing frequently referred to newspapers and other magazines, arguing with them as well as reprinting from them articles and letters about evolution. For example, one debate between Spencer and another English writer took place in the pages of the *London Daily Telegraph* and the *Brighton Daily News,* then was picked up in *Popular Science Monthly.*[30] In the course of discussing Spencer and his ideas, *Popular Science Monthly* columns incorporated excerpts from numerous publications, including the *Saturday Review,* the *Spectator, Scribner's Magazine,* the *Nation,* the *New York Tribune, Nature, Harper's Weekly,* and *Fortnightly Review.*[31] *Popular Science Monthly* observed, "We can not speak of him as a 'popular' writer, yet he writes for the people."[32] Spencer's work was reproduced widely in the popular press, according to *Popular Science Monthly,* which also accused other publications of misinterpreting him as they spread his name and ideas.[33]

Social Darwinism's vitality was due in large measure to *Popular Science Monthly.* Spencer was a close associate of the magazine's founding editor, Edward Livingston Youmans, who supported Spencer both financially and philosophically. That Youmans founded the magazine in 1872—only a year after Darwin published *Descent of Man*—was very good timing for a journal that was aimed at a general audience but carried some weighty material from a variety of physical, life, and behavioral sciences. For the magazine's owner, D. Appleton and Company, Youmans organized the ambitious International Scientific Series of books by leading figures in science. Launched in 1872, the series eventually included about seventy volumes, published in the United States, England, France, Italy, Germany, and Russia. The series included *The Study of Sociology* by Spencer, who even was central to the founding of *Popular Science Monthly.* Youmans was working at *Galaxy* magazine, where he edited its "Scientific Miscellany." Working as Spencer's American agent, Youmans attempted to have *The Study of Sociology* serialized in *Galaxy.* When the magazine was unable to cooperate in simultaneous publication with a British publication, Youmans decided to start his own magazine.[34] He intended to introduce scientific experts to general readers, and he declared in the first issue that the object was to present "papers . . . on a wide range of subjects, from the ablest scientific men of different countries, explaining their views to non-scientific people."[35] In a short time, circulation rose to eleven thousand and by 1886 was up to eighteen thousand. Youmans's promotion of Spencer has been compared to Huxley's efforts on behalf of Darwin.[36] Youmans raised seven thousand dollars for Spencer in America, after low sales of Spencer's first volume of philosophy nearly caused the author to give up the project.[37] Spencer also used the magazine to defend himself against critics, and Youmans regularly defended and promoted Spencer in his monthly commentary, "Editor's Table."[38] Youmans, like Huxley, sought opportunities to instigate sympathetic reviews in the popular press. Youmans wrote to Spencer in 1864 that he had prepared a review for the *New York Tribune,* which "circulates mainly among that class which it is important to reach, and is moreover of great influence with other newspapers."[39] In the first issue of *Popular Science Monthly,* Youmans said that the primary purpose of the magazine was to extend the domain of science beyond the traditional physical sciences: "Intellect, feeling, human action, language, education, history, morals, religion, law, commerce, and all social relations and activities, answer to this condition; each has its basis of fact, which is the legitimate subject-matter of scientific inquiry." The list sounds like an outline for Spencer's philosophy, which eventually did cover all those areas. The second major goal, according to Youmans, was to bring a high-quality scientific literature before the general public, "not the trash that caters to public ignorance, wonder, and prejudice."[40]

In the early years of the magazine, Spencer wrote articles regularly, including his thirteen-part "Study of Sociology," which was devoted largely to defining the field, its problems, and its methodology. Spencer wrote or was the subject of articles in every volume for the first fourteen years of the magazine, after which William J. Youmans, brother of Edward L. Youmans, took over as editor.[41] William had studied in England under Huxley,[42] and, although Spencer's role in the magazine declined after the death of Edward L. Youmans in 1887, it did not disappear.

The anthropologist W. J. McGee wrote at the close of the century that "America has become a nation of science."[43] E. L. Youmans was an important figure in that transformation. John Fiske (1842–1901), of Harvard, a historian, philosopher, and a leading intellectual light of the late nineteenth century, wrote that Youmans "did more than anyone else to prepare the way in America for the great scientific awakening which first became visible after the publication of *The Origin of Species.*"[44]

But Spencer was not dependent solely upon Youmans's publicity skills, and he received attention in a wide range of popular publications. For example, Spencer was noticed in *Harper's,* a middle-class magazine noted for literary quality, serializing such authors as Charles Dickens, William Thackery, Anthony Trollope, and Thomas Hardy.[45] Along with *Century, Atlantic Monthly,* and *Scribner's Magazine*, it was one of the four major popular magazines of the late nineteenth century. *Scribner's,* also aimed at educated middle-class readers, reported on Spencer, too. Like *Harper's,* it published science and travel pieces, as well as fiction and nonfiction, often drawing on established writers.[46] Spencer was finding an audience in widely read, well-regarded magazines.

In England, Spencer's appeal was shown by his appearance in such an unlikely magazine as *The Leader,* which was founded in 1850 and had a following among radical artisans. Its support came from middle-class radicals and socialists. As it became a proponent of laborers' rights, it came to fill a gap between the *Athenaeum,* which was oriented toward the arts, and the *Spectator,* which was politically conservative. G. H. Lewes, one of the original promoters of the publication, was a drama and literary critic—and a close friend of Spencer. Some of Spencer's earliest sociological studies were published anonymously in *The Leader,* where he defended the idea of evolution as early as 1852.[47] In the *North British Review,* established in 1844, Spencer was publishing even in the literary journal of the evangelical wing of the Church of Scotland. Here was Spencer in a magazine that condemned *The Origin* because of its theological implications. It was circulating to about three thousand readers by the mid-1860s, when it had become a more sophisticated and broad-based review. By the time that it ceased publication in 1871, it was rather liberal.[48]

Spencer's "Survival of the Fittest"

It was Spencer, not Darwin, who coined the term "survival of the fittest," but Darwin incorporated it into later editions of *On the Origin of Species*. Spencer was not pleased with Darwin's preeminence in evolutionary thought. On several occasions, Spencer criticized Darwin and pointed out that he had preceded Darwin in publishing work on evolution. It did not escape Spencer, as it sometimes did other writers in popular periodicals,[49] that Darwin's chief contribution was the idea not of evolution, but of natural selection, the mechanism by which evolution worked. A bit of jealousy was in the air at times, as Spencer and other writers for *Popular Science Monthly* found it necessary to show readers that Spencer had been publishing books and essays on evolution well before Darwin published *The Origin* in 1859.[50]

Spencer's and his allies' struggles to establish his primacy in evolutionary thinking reveals a problem in studying social Darwinism—Spencer's criticism of Darwin. Struggling to differentiate himself from Darwin, Spencer said that the concept of natural selection was an "untenable hypothesis," basically because of what he called the assumption that it could "pick out and select any small advantageous trait; while it can, in fact, pick out no traits, but can only further the development of traits which, *in marked ways,* [emphasis in original] increase the general fitness for the conditions of existence." Spencer argued that it was not shown how the slight variations posited by Darwin actually were providing an advantage.[51] Spencer subtly rejected an important part of Darwin's argument, and at the same time assimilated parts of Darwin's thinking into his system of synthetic philosophy. In discussing the evolution of society, Spencer said that it was "impossible for artificial molding to do that which natural molding does," apparently denying the relevance of Darwin's argument from artificial selection in domesticated animals. But, he stated, "in the absence of variety, life would never have evolved at all."[52] Variation was, of course, a critical part of Darwin's explanation of evolution.

Spencer's attempts to distinguish himself from Darwin often were labored and his points unclear. Both men clearly saw "survival of the fittest" as being cooperative as well as competitive, but they differed on the significance of natural selection as an explanation of biological evolution. This latter point was the problem for Spencer because Darwin increasingly became preeminent in the realm of biological evolution, so much so that he appeared to be gaining credit in the public mind for all of evolutionary thinking. Darwin was a scientist, Spencer a philosopher. The theory of natural selection was of limited use to a philosopher but invaluable to a biologist.

Popular Science Monthly correctly considered Spencer a philosopher first and a scientist second.[53] The philosopher's social Darwinism was far more complex than economic survival of the fittest, as Spencer attempted to embrace physical and intellectual vitality, along with individual and social progress. Most significant for Spencer and the popular concept of "survival of the fittest," however, is the fact that he was not endorsing a vicious, tooth-and-claw social order. Subsequent interpretations of social Darwinism often ignored the role of cooperation in evolution and dwelled upon competition, particularly when it was manifested as conflict. Spencer's brand of social evolution allowed for "sentiments and institutions both relaxing" from a predatory atmosphere. He attacked government welfare and embraced private charity.

Like Darwin, Spencer accommodated cooperation as well as competition in evolution.[54] He did not want the less fit, "the feeble, the unhealthy, the deformed, the stupid" to be eradicated, but he suggested some "private industrial institution" to discourage their marriage and breeding. He conceded that suffering might be necessary to decrease government welfare, which encouraged a stratum of "worthless people." However, he believed that the movement from "state-beneficence to a healthy condition of self-help and private beneficence, must be like the transition from an opium-eating life to a normal life—painful but remedial."[55]

Spencer opposed government but not private help. He believed that programs to aid the poor should promote self-help, in order that the poor might elevate themselves. His endorsement of self-help revealed a positive side of Spencer's social Darwinism. He was a critic of what he called the "pleasure-hunting life," which he believed would result in an unfit individual and, ultimately, an unfit society. Self-assertion and self-preservation, he said, benefited society by keeping the divisions of society strong, or "more fit."[56] In numerous instances, Spencer's survival of the fittest was rather benign, notably lacking in tooth-and-claw logic. Spencer denied that he wished the principle to operate identically among people as among "brutes": "The survival of the fittest, as I construe it in its social applications, is the survival of the industrially superior and those who are fittest for the requirements of social life. . . . aggression of every kind is hateful to me; . . . I have urged the change of all laws which either inflict injustice or fail to remedy injustice."[57]

Spencer explained that two "sets of conditions" were necessary in order for people living together to achieve the greatest happiness: justice and generosity. The closest that *Popular Science Monthly* came to espousing a brutal kind of social Darwinism was in an editor's column that criticized socialism's condemnation of economic competition. The problem, the editor said, was not "survival of the fittest," but human nature: "We have only to think for one moment of what the world would be in the complete absence of competition—in other words, in the absence of all means for selecting the fit and rejecting the unfit or the less fit—in order to see that competition in itself is not and cannot be evil. That evils attach themselves to it signifies nothing more than that human society is as yet imperfect."[58] Most of the article was devoted to the "golden rule": Do unto others as you would have them do unto you. The editor argued that competition served that rule by promoting the general welfare of society via orderly and *fair* competition.

Spencer, in the pages of *Popular Science Monthly,* fit evolution to society. Contrary to popular interpretations, however, Spencer was not a Darwinian, and he actually disavowed natural selection. Riding the crest of popular interest that *The Origin* generated, Spencer agreed with Darwin that both competition and cooperation were critical to social, as well as biologic, evolution. This point was lost on later eugenicists.

Sumner: Putting Spencer into Practice

Sumner was a prolific writer and lecturer, but in some respects he contrasted strongly with Spencer. The latter man outlined fairly early in his career a twenty-year agenda for completing the multitude of volumes that would comprise his synthetic philosophy. He then set about writing the intellectually weighty tomes. Sumner, who praised Spencer as the man "who has opened the way" to sociology,[59] was not so disciplined in publishing or so subservient to an agenda as his mentor. Much of his writing has survived as lecture notes, drafts of chapters, and essays that were never published, as well as in the form of wide-ranging articles for, and letters to, various newspapers and magazines. From 1869 to 1896, he wrote approximately 125 articles and letters for popular publications, including daily newspapers in New York and Chicago, and magazines such as *Collier's, Harper's Monthly, Cosmopolitan, London Economist,* and *The Independent.* The specialty publications for which he wrote included the *New York Mercantile Journal,* the *Northwestern Lumberman, Rand McNally's Banker's Monthly,* and the *Bond Review.* His debates, too, were public matters. In 1883, in New York and New Haven newspapers, nearly twenty letters were exchanged, with Sumner opposing protective tariffs and a local linen manufacturer strongly favoring them.[60]

Both Sumner and Spencer tended to publish in the upscale literary magazines most likely to have an educated audience interested in social, economic, and political issues. In *Collier's,* for example, one would find a literary orientation that attempted to rival *Harper's. Collier's,* founded in 1888, published the work of such writers as Rudyard Kipling and Frank Norris, the poetry of James Whitcomb Riley, and Henry James's serialized *The Turn of the Screw.* The magazine's content was a bit lighter than that of *Harper's,* which was viewed as both a model and a competitor, but the circulation of *Collier's* rose to three hundred thousand shortly after the turn of the century.[61] Similarly, *Cosmopolitan,* founded in 1886, was a general literary magazine, not quite on the level of *Harper's* or the *Atlantic,* but comparing favorably to them. It was oriented more toward public affairs and by the 1890s was one of the leading illustrated magazines in the nation, noted for its coverage of current events as well as its fiction, which included work by William Dean Howells and Jack London.

Compared to its competitors, *Cosmopolitan* carried more features on economic, political, and social issues, and here Sumner's writing fit very well.[62]

Like Spencer's, Sumner's popular writings were concerned with larger social issues, and "survival of the fittest" constituted only a part of his arguments. A character sketch in *Popular Science Monthly* very accurately and succinctly provided the context for studying Sumner, to whom the magazine attributed a philosophy that "denies anything arbitrary or accidental in social phenomena, or that there is any field in them for the arbitrary intervention of man. He therefore allows but very limited field for legislation. He holds that men must do with social laws what they do with physical laws—learn them, obey them, and conform to them."[63] Sumner followed Spencer's thinking in believing that society, like nature, was subject to laws, and people were obligated to follow them, and should not attempt to tamper with them. The basic law, of course, was evolution.[64] Furthering this philosophy was a major theme in Sumner's popular writing. For Sumner, the role of government was narrow. He stated, in his widely read *What Social Classes Owe to Each Other,* that government had to deal only with two primary things: "They are the property of men and honor of women. These it has to defend against crime."[65]

Folkways (1907) was the book upon which Sumner's reputation came to rest. Sociologist Charles Horton Cooley compared *Folkways,* which was the first book to become a sociological classic in America, to *The Origin* in significance. Sumner's primary contribution to sociology was the introduction of general concepts that were based upon methodical observation and collection of evidence. His sociology was descriptive and based on facts, in contrast to Spencer's abstract philosophizing.

Sumner and "Natural Law"

Sumner paralleled Darwin in relying upon natural law, not metaphysics or theology, for answers to questions about the workings of the world. But where Darwin disciplined himself to stay within the confines of empirical science, Sumner did not, putting his energy into economic policy, immigration, tariffs, and any number of legislative initiatives that he saw as naïvely defying the law of evolution. This was Sumner's distortion of Darwinian evolutionary theory, as well as the way in which he applied the Spencerian philosophy to everyday political and social issues.

Sumner's intellectual relationship to Spencer is most apparent in the idea of an "organic" society.[66] Like Spencer, Sumner declared that customs, including laws and regulations, had to evolve slowly in order to be effective: "Legislation and state action are stiff, rigid, inelastic, incapable of adaptation to cases. . . . Hence, the higher the organization of society, the more mischievous legislative regulation is sure to be."[67] In the same essay, Sumner asserted that people were limited in their power and by their antecedents. The answer was "in ourselves," and there was no escaping the "struggle for existence."[68]

Sumner believed that legislative meddling in the economy usually started with legislators and their backers, who worked in ignorance of the nature of society and economics. Typically they only made matters worse by attempting to change natural law. For example, he cautioned that regulating railroads should begin with knowledge gained by "experience and observation," and he even conceded that a regulatory commission might be a good idea—a concession that would not have been made by one espousing a merely antagonistic survival of the fittest. But Sumner warned that "blundering experiments in legislation cannot be simply abandoned if they do not work well; . . . they leave their effects behind."[69] Sumner extended Spencer's "organic society" concept by making each component of a more complex society, like the organs of more highly evolved life forms, highly sensitive to changes in any other "organ" of the society.[70]

This highlights one of the points of confusion about social Darwinism, as it was presented to the public: the "unit of analysis" problem. What was being studied, society as a whole or the individuals within society? Both Sumner and Spencer compared "organic society" to a biological organism, implying that society was the object of analysis; but they also spoke of individual fitness as being critical to the progress of society, suggesting that the essential concern was with the individual. This ambiguity invited conflicting applications of Darwinism. If the law acted upon society generally, then one easily could interpret it as advocating cooperation and regulation. If, however, the individual was preeminent, then competition and minimal government were the engines of progress.

Sumner drew not only from Darwin and Spencer but also from Malthus, who articulated the idea that a very real law affecting humanity was the ratio of population to available land. Populations would grow geometrically (2, 4, 8, 16), Malthus hypothesized, while resources grew only arithmetically (2, 4, 6, 8). Sumner called this one of the "facts of the social order . . . which control the fate of the human race."[71] Ignoring these laws meant being unable to understand the workings of society. In the laws of nature, he said, "It will be found that men are subject to supply and demand, . . . and that any correct comprehension of the existing industrial system must proceed from supply and demand."[72]

It was in this broader conception of laws that Sumner found a place for the idea of "survival of the fittest" in society.[73] For both Sumner and Spencer, the concept of natural selection, or survival of the fittest, was actually an idea of secondary importance in understanding humanity. Unlike Spencer, who was working out a whole philosophical system, Sumner was dealing only with the sociological impact of Darwin's theory. The struggle for existence was necessary, according to Sumner, because it was dictated by natural law and could not be abolished.[74] But for Sumner, to posit a struggle for existence was not to glorify men grinding one another out in bloody struggle. In fact, he condemned strife: "It is legitimate to think of Nature as a hard mistress against whom we are maintaining the struggle for existence. All our science and art are victories over her, but when we quarrel amongst ourselves we lose the fruits of our victory just as certainly as we should if she were a human opponent. All plunder and robbery squander the fund which has been produced by society for the support of society. It makes no difference whether the plunder and robbery are legal or illegal in form."[75] He did not deny that "weaker" societies had perished at the hands of stronger ones, a pattern that he saw in history when civilized and uncivilized societies clashed, with the former usually emerging as victors. Europeans dominated the world, he believed, because they had been the most enterprising people in the fifteenth and sixteenth centuries.[76]

Economic competition was, for Sumner, a law that forced individuals to develop "all powers that exist according to their measure and degree. . . . Liberty of development and equality of result are therefore diametrically opposed to each other." Individuals varied according to inherited powers, advantages of training, and personal attributes such as courage and perseverance; the results of their efforts varied accordingly.[77] Millionaires, he said, "are a product of natural selection, acting on the whole body of men to pick out those who can meet the requirement of certain work to be done." Society benefited by imposing discipline on the economic system, as competitors studied the victor's winning ways, and by insuring that those talented in special areas eventually would find their way to those areas. In this fashion he reconciled a "ceaseless war of interests" with the betterment of the whole society.[78]

The struggle for existence, Sumner said, was a struggle with nature. Moreover, "Competition . . . is a law of nature."[79] He abhorred socialism, which he saw as a system making some people pay for the self-indulgence, idleness, and ignorance of others: "We shall favor the survival of the unfittest, and we shall accomplish this by destroying liberty. Let it be understood that we cannot go outside of this alternative: liberty, inequality, survival of the fittest; not-liberty, equality, survival of the unfittest. The former carries society forward and favors all its best members; the latter carries society downward and favors all it worst members."[80] Socialism was mere sentimentalism that ignored the reality of society's fixed laws, "precisely analogous to those [laws] of the physical order." The socialist or philanthropist who saved victims of poverty was accused of "only cultivating the distress which he pretends to cure."[81] Sumner believed that hardships were the products of thousands of years of evolution of human society and that poverty was part of the whole system. "This is a world in which the rule is, 'Root, hog, or die,' . . . It is the popular experience which has formulated these sayings. How can we make them untrue?"[82]

Socialism's antithesis was individualism. Sumner called socialism a scheme to defraud an individual of liberty, "robbing him of his best chance of improving his position."[83] The complaint against socialism was the same as the complaint against undue state interference in the economy—it would impede the natural progress of society by stifling the advancement of the fittest members. The "observation of facts will show that men are unequal through a very wide range of variation," he asserted, setting up the proposition that survival of the fittest was a scientific concept based upon observable fact.[84] Even the idea that monopolies should be controlled by the state was a "sort of current dogma" that had not been adequately studied with attention to observable facts.[85] Sumner's disdain for sentimental socialism, misguided reformers, and whimsical regulation was based upon his insistence on the necessity of looking at the "facts," of treating the study of society like a physical science, with observation, analysis, and verification at the core of the search for knowledge. Any other path, he believed, was mere speculation.[86]

Sumner was willing to peel back the assumptions (which he felt commonly were paraded as facts) of human existence to a core of discomforting propositions: "Our assumption is that we should all be here, under any circumstances whatever, and that the provision for us here is, or ought to be, somewhere on hand. Unfortunately none of these ideas can be verified by an examination of the facts. We are not needed here at all; the world existed no one knows how long without any men on it."[87]

Natural Law, Natural Selection

Sumner and Spencer stressed the results of a long evolutionary process on society. They offered social reality as evidence—the existence of the poor, the existence of weaker and stronger nations, and the economic progress of the U.S. under capitalism—and in doing so borrowed the prestige of Darwin and of science. They used the language of Darwin—employing such terms as "selection" and "organism"—but not his painstaking, tedious attention to collecting data in support of a theory.

As popularizers, Youmans, Spencer, and Sumner were prominent at a time when science and social science were increasingly important in the academy and for the public. Social Darwinism justified a number of Victorian ideals: the divisions of society, the rewards of industry, the goal of "the good life," the virtues of civility and civilization. Hofstadter depicts social Darwinism as basically a defense of unregulated capitalism, a system of ideas that fit easily into the American mythology of the rugged individualist. Hofstadter recognizes the contradictory applications of social Darwinism, such as defending both socialism and capitalism, but he asserts that the American middle class's ideology of achievement made tooth-and-claw Darwinism the accepted version of the philosophy's many permutations.[88] However, Spencer's and Sumner's writing in periodicals, which were aimed at middle- and upper-class audiences, reveal far greater complexity in the tenets of the movement. Although the robber barons might seize upon social Darwinism, such an application was only one act in the grander mission of uplifting all of society. This use of social Darwinism may have reached its zenith in Andrew Carnegie's 1889 article on social Darwinism, in which the author linked individualism, social divisions, and economic competition.[89] But Sumner and Spencer reached a conclusion unlike Carnegie's, because their goal was to elaborate a coherent world view which might both explain society and establish an agenda for further sociological inquiry. Carnegie, as well as others who eschewed his simplistic view, were only defending the status quo.

Social Darwinism itself was well suited to popularization. Its core idea was rather simple: the survival of the fittest in human society. Although it had its complexities and contradictions, its essence was, and is, quite easy to convey in nontechnical language. The idea gained power and attention because it offered a good explanation of social problems, such as poverty and disease. At the same time, it provided a good defense of one's relative wealth and health. Thus, inequality could be seen not as a political or social problem but merely as the working out of natural law.

However, an incongruity arose in the association of Darwin with nonbiological social Darwinism. The nonbiological nature of the ideas espoused by Sumner and Spencer is shown in their attempts to divorce themselves from, and at times to criticize, the central tenet of Darwinism—natural selection. The social Darwinists could not divorce themselves from the Darwin name, nor would they have wanted to lose the credibility that association with his empirical science entailed. To the chagrin of Spencer, Darwin's name became a vehicle for popularizing an evolutionary philosophy. Through its association with Darwin and natural selection, the philosophy took on the aura of a science. For both Sumner and Spencer, so-called "social Darwinism" (neither of them used the term) was a secondary idea, not a primary one. Both derived their social laws from the broader concept of natural law, to which humanity, as well as the rest of the universe, was subject. Both Spencer and Sumner gave minimal credit to Darwin but were strongly identified with him. Charles Darwin was not central to the philosophy of social Darwinism in its popular origins.

Chapter 5

The Spanish-American War:
For the Sake of Empire, Not Science

The Spanish-American War took place after Herbert Spencer's philosophy of social Darwinism had crested in popularity. The Gilded Age of the last quarter of the nineteenth century witnessed all of the sins that would be expected in a rapidly expanding, generally unregulated economy: exploitation of labor, the amassing of great fortunes by a few, monopolies, market manipulation, an often unholy alliance of business and politics, to name a few. It was a jungle out there. But it was largely the economic environment and not biological theory that drove America into the conflict with Spain. Social Darwinism was as changeable as the views of, and motives for, the war. Social Darwinism was convenient but not necessary as a justification for war. People and publications blended economics, nationalism, and race to suit numerous perspectives, sometimes adding heavy doses of Darwin, at other times little or none.

Social Darwinism has been handy when historians have rummaged around seeking reasons for the Spanish-American War; indeed, there was a strain of Darwinian thought behind that war. But social Darwinism was only one element in a kaleidoscope of ideas about economics, race, and expansion. The rationales for conflict came down to: protecting American investments, enforcing the Monroe Doctrine, and teaching a deserved lesson to a corrupt, faltering monarchy. In addition, many believed that the United States was on a moral mission, furthering civilization and its virtues, while manifest destiny entered its next stage as the nation moved beyond the continent. So social Darwinism, at the very least, had to fit into a complex array of ideas and motives. Richard Hofstadter, in *Social Darwinism in American Thought*, established a theme for many subsequent historians of the war: the significant impact of social-Darwinian thought as a justification of the conflict. Hofstadter was more concerned with tracing the existence of social Darwinism in America than he was with describing the contradictions and complexities of that general movement.[1] He did the former admirably. However, the coexistence of a philosophy and an event does not mean that the philosophy contributed to the event, or that the event helped to establish the philosophy. Hofstadter admitted that expansionists were not just waiting for a good philosophy to support their ideals. But he construed social Darwinism so broadly that it was synonymous with "Anglo-Saxonism." This is a problem because "Anglo-Saxonism" may be equivalent to ethnocentrism or, more severely, racism—both of which existed well before Darwin. And the existence of racism in the 1890s does not necessarily mean that it was Darwinian in nature.

The War

Tension between Spain and the United States had been building for several years before the outbreak of war in 1898. In February 1895, American sugar planters funded a revolt of Cuban insurgents against their Spanish masters. Spain brutally quashed the revolt by putting the peasant population into concentration camps in order more easily to pursue the guerrillas. What began as an economic issue quickly became a humanitarian one, for many Cubans died as a result of conditions in the camps. The New York press, especially Joseph Pulitzer's *World* and William Randolph Hearst's *Journal*, sensationalized the maltreatment and assailed Spanish barbarism. President Grover Cleveland opposed military action, but he could not match the vigor or the reach of the "yellow press," which clamored for war.

Congress became involved in April 1896 by offering to be an arbiter in the conflict between Spain and the Cuban insurgents. Spain refused the offer because the U.S. goal was Cuban independence. By the time a moderate premier was inaugurated in October 1897, the American public was in the mood for war. Atrocity stories abounded in the press, feeding the war sentiment despite the fact that the Spanish offered home rule to Cuba, as well as an end to the concentration camps. President William McKinley believed, in retrospect, that a peaceful solution to the disagreements might have been found; however, the public and Congress wanted war, and the president acceded to that wish.[2]

The demeanor of the popular press in New York was exemplified by its response to an episode in which the Spanish minister to the United States privately characterized McKinley as feeble. The letter got into Hearst's hands, and he published it in his *Journal,* heightening tensions. Hostilities appeared inevitable when the battleship *Maine* was destroyed in Havana Harbor in February 1898; debate continues as to whether a Spanish torpedo or an explosion in the ship's own ammunition magazine was to blame. The war began formally on April 19, 1898, when Congress authorized McKinley's use of military force to throw Spain out of Cuba. By summer, McKinley was demanding that Puerto Rico be turned over to the United States and that Cuba be granted independence. The conflict was short, with Spain signing an armistice on August 12 and a peace treaty on December 10.

The war did not end so quickly in another part of the disintegrating Spanish empire, the Philippines, where the United States fought Filipino insurrectionists well into 1899. McKinley had declared that the Philippines were to be developed, not exploited. He and other leaders supported the idea of holding the islands until the natives were deemed capable of governing themselves. It was 1946 before they appeared ready. The ratification of the treaty in 1898 involved lengthy debates between imperialists and anti-imperialists. The former argued that acquisition of new territory simply meant taking advantage of economic opportunity and spreading the influence of the United States. Anti-imperialists depicted the annexation of the Philippines as contrary to the American ideal of self-government and to the tradition of not going beyond the continent for territory.

A Thread in History

Hofstadter notes that social Darwinism was not the "primary source of the belligerent ideology and dogmatic racism of the late nineteenth century." But he calls it a "new instrument in the hands of the theorists of race and struggle."[3] Hofstadter explores the ideas of an elite social stratum, composed of professors, political leaders, educated clergy, and a few leading military men. Richard Welch, in *Response to Imperialism,* finds that the academic and scholarly communities were united in opposition to the war. These are the very groups so often cited by Hofstadter and others as embracing the Darwinian rationale for conquest. Welch relies heavily on comments by Theodore Roosevelt in exploring the social-Darwinian thought of the period, and he cites Roosevelt as an example of such thinking. Welch finds that racism played a large role in the war. Like Hofstadter, he defines social Darwinism very broadly.[4]

Walter LaFeber, in *The New Empire,* says that the first source of inspiration for those who advocated military force was social Darwinism, followed by Nietzsche, the triumph of Bismarck in western Europe, and concerns about the declining physical vitality of a nation without a frontier. LaFeber, too, attaches social Darwinism to a few thinkers, not the many.[5] David Healy's *U.S. Expansionism* treats social Darwinism similarly, as one among several factors, and he cites leading intellectual figures. But for Healy, the idea is an extremely vague one encompassing all sorts of competition, whether military or economic, and including racism and nationalism.[6]

Even the history of science identifies proponents of a sweeping sort of Darwinism. Stephen Gould states:

> Recapitulation [the notion that lesser races would degenerate into an uncivilized state with-
> out the guidance of superior races] had its greatest political impact as an argument to justify
> imperialism. . . . During the Spanish-American War, a major debate arose in the United States
> over whether we had a right to annex the Philippines. When anti-imperialists cited Henry Clay's
> contention that the Lord would not have created a race incapable of self-government, Rev.
> Josiah Strong replied: "Clay's conception was formed before modern science had shown that
> races develop in the course of centuries as individuals do in years, and that an underdeveloped
> race, which is incapable of self-government, is no more a reflection on the Almighty than is an
> underdeveloped child who is incapable of self-government."[7]

In one of the best works on the history of social Darwinism, Robert Bannister states simply that biological racism, independent of Darwin, drove the imperialist urge. He says that Darwinian ideas could be found among both anti-imperialists and imperialists, and that both groups believed in the superiority of Anglo-Saxons.[8] Thomas Gossett argues, in *Race: The History of an Idea in America,* "Social Darwinism provided ready and seemingly invincible arguments for the expansionists of 1898."[9] Morton White recognizes that the idea was primarily Spencerian, not Darwinian, but he and Schlesinger consider only the intellectual circle of thought. In the same work, *Paths of American Thought*, Donald Fleming asserts that American thinkers were invoking Spencer "to put the stamp of the cosmos upon the advance of the Anglo-Americans to world dominion over lesser breeds."[10] Paul Boller, in *American Thought in Transition,* like Fleming, assigns a significant role to social Darwinism, while stressing the economic motive. For Boller, social Darwinism, in its application to imperialism, was very much a race doctrine. Many people, he says, believed that freedom was an accomplishment of the fittest races, which usually meant Anglo-Saxons.[11] Other historians find a similarly obvious, but vague, kind of social Darwinism. Merle Curti, for example, in his classic *Growth of American Thought,* says that social Darwinism was used as a reason for expansion, and he points out the very important role played by thought about superior races and expanding civilization.[12]

Historians have found other catalysts for the war. David Trask says that imperialist sentiment alone did not account for the decision to go to war, and he cites the desires to expand trade and to throw Spain out of the hemisphere. Politics, of course, was present. Trask states, "McKinley chose to fight because he could divine no means of weathering the public enthusiasm for support for Cuban independence."[13] Marcus Wilkerson, in *Public Opinion and the Spanish-American War*, finds that newspapers concentrated largely on the ideal of freedom, with some anti-European sentiment thrown in.[14]

In these studies and others, both economics and social Darwinism are persistent themes. The economic motive has been portrayed in a variety of ways, from blind greed to humanitarian assistance. With or without the social Darwinian crutch, this was the most significant factor leading to American involvement in hostilities. The economic reasons for American action were outlined by politicians, clergy, academics, and popular periodicals. If social Darwinism had been a key justification for war, the economic argument would have been the most logical point at which to inject the "survival of the fittest," but usually that did not occur.

Survival of the Richest

In its simplest form, the appeal to superiority had only tenuous connections to Darwinism. Instead, superiority was defined broadly as economic progress. The quest for empire—taking Cuba—was perceived as a natural function of a growing civilization and its economy, rather than as an effort to elevate an inferior race. Numerous popular articles about the war could be interpreted, if very liberally, as using social Darwinism to rationalize imperialism. However, the Darwinian remarks often were of secondary or tertiary concern. What might pass for Darwinism often involved nothing more than equating commercial growth with the advance of civilization. In its other forms, the economic justification postured as Darwinism when imperialism was defined simply as an economic act, when races or nations were compared economically, or when economic opportunism was touted as a virtue. This vague social Darwinism was evident in a number of popular publications aimed at the upper-middle and upper classes. For example, an article in *Atlantic Monthly* was explicit about racial traits but said nothing of Darwin, Spencer, or science. It charged that Cubans were "like a race of slaves. . . . but the race as a whole is peaceable and well disposed. . . . It is unintelligent, moreover, to blame the Cuban people for the bad qualities forced upon their character during Spanish rule, when deception became almost necessary." The writer argued that Cuban businessmen wanted *permanent* American control in order to "enhance enormously the value of land and the volume of business."[15] The article stated that Cuban dependence upon America was for the island's own well-being. The author equated the social and political shortcomings that grew out of Spanish oppression with the passing on of biological traits. There was no real distinction between biological and political traits.

A similar idea surfaced in *Atlantic Monthly* in December 1898, in an article on control of the tropics. The writer was Benjamin Kidd, who in 1894 wrote *Social Evolution*, a book with substantial popular appeal, which won acclaim in both England and America. In the book, Kidd argued a basic Spencerian idea that competition would encourage the growth of society, or of what Spencer would call the "social organism." Kidd portrayed religion as an irrational system that basically served the purpose of getting people to behave in a socially responsible way. His ideas were unpopular with many rationalists, sociologists, proponents of laissez-faire, and even other Spencerians. However, this did not diminish the popularity of his book.[16] Kidd believed that the national quarrels within Europe really amounted to a centuries-long conflict between "the latin type of civilization, represented by the southern [European] races, and that type of civilization which has been developed in Northern Europe."[17] The Spanish-American conflict, he said, was only the latest episode in this struggle. But U.S. expansion was an economic urge, not a biological one: "The people of the United States will be driven to seek the widest possible outside market for their industrial productions, . . . for they will be the leading representatives of definite principles in the development of the world."[18]

Kidd's analysis of the relationship with the tropical lands was a study in imports, exports, and crop production. Kidd mingled race, nation, and even language, referring to the "English-speaking races." A clear definition of race eluded him, as he generalized instead about the subject in the context of vast geographical regions, without ever presenting race as a biological issue.[19] As he combined the racial and economic arguments in defending U.S. expansion, Kidd contended in the *Atlantic* that "we of the more vigorous races" had been busy colonizing the world and "taming the temperate regions." But he believed that this era was coming to an end and the age of economic expansion was at hand. Kidd said that trade with tropical regions was an aspect of the destiny of the United States.[20] In outlining the transition from geographical to economic expansionism, Kidd was a social Darwinist in that he relied upon Spencer's ideas: "The United States is the highest, and yet the youngest, of all *political organisms* [my emphasis],—an organism with a promise and a potentiality behind it of which there has been no previous parallel."[21] Although the idea of "political organisms," and the implication of social evolution, were pure Spencer, the article's primary argument was very straightforwardly economic, with Kidd analyzing American trade and concluding that one-third of American imports in 1895 were from tropical regions. In order of importance, Spencerian evolution ranked behind about $350 million in trade between the United States and the tropics.

An article in *Forum* also used Kidd to elevate economics over science as a sufficient justification for imperialism. The *Forum* offered a symposium on a variety of issues, which encompassed economics, politics, religion, and education. Its debates and clear writing helped it find a place in schools and college classrooms. By the end of the 1890s, with a circulation of about twenty thousand, it was a prestigious and influential journal whose contributors included Theodore Roosevelt, Woodrow Wilson, and other well-known academics.[22] It was in the same circle of magazines as *North American Review,* from which the *Forum's* first managing editor was hired, and the *Atlantic,* where the *Forum's* editor went in 1895.

In an article on "Isolation or Imperialism," the author said that Kidd's *Social Evolution* identified two attributes of "our race": individual initiative and "social efficiency." "The Tropics are peopled with millions of low social efficiency; and it seems to be the fate of the black and yellow races to have their countries parceled out and administered by efficient races from the Temperate Zone. If such administration be just, wise, and humane, . . . it will be for the upbuilding and enlightenment of the peoples of the Tropics, and the advance of the blessings of civilization over the world."[23]

He pleaded neither race nor money as the higher motive but simply stated that the United States should hold the islands in order to prevent a power scramble in the area, as Europeans competed for position. The American expansion was called the "new imperialism" and would be based upon Anglo-Saxon principles.[24] In his proposals for settling the issue of the Philippines, the first tenet was a treaty of arbitration among competing interests in the Pacific. The second item was to treat coal as contraband of war. The third condition was to open to commerce all countries acquired by the United States. In short, the issue was economics. All else—peace, civilization, law—was a means to economic ends.

Atlantic Monthly was consistent in publishing articles that focused on expansion as an economic issue, casting only an occasional sideways glance at the scientific—perhaps Darwinian—justification. Social Darwinism was not critical to the primary argument of promoting civilization through economics. One article stated that the goal of expansion was economic gain and that the expansion of civilization would be a commendable, but not primary, benefit. The lack of emphasis on the ability to uplift lesser races was explained away by "reversion," the tendency for the Negro to "revert [to a wild state], as soon as he is left to himself" without the guidance of Caucasians.[25] Another article, "Can New Openings Be Found for Capital?" touted the capitalist position. The writer, Charles Conant, who was prominent in financial and journalistic circles, was concerned with the problem of "excess capital." In 1896–1905, he wrote several books on economic issues, including *The United States in the Orient: The Nature of the Economic Problem* (1900). At the time of the Spanish-American War, he was the Washington correspondent for the *New York Commercial Bulletin*, and in 1902 he became treasurer for Morton Trust Company. Thus, he was well suited to communicate the economic argument to a popular audience. Conant's detailed economic analysis provided a list of outlets for American capital: electricity, extension of railways over Africa and Asia, equipping those continents with heavy machinery. But there was no direct reference to imperialism as a necessary prelude to utilizing the outlets. The movement of capital involved international economics, not war.[26]

Conant made a similar argument in the *North American Review,* this time with a touch of Darwinism: "The law of self preservation, as well as that of survival of [the] fittest, is urging our people on in a path which is undoubtedly a departure from the policy of the past, but which is inevitably marked out by the new conditions and requirements of the present."[27] However, the Darwinism was thrown in without any reference to biology or society, only as an approach to an economic issue, which was the accumulation of capital. The imperialistic urge, Conant stated, was the "result of a natural law of economic and race development." The natural law to which he alluded probably was the Spencerian idea of evolution as a cosmic, metaphysical force. Spencer believed that humanity was evolving toward a higher state and that "survival of the fittest" was a positive law which promoted the progress of humanity. Conant, drawing on this general concept of evolution, applied it equally to any aspect of the human condition—biological, sociological, or economic.

When the *North American Review* flirted with a similar blend of imperialism and economics, it suggested some kind of social Darwinism. The author, John Barrett, former U.S. minister to Siam, deemed Filipinos "unprepared" for democracy, but he did not say they were unfit. The first reason for taking the Philippines, Barrett said, was to extend commerce and trade. In a long list of reasons for U.S. expansion, all were related to commerce and none to biology. Another part of the same article, written by another author, pointed out that "intercourse with superior races . . . lays the foundation of civilization."[28] But the expansion of civilization was gauged economically, not racially.

Even a clergyman, the Reverend Lyman Abbott, joined in the chorus of economic arguments. Abbott was a moderate reformist and one of the most influential clergymen of the period. As editor of the *Outlook*, Abbott had propagated the liberal theology of Henry Ward Beecher, who preached a "Christian evolution" in which theology would be enlarged by evolution, while religion remained fixed and essential to humanity. For example, Abbott proposed that immoral acts actually represented regression into an animal state, and that God's greatness would not be diminished by the existence of original sin. Abbott had discarded the traditional concept of sin, although his theistic evolution still held sin abhorrent; he believed that Christianity was made more powerful by being restated in evolutionary terms. In this view, the Bible became a record of humanity's moral and spiritual growth, and sin became a relapse into an earlier stage of development rather than an implied libel of God. The ultimate goal of Abbott's evolutionary Christianity was the establishment of God's kingdom on earth.[29] Abbott wrote in the *North American Review* that enterprise actually was a characteristic of the "Anglo-Saxon race."

Advocating an English-American alliance to promote economic development, he gave three reasons for the partnership. The first was "commercial principles." He believed that the United States and England could be polite rivals who would "lead the world commercially." The next two reasons were political and moral advantages. The ethical standards of the United States, Abbott said, were Christian: "Its ruling force in the country, educational, political, and on the whole commercial, is not Celtic, nor Slavic, nor Semitic, nor African, nor Mongolian, but Anglo-Saxon."[30] His list revealed a strong allegiance to economics, but his idea of race was a mixture of religion, language, and geography—not biology. He concluded: "Invincible against enemies, illimitable in influence, at once inspiring and restraining each other, these two nations, embodying the energy, the enterprise, and the conscience of the Anglo-Saxon race, would by the mere fact of their co-operation produce a result in human history which would surpass all that present imagination can conceive or present hope anticipate."[31]

Exalting America

Nationalism often was entwined with isolationism, with Anglo-Saxons cast as the ones who would further world civilization, remaining aloof from the decadence of old Europe and civilizing the barbarians everywhere else. The nationalist rationale for war with Spain also incorporated social Darwinism. Nationalism places nations in competition with one another and puts political "organisms," to use Spencer's term, in competition with one another. But, upon closer inspection, "social organisms" and "nationalism" take different directions in Spencer's evolutionary philosophy. He believed that evolution was a natural law, a process that could not suddenly be changed by such devices as the introduction of a new set of laws via "paper constitutions," which he disdained and believed could sidetrack social evolution only temporarily. Imposing a written set of laws or ruling people by force, Spencer believed, did not promote evolution toward a higher level of civilization, because such action would constitute an interruption of the natural evolutionary process. In other words, such an imposition might appear to be of value but in fact was not, because it was done outside the natural stream of evolutionary progress. A sudden takeover of the Philippines, as advocated by nationalists, was contrary to Spencer's ideals, because such action would disrupt the natural evolution of Filipino society.

Nationalism did not need social Darwinism and usually made no pretense of embodying social Darwinism. An *Atlantic* writer, discussing U.S. problems with England, said, "A serious danger arises from *national vanity*, [emphasis in original] as a popular failing in countries that are democratically governed in form or in fact." The writer believed that commerce and religion were the chief reasons for international conflict.[32] Even when nationalists adopted racial themes, social Darwinism was unnecessary. For example, "A Century of Anglo-Saxon Expansion," in the *Atlantic Monthly,* explained world history and progress in terms of race. The Anglo-Saxon race, "in itself the most wonderful of all time," was destined for "kindly domination" of the world. After a century of annexation and growth, the author said, the Anglo-Saxon race obviously was the most vital, energetic, productive, and intellectual race ever to inhabit the earth. The author predicted that the twentieth century would see an even greater expansion of the Anglo-Saxons, which would go hand-in-hand with founding a "united commonwealth of all nations."[33] The virtue of race, like nationalism, was an assumption, not a scientific point to be argued.

In addition, writers in the *Atlantic Monthly* stated, history was supporting America. Asserting that "the United States has been one of the greatest and most successful colonizing powers the world has ever known," Lawrence Lowell, a lecturer at Harvard who later became its president, wrote: "Finally, we must not forget that the Anglo-Saxon race is expansive. . . . It seems altogether probable . . . that if the war with Spain had not broken out, the question of expansion would have arisen in some concrete form before many decades had passed, and that it would ultimately have been answered in the affirmative."[34] Interestingly enough, Lowell was an antiexpansionist whose argument neatly combined economics, historical inevitability, and racism. The racism, however, was an artifact of Lowell's concepts of economics and historical inevitability. He deduced Anglo-Saxons' power from their economic success, and he assumed historical inevitability, which was presented as a fact. Thus, the social-political phenomena of economics and the false logic of inevitability were used as foundations for "discovering" and asserting a biological phenomenon—racial superiority. As was the case in so many popular writings that supported expansion, social Darwinism followed rather than preceded nationalism.

Harper's magazine ran a series of articles that illustrated very well the nationalist rationale for territorial expansion. For nationalists, American expansion was explained not so much by racial superiority as by historical and divine forces: "The real motive which may dispose American opinion towards a policy of territorial aggrandizement is that impulse which every great nation feels to keep abreast of other great nations. . . . [The motive to expand] springs from the wish to bear a part in the work of developing the backward parts of our earth and civilizing its ruder or lower races. . . . [E]very such people conceives it has a mission to propagate its peculiar ideas and its . . . civilization."[35] But the idea of "ruder races" was not developed in this article or others. Again, it was a presumption that accompanied the nationalistic urge.

Harper's illustrated the presumptions about race and nation a few months earlier, in an article by Professor Albert Bushnell Hart, a historian at Harvard University and an imperialist. He argued that the "land-hunger" of Americans put the United States on a collision course with Cuba, because of Americans' "natural, hearty, and irrepressible desire to make a large country larger [and] their conviction that Anglo-Saxon civilization must prevail over Latin civilization where they come in conflict."[36] In another article, Hart reiterated the primacy of manifest destiny, but gave it a humanitarian twist:

> In 1898, moved partly by humanity, but more by manifest national interest, the United States has compelled Spain by force of arms to leave Cuba to the Cubans, and to cede Puerto Rico outright. . . .
>
> . . . The United States has heretofore found little occasion to assert its dignity as a World Power: our strength is unquestioned. . . .
>
> . . . [A]nnexations, interventions, colonies, and international influence are not new factors in our national life. . . . The advance into the West Indies is as inevitable as it was into Texas and California.[37]

So he explained the U.S. push as a nationalistic impulse. The racial implications followed from the fact that the dominant "race" in America was Anglo-Saxon. So if one were talking about American progress, manifest destiny, or economic expansion, one naturally was talking about Anglo-Saxons and thereby was speaking of "race," as it was defined at the time. Darwin was incidental to the idea.

The issue of racial characteristics emerged by way of ardent nationalism and a desire for economic progress. It usually was the case that the argument for expansion was economic or nationalistic; the latter concern is implicitly economic, inasmuch as a nation looking out for its own interests and the welfare of its citizens often is doing so by guarding material welfare and promoting the growth of wealth. When Kidd, for example, made his economic argument, the racism was couched in terms of economics, not biology.[38]

A companion piece to Kidd's in the *Atlantic Monthly* was racist, too, but a close reading reveals an ill-defined notion of race. In discussing what poor slaves the Dutch colonists had found some Negroes to be, the author treated blacks harshly, mentioning reversion to barbarism once the bonds of Christianity were removed, and the apparent inability of education to improve the race. However, he said it was possible that the Dutch were simply poor managers, not that West Indians were defective by nature. Only three paragraphs, in a seven-page article, considered biological factors. The rest was taken up with economics.[39] But the structure of the article reflects the common thinking. The race issue was part of the larger economic problem. The article exhibits another trait common in the racial argument: inconsistency. The concept of race was knotted up in arguments not only about economics, but also about religion versus superstition, civilization versus barbarism, energy versus indolence, and adaptability versus rigidity.

Racism without Darwinism

Racial differences were presumed in 1898, and racial distinctions that degenerated into racism did not need the support of science in order to find acceptance across society. When race came to the front of the imperialism debate, racism was assumed and accepted, not explained. The assumptions about race are evident in the way it was equated with concepts that no longer are accepted as necessary correlates of race. Various social and political conditions were viewed as functions of race. Democracy and personal liberty, for example, were seen as ideals peculiar to Caucasians, especially Anglo-Saxons. Ignorance of such enlightened government was associated with people who were not Anglo-Saxons.

Two of the leading literary magazines, *Harper's* and *Atlantic Monthly*, reflected the assumptions about racial distinctions. The magazines were writing for an educated, middle-class audience and engaged major intellectual figures to provide readable, credible articles. When *Harper's* magazine stated, "Political and race elements in Cuba have been much confused," it was showing the problems involved in using the word *race* as a term of convenience, in whatever manner best fit the prejudices of the individual writer.[40] An article in *Atlantic Monthly* illustrated the non-Darwinian concept of race. No biological definition of race was employed; instead the term was defined politically and geographically. The article, and others, divided the Anglo-Saxon "race" into "two great divisions," England and America—a definition which further supports the idea that race was defined not biologically, but geographically.[41] *Harper's* came to a similar conclusion: "The common aims and aspirations of the United States and Britain, the bond of race, of language, of religion, and of government, indicate for them a common destiny." Race was everything but biological.[42]

Atlantic Monthly appealed time and again to racist impulses, but did so without bothering to analyze scientifically the logical or empirical foundations for assertions about racial distinctions.[43] The pages of the *Atlantic Monthly* hosted much discussion about an "evolved" political-social entity. During the conflict with Spain, an article titled "The American Evolution: Dependence, Independence, Interdependence" seemed Spencerian in its view of evolving society. But the concept of race made no pretense of scientific or philosophic grounding. The Anglo-Saxon "race" again was divided into two branches, which were separated by an ocean; both were destined to "civilize the globe." The article vaguely defined race by language and geography, and a teleological-evolutionary viewpoint was evident in the article's contention that social evolution was directed toward greater civilization, "one grand whole" across the globe. Anglo-Saxons would be the leaders in this evolution: "The welfare of the world depends upon their [American and English] accord."[44]

Anglo-Saxons were not the only ones divided by geography. *Harper's* divided blacks by national boundaries also, reinforcing the idea that race was defined by geography and national borders. Although American and Cuban blacks were not considered as different races, their accomplishments in politics and economics were attributed to national borders, with Cuban blacks seen as being in advance of American blacks. The fogginess of the idea of race was displayed by the differentiation of the "American race" and the "Anglo-Saxon race." Blacks, the article said, were attempting to assimilate into the latter, not the former. Furthermore, racial weaknesses were attributed to environment, not to innate biological differences. This was the reasoning when Spanish rulers were blamed for the moral failures of Cubans.

In spite of the fact that "race" was a term of convenience that lacked clarity, the hierarchy of races was quite clear. In equating race with political structure, subordinate and superior races were correlated with lesser and greater degrees of democracy in a political system. A *Harper's* article on colonization explained the relationship between race and government:

> The republican form [of government] has always halted at the edge of barbarism. It makes too heavy demands on men to prosper among any barbaric people. Probably the majority of Americans who have thought of the matter believe that the principles of our government are of universal application. Doubtless also many Americans believe that our political form possesses latent and inexhaustible virtues which need only contact with other races to transform them into self-governing and prosperous communities. . . . Our continental optimism is vigorous enough to cross oceans and ignore racial bounds. . . . Whatever civil service is demanded in ruling subordinate races . . . , that service will be construed as in harmony with the republican form.[45]

John Barrett, recounting his experiences as U.S. minister to Siam, had a more liberal view of race. He argued that Asians too quickly were labeled barbarians, noting, "Some uncomfortable experiences are remembered, but they were not due to any racial, tribal, or characteristic maliciousness. . . . The severest critics of Asiatics are those who see them only in passing." He found "more to commend than to censure in the character of the Filipino." He believed Filipinos fully capable of self-government, if they had the help of American training and experience.[46] But even in this more liberal pronouncement, Barrett reinforced the idea that races had peculiar characteristics, that race was geographical, and that Americans were superior. But he did not use, or need, Darwin or Spencer to come to that conclusion.

Thinking about race was mixed up with distinctions based on politics, economics, and geography. Even for liberal thinkers such as Barrett, racial differences were assumed, not scientifically explained.[47] This does not mean that social Darwinism was nonexistent. Darwinian and Spencerian ideas were part of the debate, but they were not the foundation of prejudices concerning racial distinctions.

Social Darwinism and Racism

The coexistence of Darwinian thought and racist thought is undeniable. The issue, though, is how much Darwinian thinking contributed to racism, which in turn helped to rationalize the war. If Darwinian and Spencerian ideas were linked with racism in a cause-and-effect relationship, there should be no ambiguity. But such an unambiguous relationship cannot be shown. By the late nineteenth century, evolution and racism were concepts that were widely embraced. Both had ancient roots, and both were profoundly affected by economic, political, and social conditions in Europe and America. The way in which these general ideas bled together was shown very well in *Popular Science Monthly,* Spencer's primary conduit for publicity in America. In "The Negro Question," a writer asserted that the debate about races had nothing to do with individual exceptions but was an issue of "race in the aggregate." The first Darwinian step was taken with this approach. The writer did not use the individual as a unit of analysis, but instead used the group as a unit of analysis, just as Darwin had used species, not individuals within the species, as his unit of analysis.[48]

But the writer struggled with a taxonomy that demanded discrete boundaries between species: "We find in the South the presence of two distinct peoples, with irreconcilable racial characteristics and diverse historical antecedents. The Caucasian and the negro are not simply unlike, but they are contrasted, and are as far apart as any other two races of human beings. They are unassimilable and immiscible without rapid degeneracy. Ethnologically they are nearly polar opposites."[49] The writer wanted to separate races in the same way one would separate species of animals, as was shown by his assertion that the races were "irreconcilable" and "unassimilable." Here was a veneer of science, with connections to Darwinian thinking and the adornment of scientific language. The author, however, sinks into confusion, trying to establish a severe taxonomy within a species. In order to support the idea, he would have had to show the existence of at least two races—and by his implication, species—of human beings, but his argument was founded largely upon his own assertions about behavioral traits, not on biological evidence or criteria.

Social Darwinism was more obvious in other publications, with such ideas as the "racial competition carried through countless ages," industrial "survival of the fittest," and the ascendancy of "blue-eyed races" over Celtic and Latin races.[50] The survival of the fittest emerged in its most brute form: "It is a theory as old as man that the land belongs to those who can till it, the mines to those who can work them, the watercourses to those who can use them—and who possess the force to hold their own. . . . I can see but one policy to pursue—that of free trade in the Philippines, permitting the islands to find their place under the full stress of competition."[51] However, the writer was not concerned with racial differences, but with commerce. Race was an economic issue, not a biological one.

Sen. Henry Cabot Lodge wrote that Spain's problem was simply being "unfit to govern, and . . . unfit among nations." The governing principle was, in other words, survival of the fittest nation. Lodge, adopting a Spencerian view, declared, "The movement against Spain was at once natural and organic, while the pause on the seacoast was artificial and in contravention of the laws of political evolution in the Americas."[52] Lodge was an adherent of the "Teutonic origins" school of thought, which emphasized the contributions of Teutons to civilization. Though a national-ist and an advocate of immigration restriction in 1890, a year in which he loaded the *Congressional Record* with racist comments, that same year he also championed a bill that would have guaranteed blacks the right to vote in federal elections. Lodge, who was elected to the U.S. Senate in 1893, was a protectionist and an expansion-ist. He considered international affairs his specialty, and other important figures of the era accepted his judgment on such issues.

When Spencerianism was interpreted most fiercely, it could not be doubted that the writers meant survival of the fittest in a very harsh way. When Rear Adm. Stephen B. Luce touted "The Benefits of War," he did so with reference to "eco-nomic laws of nature," purges of nations, and purifying forces. He said that self-preservation was the "supreme law" of the world, and that "strife is continual and everywhere in this wicked world." But he had only the vaguest conception of race, and like others he referred to "English-speaking races." He focused on economics, not race, and all other issues were aspects of economics, not biology.[53] The tough Spencerian had no biological definition of race. Luce, like Lodge, was well known and highly respected. He was credited with being the man who "taught the navy to think" and was the founder and first president (1884–86) of the first Naval War College in Newport, Rhode Island, providing officers instruction in command, his-tory, international law, and foreign policy. Luce was visible not only as an educa-tor but also as a contributor to the *North American Review* and the *Naval Institute Pro-ceedings.*[54]

In *Popular Science Monthly,* a writer who interpreted Spencerianism in a way similar to Luce found the United States to be a model of dynamic evolution, in contrast to other nations, particularly China: "These nations have grown old as many men grow old, their prejudices become rigid, their conceits hardened, their beliefs inflexible. They have reached the limit of their narrow line of development [evolution], and crystallized there." The writer argued that war was an "efficient civilizing agent" but was being supplanted by commerce as a carrier of civilization. Again, the Spencerian idea was playing both sides—war was good, war was bad—but in either case the presumption was that social evolution was at an apex or near it. It was incumbent upon the most civilized people to enlighten the less civilized: "War still exists, but it has largely lost its function as a civilizer so far as enlightened nations are concerned. . . . Yet its active power . . . continues."[55]

John Proctor, of the National Civil Service Commission, gave Spencer a different twist when he said that the U.S. should retain the Philippines for humanitarian reasons. He even cited Benjamin Kidd's *Social Evolution,* along with the idea that "our race," which he contrasted with people in tropical lands, was possessed of great individual initiative and "social efficiency."[56] Proctor earned a national reputation through his fight for civil-service reform and his articles in scientific and general-interest magazines. His thinking on race may have been influenced by his association with Harvard geologist Nathaniel Shaler, who in the 1870s was state geologist of Kentucky, where Proctor assisted him, and who was a major figure in geology at Harvard, where Proctor studied the subject. Shaler promoted the idea of racial "retrogression," which meant that different races had evolved over time, and at some point in prehistory race characteristics became permanent. He believed that retrogression to a more primitive society occurred when blacks broke ties with whites.[57] Proctor's writing showed similar assumptions about the hierarchy of races and the effects of evolution upon cultures. Proctor was, not surprisingly, especially interested in the impact of territorial expansion on U.S. interests. As a nationally known figure, Proctor brought a Spencerian perspective into the debate about the Spanish-American War, including its racial implications.

Obviously, there was some embracing of racial and national "survival of the fittest." But in that kind of thinking, race, nation, society, and geography were indistinguishable. If this were not problem enough in attempting to trace a distinctive idea with any precision through the period, the same Spencerian arguments such as those used by Lodge were used by people who were opposed to U.S. expansion.

The Anti-Imperialists

The case for the Spanish-American War as a conflict based on Darwinism, it has been argued so far, is weakened by two facts: that social Darwinism easily could be adapted to very different points of view, and that racism was defined so broadly that usually it had little to do with biology. When race was identified with the Spencerian idea of an organic society, there still remained no distinctions among biological characteristics, national borders, language, or political systems.

Anti-imperialists employed Spencerian ideas to argue that the assimilation of other people would burden the U.S., because such action necessarily would lead to the addition of new states to the union, along with new citizens who would be less able to govern themselves:

> The Philippine Islands . . . must, unless we are to violate the *organic law* [my emphasis] of the land and hold and govern them perpetually as conquered provinces, be erected . . . into several States. . . . The possession of the Philippine islands, Cuba, Hawaii, the Caroline islands, the Ladrone Islands, and Puerto Rico will not satisfy the aggressive spirit of imperialism; in fact, it will, according to the uniform experience of other nations, stimulate the desire for new acquisitions, and we will almost certainly go on, unless checked by the armed opposition of other powers, until we have fastened upon the United States a black and yellow horde of conscript citizens to debauch the suffrage and sap the foundations of our free institutions.[58]

A *Popular Science Monthly* book review lashed out at the "craze for expansion" and militarism, which was costing lives and money.[59] And Spencer himself criticized imperialism:

> No one has so often insisted [as Spencer had] that "the ethical process" is hindered by the cowardly conquests of bullet and shell over arrow and assegai, which demoralize the one side while slaughtering the other.
>
> . . . I am not aware that any one has more emphatically asserted that society in its corporate capacity must exercise a rigorous control over its individual members, to the extent needful for preventing trespasses one upon another. . . . So far from being, as some have alleged, an advocacy of the claims of the strong against the weak, it is much more an insistence that the weak shall be guarded against the strong.[60]

Anti-imperialists did not need Spencer, any more than racists needed Darwin. David Trask has argued that anti-imperialist sentiment was even stronger than the imperialist impulse during the period. The ultimate decision to go to war, he said, came down to President McKinley's inability to fight the public mood in favor of Cuban independence. If Trask is right and public opinion was the decisive force for war, then the ideas circulating in the public and supporting hostilities with Spain take on even greater importance. Whether for the sake of markets, empire, or social evolution, the rationales for war reflected what Trask called America's "paradoxical combination of confidence and insecurity."[61] Social Darwinism demonstrated not only that paradox, but also the malleability of Darwin's and Spencer's ideas. The justifications for war, in addition to the Spencerian one, all were used by expansionists and then simply turned inside-out for use by anti-imperialists. The economic argument for empire could be turned around simply by citing the British experience and the drain on resources resulting from colonizing lands populated by impoverished and ill-educated people. The anti-imperialists could cite Spencer in arguing that forceful assimilation of unlike people into a nation was a violation of the natural evolutionary process and a backward step in social evolution because of the potential for ethical relapse.

Darwin, Etc.

Americans did not need Darwin or Spencer in order to justify war with Spain. Social Darwinism obviously was alive and well, but only on the edges of the mass of rationalizations for war. The arguments offered up for popular consumption were economic, nationalist, or racist and usually lacked any pretense of scientific theory or fact. That nonwhites were inferior was assumed; this was not an issue for debate. Similarly, many of the articles presumed that it was only rational to pursue economic self-interest and, by extension, national interests. What inflated the social-Darwinian impact was the vagueness of the concept in the popular mind and the fuzzy thinking about race. Popular social Darwinism adopted many forms and prejudices that went well beyond Spencer's philosophy. The evidence simply leads to the conclusion that social Darwinism was "in the air." It was an idea that had been assimilated very broadly and deeply, so much so that it was equally useful to both imperialists and anti-imperialists. And often it was nothing more than a crutch for prejudices, not a catalyst for racism. The Gordian knot of racism and social Darwinism cannot be cut into two neat strands of science and social prejudice. As a result, two very vague ideas, social Darwinism and race, became hopelessly entangled. If one wants to divine social Darwinism running beneath the clutter of ideas, it is possible to do so. Jutting most prominently from the assortment, however, were economics, nationalism, and racism—sometimes with and often without Darwin.

Chapter 6

Eugenics: The Political Science

> Thus, man has been given a new responsibility for controlling human
> evolution, a responsibility he did not expect and which he is as yet wholly
> unprepared to discharge. Eugenics desires to prepare public opinion for the
> discharge of this new responsibility.
> —Conference of Publicists of the American Eugenics
> Society, New York City, Dec. 11, 1937.

A eugenicist and an attorney teamed up in the late 1920s to provoke a little attention for the eugenics cause. The eugenicist, Leon F. Whitney, had recently published
a book, *Sex and Birth Control*, that promoted race improvement by contraception.
The attorney, Clarence Darrow, a few years earlier in Dayton, Tennessee, had pulled
off a very successful publicity stunt for the sake of evolutionary science—the defense of John Scopes. Now eugenics needed some help. Darrow told Whitney to
find some unwanted children, give the parents a copy of the book, and get arrested.
Darrow would come to the defense.

Whitney found a "degenerate" family in New Haven, Connecticut, and, in the
presence of a town selectman, gave the father a copy of the book. Whitney then
went to the police, said he expected to be arrested, and probably erred when he
let it slip that Darrow would be the defense attorney. The police chief said he would
have to consult the local bishop. The chief called Whitney later to tell him how good
the book was. Whitney reported that hundreds of copies of the book were being

sold in local drugstores, but town officials never got upset enough to arrest him. Apparently Whitney's mother was the only one who was upset by the episode, and her grief was over the possible arrest, not the book. "All that effort for nothing," he lamented.[1]

Even though Whitney could not get arrested, he had the right instincts about getting attention. The eugenicists spent the next decade whipping up publicity for their cause, which was to improve the human race by selective breeding. As they aggressively pursued publicity and policy change, the eugenicists routinely referred to their "movement," implying an activity that is political or social and not just scientific.[2] This chapter explores the movement's activities that turned evolution and genetics into a political campaign which was a lever for prying into legislation and social policy. The energy spent on publicity and politics also may have benefited the eugenicists by deflecting attention from substantive issues concerning their science—issues of methodology, such as generalizing from very small and unrepresentative samples and measuring poorly defined concepts, such as intelligence or feeble-mindedness; and the morality of who was to make the decisions about the fate of the "unfit." With the coming of eugenics, social Darwinism's journey from abstraction to application was complete. If social Darwinism provided a few people with the scientific rationale for conquering geographical frontiers, then the eugenics movement was the logical foundation for extending conquest to yet another frontier—the biological one. Americans always have been conquerors, especially of wilderness, as is shown in the myths of Wild-West heroes, Daniel Boone, and Davy Crockett.[3] The eugenicists fit into this tradition of American mythology by venturing into the frontier of human sexuality and reproduction. They brought the logic of science and an era's passion for engineering to that which was the domain of passion and impulse.

Darwin's natural selection itself had evolved from biological theory, to social, political, and economic theory, until finally it provided the intellectual foundation for creating a "better" human race. Alfred Russel Wallace, writing in 1890 in *Popular Science Monthly,* provided evidence of Darwin's support for what later became eugenics: "In one of my latest conversations with Darwin he expressed himself very gloomily on the future of humanity, on the ground that in our modern civilization natural selection had no play, and the fittest did not survive. Those who succeeded in the race for wealth are by no means the best or the most intelligent, and it is notorious that our population is more largely renewed in each generation from the lower than from the middle and upper classes."[4] Leonard Darwin accepted the family's place in the parentage of the field of eugenics when he dedicated his 1926 book, *The Need for Eugenic Reform,* to his father. Darwin's natural selection had been turned into a program to segregate people by race and intelligence, dubious standards already recognized as difficult to measure validly and reliably.

The eugenics movement in the United States in the 1920s and 1930s was a political movement cloaked in science. Racism was nothing new, of course, but a science dedicated to racism—though not announced as such—was new. Darwin's theory of natural selection was one of the ideas of the nineteenth century that dramatically increased the credibility of science. The new field of statistics was being used in the early twentieth century to gain genuine insights about the distribution of various traits across plant and animal populations.

Changes were taking place, and they were threatening—people from unfamiliar cultures coming to America, industrialization and urbanization, and the devastating Great Depression. Under such circumstances, people are understandably defensive, and one defense is to bar the door to strangers. Waves of immigration in the late nineteenth century and World War I heightened xenophobia. This immigration also broadened the focus of racism from a primary concern with blacks and Orientals, to include people who were Caucasian but were not of western European descent. Skin color no longer was a sufficiently discriminating criterion for separating people, so "differences" needed more sensitive tests and had to be defined more sharply in order to justify discrimination.

In the United States, eugenics reached its political pinnacle with the passage of legislation in 1924 that restricted immigration of people deemed "less desirable." Eugenicists offered an apparently scientific rationale for anti-immigration sentiment, as well as for an emotional and economic issue. The Immigration Restriction Act of 1924 not only restricted immigration, but also created criteria for selecting those who could enter, designating 1890 as the census year for immigration quotas.[5] The use of 1890 more severely restricted the influx of people from eastern and southern Europe. These were the "types" who were less desirable because they were less Nordic.

No matter where the immigrants came from, they brought with them a vision of the New World that included both a consciousness of the world left behind and an awareness of the newness of their adopted land.[6] This dual aspect of their visions fit very well with the eugenic mission of recreating the human race, an idea that implied the decadence of the Old World and the existence of an Eden-like new world in which humanity could be purified. Ethnographers have found on every continent a myth of a couple who survive catastrophe and begin a new cycle of humanity.[7] For eugenics, the myth took on a more scientific and democratic tone, because it would be a number of couples, not just one, and these couples would be selected by scientific principles. Although such an approach skirted the traditional myth that included God, the eugenic conclusion was a restatement of either Genesis or the Flood.

The Founders

Francis Galton, cousin of Charles Darwin, originated the term "eugenics." In *Hereditary Genius* (1869), Galton said that upper-class parents would pass on to their children those desirable traits that made the parents successful. He was convinced that society needed to promote the reproduction of its better members in order not to be swamped by the unfit, for which urban slums were seen as a prime breeding ground.[8] As a young man, Galton traveled extensively in Africa, and those travels confirmed for him the existence of inferior races, although ultimately work on race distinctions formed only a very small part of the content of his professional writings. He termed his field of study *eugenics,* taking the term from a Greek root meaning "good in birth" or "noble in heredity."[9]

By embarking on a course of study that involved heredity and statistics, Galton was venturing into two fields that had received little attention. The study of heredity had not been given a lot of attention because it was so poorly understood.[10] While Galton was not a mathematician, he was committed to showing that heredity could be dealt with in such a fashion. His work with the distribution of human characteristics along a normal curve was highly innovative and departed from the standard science of the day that focused on gathering data and describing it.

Galton's most important student, and his successor as the central figure in the emerging field, was Karl Pearson, a biologist-statistician. Pearson believed that Great Britain was in a state of deterioration as a result of rampant breeding by the lower classes, combined with the tendency of the better classes to have smaller families. Criticizing this tendency of upper-class families in the late nineteenth century, Pearson noted that neither Darwin nor Galton would have been born, had their parents been as constrained in family size as typical contemporary men and women of the English upper crust. Pearson was in tune with the imperialist times. Like many other intellectuals, he interpreted Spencer's social philosophy to mean competition among nations rather than individuals, and he equated fitness with a form of nationalist socialism in which people were subordinated to state interests.[11]

Pearson deepened his impact on heredity studies when, in 1895, he began offering a statistics course in University College, London. The journal *Biometrika* was founded in 1902 by Pearson, Galton, and Walter F. R. Weldon, a zoologist who collaborated extensively in research with Pearson. In 1911, upon the death of Galton, University College was given forty-five thousand pounds to establish the Galton Eugenics Professorship. Pearson assumed the post, in accord with Galton's wish, and became head of a new department of statistics. The new department increasingly stood at the center of the study of statistics in England, and by World War I it was devoted largely to the study of eugenics. Much of what was produced was flawed both methodologically and in underlying assumptions about the data. In the early twentieth century, however, this was the only British institution engaged in systematic study of eugenics, so it became the standard bearer of the field. Although Pearson was criticized for his speculations and for some of the questionable measurements of even more questionable traits, such as intelligence, many would have conceded the point made by geneticist J. B. S. Haldane about Pearson's work: "His theory of heredity was incorrect in some fundamental respects. So was Columbus' theory of geography. He set out for China and discovered America."[12]

Eugenics in America

At the turn of the century, American culture exhibited special enthusiasm for engineering and technology. Railroads had traversed the continent, and the Panama Canal was linking oceans. Such engineering feats reflected not only genuine accomplishments, but also the grandeur of the visions associated with the engineering perspective. If engineers could conquer such incredible geographical obstacles, then why not human society as well? Regulation and reform were at the heart of the Progressive movement, which was guided by the assumption that good government not only was possible but even could improve society. Railroads, banks, and insurance were put under regulation. States created labor boards to bring order out of chaos and to civilize the labor-industry clashes. Frederick Taylor's *The Principles of Scientific Management* (1911) put the stamp of efficiency on labor-management relations. And Ivy Lee, a pioneer in creating the profession of public relations, engineered nothing less than public opinion.

Even utopia could be engineered, as architects and planners launched into building communities that would be antidotes to the ailments of urbanization. Pullman, Illinois, for example, was to be a model community. Its creator, George Pullman, inventor of the Pullman railroad car, had planned to build a new factory outside Chicago and decided to build a town, one in which his workers would not have to suffer the tenements and temptations of the city. Billed as the town where "everything fits," he planned a city complete with schools, post office, bank, library, and church. The town design also was an attempt to control contentious workers in the Pullman factories. With the company providing everything, Pullman hoped to quell dissent and to create to a stable, docile workforce. The effort did not work, as strikes continued; and in 1898 the Illinois Supreme Court ruled that the company did not have the legal standing to build a city. And some criticized the concept as undemocratic—benevolent but feudal. Other such cities were attempted in the United and Europe.[13]

The engineering vision was enticing: technology would conquer the continent; architects would create not just buildings but whole communities; government would use regulation to create a better, more just, economy and society. It followed that the individuals who comprised the communities, drove the economy, and traveled the continent also could be engineered.

Eugenics gained momentum in the United States when, after the Second International Conference on Eugenics, held in New York City in 1921, the American Eugenics Society (AES) was organized.[14] The AES budget was only a few thousand dollars at first, but it was supplemented by substantial gifts from donors such as John D. Rockefeller, Jr., and George Eastman. The budget soon was up to forty thousand dollars a year. Building transcontinental railroads and joining oceans paled in comparison to the vision of the eugenicists. The founding members stated that the eugenics movement was "like the founding and development of Christianity, something to be handed down from age to age."[15]

Given what the eugenicists figured to do unto others, that was an ironic parallel to draw. But their ambitions went far beyond mere science—they intended to change humanity and to revolutionize humanity's self-perception. Whereas Christianity made the individual matter and gave intrinsic value to each person, the eugenicists were going even further—the components, the genes, of the individual were what really mattered, and not for the sake of the person but for the sake of humanity's future. Like Christians, the eugenicists believed that sacrifice for the sake of others was noble. But it seems always to have been other people who needed to be sacrificed for the good of humanity, not the eugenicists themselves. For example, members of the Society for Racial Hygiene in Germany had to take an oath not to marry, should they be unfit. But apparently, not one of the society's thirteen hundred or so members ever admitted to such defects.[16] The eugenicists had entered a shadowy realm blending science, politics, and religion—realms that Thomas Huxley had fought fiercely to segregate. They drew credibility from science, sustenance from politics, and righteousness from religion.

The movement was organized loosely around various committees and associations, some devoted to science, others to ideology, and some committed simply to good citizenship. The structure of the movement itself was akin to that of a political party, with common interests and competing factions jostling for public attention and issuing proclamations of concern about American society and the future of civilization. Policy formation and information dissemination were central to the movement. Although scientists had engaged in such activities in the past, these had not been given primacy in the missions of the individuals and organizations involved. One of the first actions taken by the American Eugenics Society was political—forming a subcommittee on selective immigration.[17] This move, in conjunction with the stated promotional purpose of gaining "widespread cooperation," set an agenda for the group's politics and publicity in the 1920s.[18]

Publicists from the Beginning

For the eugenicists, policy making and publicity were as important as the scientific mission.[19] Thus, compromises had to be made in order for policy, publicity, and science to work together effectively. Even before it formally was created, the American Eugenics Society was a publicity machine. Its predecessor, the Eugenics Committee of the United States of America, which was composed largely of scientists, was formed with the idea of advising government and spreading popular information about eugenics. Leon Whitney, a founding member of the AES, wrote some years later:

> Our basic idea was to acquaint the public with what eugenics really was. And we did it. Hundreds of thousands of dollars worth of free publicity resulted from our efforts: I can't say that "eugenics" became a household word but surely one heard the word used far more frequently than one hears it now, 35 years later. . . .

With only a small amount of money to start with, our directors in the American Eugenics Society had to figure the means of making Eugenics a household word and as I think back, I'm sure we did a tremendous job. Irving Fisher [AES member and Yale economist] said, "There are four bases for success in such a movement: 1) a plan, 2) workers, 3) money, and 4) prestige."[20]

Those bases sounded more political than scientific. By the end of the 1920s, the AES had developed an ambitious, detailed publicity plan. Its Popular Education Committee, in its annual report for 1930, stated that the goal of the society was to be "national in influence," an ambition that was political, not scientific. The committee enumerated the print media outlets and outlined a strategy for getting into them: "a. Newspapers—2,000 papers in U.S.; 300 with circulation of 24 million. Follow up articles thru clipping service. Try for daily news events and also daily supplement stories. b. Magazines—get articles with prestige names." One section was devoted to "Special Short-time 'Stunt' Projects," and included a "fitter families contest," sermon contests, essay contests, exhibits, and community surveys. The report concluded: "With something definite for the state committees to do, our Society will also gain valuable publicity. Movements like ours are often seemingly inactive not because of lack of interest but because of lack of national organization of that interest. We could run a one-page 'dittoed' news sheet to all the state chairmen each month to act as a stimulus to them and to the Society."[21]

From its inception, the AES showed considerable savvy about stunts that would promote eugenics. A couple of the most noteworthy enterprises along this line in the 1920s were the fitter families contest and the sermon contest. The AES used both to build a constituency and to go beyond broad media audiences.

The fitter families contest was an innocuous way to promote eugenics. After all, who could find offense in promoting good health? At the same time, the contest was pitched at a level that appealed to traditional values, inasmuch as it was not individual selfishness but concern for one's family that was at stake. And, finally, it was a great way for eugenicists to collect data while running a publicity campaign. The first contest was at the Kansas Free Fair in Topeka in 1920, and soon the contests were being held in seven to ten states per year. In order to participate, families had to have medical and psychiatric examinations and an intelligence test.[22] As propaganda, the contest was a great success. Whitney wrote that "the publicity was out of all proportion to what it cost. . . . All the newspapers were glad to cooperate. . . . No activities of the society got so much publicity."[23] In addition, the AES obtained data on the families: the names of three generations, sex, age, marital status, cause of death of family members, birthplace, "consanguinity," and education. The contest classified families by size (small, medium and large) and scored them on psychological and physiological criteria.[24] At state fairs, the contests often were conducted in the "human stock" section,[25] making them sound rather like the prize bull or lamb contests. In the Waco, Texas, fitter families contest in 1927, in which the winning families were awarded medals, the categories also included "incomplete families" and "individuals," who ranged from a fifty-two-year-old woman to a nineteen-year-old man. Families were awarded trophies and medals, even, at the Kansas Free Fair in 1924, by the governor himself.[26]

AES Political Goals

The early policy goals of the AES were developed in tandem with the publicity efforts, and those goals revealed a radical program cloaked in the respectability of scientific language. The eugenicists were very much akin to modern proponents of a large, socialist welfare state, in that a great deal of faith was put in the ability of government to solve problems for individuals. But the radicalism of the eugenic political program lay in the amount of power they wanted to give the state for enforcing good breeding among citizens, especially with regard to sterilization and institutionalization of the "unfit."[27] It is important to emphasize the radicalism of their program, which would invite the sort of authoritarian state that was coming of age at the same time in Nazi Germany, because this extremism was finding an audience in America; and, of course, it was presented not as fringe politics but as rational discourse on policy.

The eugenicists did not see themselves as radicals but rather viewed their program as a natural extension of the ideals of democracy. This was illustrated in eugenicist Frederick Osborn's outline for an elementary text, which devoted a chapter to "Eugenics and Democracy." Osborn left a Wall Street career in the late 1920s and settled into an office at the American Museum of Natural History, which was run by his uncle, paleontologist and eugenicist Henry Fairfield Osborn. Frederick Osborn began reading demography, genetics, and psychology, and came to oppose the racist and anti-immigration policies that were at the core of mainstream eugenics.[28] Osborn's chapter on democracy was projected to include a discussion of eugenics: "The new philosophy of eugenics would diminish social class stratification. Democracy offers greater possibility for eugenics as a natural process than do other forms of government. Distribution of births [is] always a matter of individual decisions, so democracy offers [the] greatest possibility for successful application of eugenics."[29] So, even in rejecting racism, science and politics were yoked together to drag forward the idea of human betterment.

The AES state legislative program included proposals for a minimum age for marriage; allowing first cousins to marry only with the approval of an expert in heredity; providing more money for institutions for the feeble-minded, the insane, epileptics, and "defective" delinquents; and state authorization for approved physicians to sterilize the insane, the feeble-minded, epileptics, and those with inherited blindness or some "other very serious inherited defect." The AES also advocated widening the grounds for divorce to include insanity, epilepsy, feeble-mindedness, desertion, and sterility (except for age). The federal legislative program called for increasing the tax exemption per child to fifteen hundred dollars, restricting immigration to "those who are superior to the median American in intelligence tests as well as fulfilling such other qualifications as are now imposed," and extension of deportation privileges.[30]

Energy was spent at all levels of government, from lobbying President Calvin Coolidge for support, all the way down to organizing at the county level. One document, "A Constructive Program for Eugenics Work in Nassau County," New York, began with an anecdote concerning two sisters with "only two years' difference in age; one is highly erotic, bringing scandal to the neighborhood by her wayward behavior, and the other is secretary of an educational institution, working hard but vainly to keep her sister from going to the bad." It outlined a county program, the first item being the prevention of procreation of "grossly defective and wayward strains." The document said that sterilization legislation alone was inadequate. The time might come, however, "when castration of the male and ovariotomy will be accepted as within the province of the state and these operations would, at once, tremendously diminish the amount of crime." The second suggestion was for eugenics education in Nassau County. "But while we are considering the elimination of the defectives we must not forget the possibility of improvement at the better end of the series." This was proposed as a series of lectures pitched to high school students.[31]

Charles Davenport, director of the Bureau of Eugenics at Cold Spring Harbor, New York, was chairman of the board of managers of the "Nassau County Association," which intended "to promulgate and assist in the enforcement of uniform laws for the protection and safeguarding of the public health."[32] Davenport advocated that a "clear cut presentation of the facts as to the results of reproduction of imbeciles be placed in the hands of each state legislature to the end that at least female imbeciles be in general prevented from reproduction either by restraint during the reproduction period (say from 15 to 45) or by sterilization." He believed that every state ought to have a program for studying the "pedigrees of the feeble minded . . . not merely to confirm the laws of heredity of imbecility but to determine the main blood lines of imbecility coursing through this country."[33] Davenport began his career as a biology instructor at Harvard, which he left in 1899 for the University of Chicago. Davenport demonstrated his organizational and publicity skills when he persuaded the Carnegie Institution of Washington to support a eugenics laboratory, which was built in 1904. Davenport left Chicago to direct the institution in Cold Spring Harbor, about thirty miles from New York City, and remained there for the rest of his life. The institute contributed substantially to the growing fields of biometry and genetics, in particular with Davenport's studies of poultry and canaries. But he wanted to extend his inquiry to humans, and he did so by collecting data on family pedigrees, as he applied Mendelism to people. Like other eugenicists, Davenport equated race with behavior. He considered good human stock to be the middle class, and he favored a selective immigration policy. For example, Davenport believed that the influx of people from southeastern Europe would make Americans "darker in pigmentation, smaller in stature, more mercurial . . . more given to crimes of larceny, kidnapping, assault, murder, rape, and sex-immorality."[34]

Political activism by eugenicists on occasion went even to the highest office in the nation. Raymond Pearl, of Johns Hopkins University, asked President Calvin Coolidge in 1925 to give serious consideration to a bill "To Establish a Laboratory for the Study of the Abnormal Classes." Pearl wrote, "It seems to me unlikely that any adequate solution of the economic and social problems presented by the criminal and defective classes will be reached until we have a better knowledge than we now do of the factors which are fundamental to these problems."[35] Pearl wrote to Secretary of Commerce Herbert Hoover in 1922 to congratulate him on election to the National Academy of Sciences: "You will, perhaps, remember that I always used to say to you that, if you had chosen to devote your life to scientific research, it was my opinion that you would have made as brilliant a success, or perhaps even more brilliant in that field than in the field you chose. I interpret this election to the Academy as an independent confirmation of my views on this subject."[36] Pearl also managed to get a meeting with President Hoover in 1929, a meeting he requested merely for "personally renewed assurance of my faith in and loyalty to him," not for any request or propaganda. Hoover was sympathetic to eugenics, for the White House went to the trouble in 1931 of correcting a *Cosmopolitan* magazine remark that Hoover believed that all deficient children suffered from malnutrition. The White House said that Hoover's views were to the contrary and that the magazine's remark was in opposition to "all scientific knowledge of heredity."[37]

Congress sent one eugenicist, Harry Laughlin, to make observations in Italy, since so many Italian immigrants were pouring into the United States. Mussolini himself entertained Laughlin. In recounting the episode, Whitney wrote: "Dr. Laughlin told me about examining the emigrant in Italy. As the troops marched by, it was obvious that they were a splendid lot of physical specimens. Dr. Laughlin said, 'Il Duce, we'll take all of those men into America without a physical examination.' Mussolini smiled and said, 'We don't let men like them leave the country.' Which warns us not to judge the quality of people in any country by its representatives here."[38]

The political instincts of the eugenicists also showed in their instructions to student research assistants, who sounded more like campaign workers than scientific understudies. A form was given to the students that provided an imaginary dialogue, guiding them on how to approach people on becoming members of the AES. The students were basically salesmen, pitching "A Eugenics Catechism" and other pamphlets pertaining to the cause. Students needed to have basic knowledge of the cause and exude confidence, the instructions said. Concise, simple answers were provided to questions about the nature of the AES, why one should join, the advantages of membership, and how to become a member. The catechism stressed good salesmanship principles: encourage and anticipate questions, provide printed material, promote the advantages of membership. The first two sample questions in the catechism said nothing about science, but emphasized social good and the "missionary role," and compared the movement to voting:

> Prospect: Oh, yes, I have heard of the American Eugenics Society. What is it? . . .
>
> You: The American Eugenics Society is an organization of thoughtful people of the United States bonded together for the benefit of humanity to do what it can to raise the hereditary endowment of the human race to the end that the human race may become happier.
>
> Prospect: But why should I join the Society? . . .
>
> You: The fact that you are a member of the Society means that you are interested in the work of race betterment. It means that you become a missionary for this work and that your influence will be spread widely. . . . It is very much like asking the question, "Why should I vote on election day?"[39]

Preaching Progress

In the late 1920s, the eugenicists further refined their publicity efforts with a particularly clever stunt—a sermon contest. The AES offered a five hundred dollar prize for the best sermon preached, and more than five hundred sermons were sent in.[40]

The sermon contest showed how just about anything could be adapted to the eugenic message. It also took eugenics propaganda to a more effective level, the interpersonal one, as opposed to the mediated message. With the sermon contest, people were hearing about eugenics from someone they knew and trusted, and who was skilled at communicating at the level of the audience. A 1928 letter to ministers included a questionnaire about families in the church. It had to be completed and returned with any entry submitted for the contest. The questionnaire sought information on parish families, including the number of living children, occupation of the father, and the family's church activities.[41] The cover letter said that the AES was interested in finding out "whether the kind of people who maintain our churches are increasing or decreasing."

Eugenics employed several myths embedded in Christianity and other religions. The consequence of ignoring the laws of eugenics was biological apocalypse, akin to the wholesale destruction promised for those who ignored God's laws. Eugenics was renewal and regeneration, and like Christianity it promised rebirth.

The sermons collected by AES interpreted eugenics as a beneficent science, which, like religion, would elevate humanity above its innate decadence. One minister supplied eugenical statistics with his sermon. The preacher's enthusiasm for eugenics had no bounds, and he found it the perfect complement for Christianity:

> The aim of eugenics and the aim of the Christian church are one in that both seek to bring the Kingdom of God down to earth and to people it with an abler and happier and more wholesome humanity. "The aim of eugenics," wrote Francis Galton, "is the production of a more healthy and vigorous, and more able humanity." What is our Christian dream of the Kingdom

if it is not to realize a new social order peopled with men and women, with not only the spirit of Christ but with capacity to grow into the full measure of the stature of Christ? . . . The principal business of the Eugenists [sic] and our principal business as Christians is to make that dream a reality. The method of Eugenics is the method of science. Working on the basis of well-established laws of biology, it brings science to the aid of the church. . . .

There are two directions in which men may work in seeking to realize the Kingdom of God. They may work on the environment. . . . Or they may work on the factors of heredity. . . . Both are necessary. Jesus told both the parable of the sower and parable of the tares together. A good Harvest is a product equally of good seed and soil. . . .

Eugenics will be a great aid to the Church in the Church's practical program of social service. . . .

The Church is fighting, too, against the inroads of an increasing feeble-mindedness in society. . . .

The Church needs the aid of Eugenics again, in its fight against poverty. . . .

Moreover, the Church needs the aid of Eugenics in her fight against crime.[42]

He recounted the story of the notorious Jukes family, which was an example of the "bad seed." From the "shiftless, lazy, drunken fisherman" were descended five generations of "feeble-minded, idle, pauper, criminal specimens." Of 1,200 total descendants, 310 were professional paupers, 440 "viciously diseased," half the women prostitutes, 197 convicted criminals. The family, he stated, was a "sample of many others." He compared it to the Jonathan Edwards family, "world famous in its yield of good stock," including judges, divines, theologians, senators, authors, college presidents, and inventors. He concluded, "The Kingdom on earth can be realized only among the sort of people who have come down to us from the Edwards line." Another minister declared, "The Bible is a book of eugenics. . . . Christ was born of a family that represented a long process of religious and moral selection."[43] Others found a similar compatibility between Christianity and eugenics: "The religion of Jesus is concerned more with the nature of man than with his nurture. And so is Eugenics."[44]

In 1929 there was also a contest for the best essay on the causes of the decline in birth rates among "Nordic" people. The problematical issue of defining race was revealed in the terms of the contest, which stated, "The Nordic race is defined as covering the Scandinavian countries south of about 63 [degrees] N. lat., the Netherlands, England, Scotland, North Ireland, and the German States of Schleswig-Holstein, Mecklenburg, Hannover and Westphalia." Race was defined geographically or by nationality, not by any biological criteria, which one might think an allegedly biological science would demand.[45] Of course, biological criteria for defining race have been difficult to establish. Davenport, for example, shared with many others the common idea that race was simply ethnic or national identity[46] and gave it little more consideration beyond that.

Not all of the publicity stunts worked so well. *Eugenics* magazine reported in September 1929 that the "eugenical information service" was terminated because, according to Davenport, only 10 percent of the people for whom they performed a prediction about offspring thanked them, and 0 percent told the service what happened.[47] But, despite occasional failure, the eugenicists were quite astute about organization and communication. Their sermon and fitter families contests, as well as local eugenic organizations such as those in Nassau County, New York, all showed an ability to organize and proselytize. Such efforts were grassroots political campaigns, enlisting parents, clergy, and prominent citizens as eugenic precinct captains.

Missionaries

Politically minded scientists were nothing new. It was common, even expected, for nineteenth-century scientists to seek public audiences. In England, Huxley reigned as the era's foremost public scientist.[48] In the United States, the Darwinian Asa Gray and anti-Darwinian Louis Agassiz were similarly sensitive to, and manipulative of, public opinion. But the eugenicists were unique in that they not only generated publicity as individuals, but also included it as an important dimension of their professional organization's program. The AES was singularly dedicated to race betterment, and publicity was named among the goals of the organization and those of its predecessor, the American Eugenics Committee.[49]

In addition to promoting contests and building organizations, the eugenicists maintained and nurtured ties with a broad range of newspapers and magazines in its flurry of scientific, political, and public activities in the 1920s. Eugenicist Herbert Jennings's correspondence included such diverse connections as *Popular Science Monthly, Science Magazine,* the *Nation,* and publisher E. W. Scripps.[50] Upon occasion, the connections were well timed. In 1923, the year before passage of the Immigration Act, the managing editor of the *Survey* said that he would publish a Jennings article on the immigration issue "when the new session of Congress throws the emigration question into relief once more."[51] The *Survey,* self-described as a "cooperative journalistic venture of socially minded men and women," also wanted Jennings to evaluate eugenicist Harry H. Laughlin's testimony before the House Committee on Immigration concerning the "'dumping' of social inadequates."[52] The *Survey* did not circulate widely, but it was highly regarded among intellectuals and fit the eugenicists' publicity tactics nicely because it was dedicated to publishing articles about social studies and reform movements. The magazine's associate editors often were activists in social causes, and in the 1930s the magazine narrowed its focus further, becoming a professional journal for social workers.[53]

Pearl and Jennings were particularly adept at cultivating publicity. Pearl was a member of H. L. Mencken's "Saturday Night Club," a social group that met for beer and music.[54] For eugenicists, this meant access to a sympathetic ear from the influential editor of the *American Spectator*. But Pearl also corresponded with editors at the *Baltimore Sun,* where Mencken worked; *Harper's Magazine*; and the *Saturday Evening Post.*[55] At times, Pearl even sounded like Mencken: "My own feeling is that it is about time some scientific man did something besides pussyfooting on the question of religion and science."[56] And, writing to Mencken, Pearl groused: "It has seemed to me for a long time that there is a dreadful lot of bilge talked by the self-constituted leaders of the eugenics movement."[57] Not all was work between the two, as was indicated by a letter from Mencken, who reported from Tennessee during the 1925 Scopes trial that the Chattanooga populace was debauched and drunken, but that the city was full of good Scotch whiskey.[58] Editors pressed Jennings to write reviews and articles for the *Nation* and the *Survey,* which he did. The *Nation* also asked Jennings to write for the series "What I Believe," which was described as being by men and women of "high standing in the field of abstract thought." Such an invitation, particularly coming from one of the more liberal, intellectual publications, was useful to Jennings and the eugenicists not only for the publicity but also as a means of bestowing intellectual legitimacy on their ideas.[59]

In the 1930s, a new medium was capturing the national imagination and market. Eugenicists were ready to spread their gospel by radio. In fact, Jennings was able to take advantage of the cross-fertilization of media, with his success in print serving as a springboard to radio exposure. In April 1931, the editors of *Parents' Magazine* prepared a radio script that referred to Jennings's book, *The Biological Basis of Human Nature,* which a few months earlier the magazine had judged the "outstanding scientific contribution of the year toward the understanding of heredity." In addition, the editors had selected it as one of three outstanding books for parents in 1930. The script was sent out nationally to about one hundred stations, and the magazine said that the material was used regularly.[60]

Frederick Osborn also took to the airwaves, but with an issue much more controversial than that which Jennings faced. A 1940 radio script for the "Adventures in Science" series on CBS had Osborn discussing the issue of population decline in Europe:

> England muddled along, trying to figure out what to do. Germany began paying people to have children. At the same time they vigorously suppressed practices used in German cities to limit families. The German system worked, the birth rate went up. But it worked mostly with the poorest and most ignorant people. . . .
>
> . . . American parents are increasingly coming to believe that they should not have more children than they can take care of. . . . [L]ocal communities, states, and the federal government itself are doing more each year to help children with their health, their education, their recreation, and their nutrition, without adding to the expenses of the parents. That is sound population policy on the positive side. . . . The only trouble with these budding American population policies is that they don't go far enough.[61]

Though Osborn was steering clear of Nazism, he was advocating a very large role for the government in the rearing of children. The last sentence suggests that he may not have seen any outer limits for governmental power in this arena.

The Promise of Science

Extravagant hopes, claims, and visions for science were not peculiar to the eugenicists, although their promise to recreate humanity may have been the most grandiose of scientific dreams. In the 1930s, popular science magazines such as *Scientific American* and *Science News Letter* depicted science as highly credible and compelling, a way of discovering and creating knowledge in order to solve social ills. There were heroes, technological marvels, and endless praise for the scientific attitude.

Scientific American portrayed a muscular science, emphasizing the applications of science but offering an eclectic mix that included astronomy, life sciences, physics, chemistry, and social sciences. The weekly *Science News Letter* was part of the nonprofit Science News Service, founded by newspaper magnate E. W. Scripps to popularize science. Relentless progress was a favorite theme in the magazine, which included sociology, anthropology, political science, economics, public health, chemistry, physics, biology, medicine, and technology. Both publications endorsed the idea that the answer to any problem only awaited the right scientific method. The success of science marched through their pages, cloaked in white lab coats at academic labs and the well-cut business suits of research leaders at General Motors and other giant companies. Albert Einstein and Thomas Edison represented the pinnacles of pure and applied science. *Science News Letter* presented each scientific advance, event, or publication without question or criticism, occasionally lambasting the lack of government spending on science and the vast sums spent on the military. *Scientific American's* longer, more involved articles were similarly uncritical but sometimes offered differing points of views of such controversial issues as eugenics.

In a climate that included such opinions, eugenics could flourish even when its racial goals became more obvious. American eugenicists' focus on feeble-mindedness, however, helped to deflect attention from the potential for Nazi-style racism. Moreover, eugenics had the imprimatur of government, via federal immigration legislation and state sterilization laws. Government, social prejudice, and empirical method, however flawed, made eugenics scientific. And science was viewed as credible and effective.

The Decline of Eugenics

By 1937, the "Conference on Education and Eugenics" was suggesting that eugenics courses in higher education "probably . . . should not be given under the name of eugenics. It might be called 'Human Environment, Heredity and Eugenics.'" Some believed that the best way to propagate the faith was indirectly: "[The] eugenic approach must be made through the environment of the student, economic, cultural, its aspiration for social justice, and the proper atmosphere in all the social sciences. In other words, eugenic propaganda will go furthest if it is treated as incidental to all other social advance. If the eugenicist is to save his soul, he must first lose it."[62]

Losing one's soul meant forgetting about the scientific aspects of the idea and devoting oneself to publicity and political efforts, leaving the laboratory and joining the ranks of eugenical evangelism. The idea of aggressive publicity was prominent in the report, with at least two conference participants advocating a "eugenic attack" that would be made indirectly, by building a campaign on campuses and among families. The indirect attack was supported elsewhere. Albert E. Wiggam, an enthusiast who was not trained as a eugenicist but who wrote numerous popular tracts on the subject, said he had probably written more on the subject than anybody else: "I may appropriately say that in my belief the most effective way to write about eugenics is not to write about eugenics at all." He cited articles in *Harper's* and *Good Housekeeping* on subsidizing marriage and on whether or not people should marry—articles about eugenics that never mentioned the term.[63]

Eugenicists remained committed to the belief that public institutions could solve social problems. A conference report on eugenics and education referred to schools as "community supported agencies," and stated that society could look forward to "adoption of the conception of the school as essentially *the* [emphasis in original] child welfare agency of society."[64] If society were reticent about following the path of eugenics, then the answer was more eugenics, not less. And the way to apply it was to manipulate social conditions via government policy: "According to the new view the remedy for this [failure of society to follow eugenic principles] is not less eugenics but more. It lies in shifting the center of effort away from the individual to the social environment. The thing to do is to create social conditions which make it easy for desirable types of people to have large families and at the same time create conditions which lead undesirable types to have few children."[65] By the mid-1930s, some eugenicists simply had made science secondary to publicity. A program outline said, "The *first* [my emphasis] aim of a eugenics program must be to develop an intelligent and aroused public opinion."[66]

The lingering Great Depression, the rise of Nazi Germany, and the outbreak of World War II crippled the eugenics movement. The eugenicists knew in the 1930s, well before the war, that Nazism was bad news for their ideals, and they worked to distance themselves from that movement. In addition, war meant a drying up of donations, which had provided a substantial part of their funding.[67]

Raymond Pearl knew that the "Jewish question" was problematical. He admitted that there was no good definition of race, and he opposed Hitler. Pearl recounted an episode in which a committee of eight or ten anthropologists convened in the mid-1930s for the purpose of making a brief, accurate statement on the issue of race.

They intended to give it to the "public press," with an eye toward combating "mischievous notions," including those of Hitler. The committee never came up with an agreement.[68]

There lay the dilemma. Hitler had taken the eugenic ideals to their logical extreme of purifying the race. Where did the eugenicists draw the line? If eugenicists issued a blanket condemnation of Hitler, they risked self-condemnation. But they were unable to distinguish between Hitler's racial purity and the racial improvement espoused by American eugenicists, and attempts to do so risked causing more confusion among laymen.[69] The eugenicists also struggled with what Daniel Kevles called the "eugenic paradox": success in a Darwinian sense was a high fertility rate, but in the United States and Great Britain, the high fertility rates existed among the lower classes.[70] The eugenicists could blame misguided social policy for the proliferation of the less fit, but doing so revealed another paradox in their thinking. They were advocating policies that would give government unparalleled control over people's lives, but philosophically they were stressing the power of the individual to survive and thrive by his own devices.

A eugenicist finally did recognize the problem in espousing state intervention to assure good breeding—or no breeding. In 1936, Jennings devoted an address at Oxford University to attacking a popular book, Alexis Carrel's *Man the Unknown,* which Jennings said tended "to secure for the book a welcome as supplying the biological philosophy for a fascist state. This may turn out to be the most important feature of the work." He concluded: "But there is little ground for the hope that a Central Council of the sort proposed by Carrel will provide a solution for the major difficulties of mankind. It might however become an instrument for imposing the will of the powerful on the rest of humanity." Jennings understood that a "Central Council" could have too much power, but he skirted the issue of the morality of the state-run sterilization programs that had been the core of eugenic legislative programs.

When all else fails, blame the messenger. In the Oxford address, Jennings stated, "We must free ourselves from the mass of illusions, errors, and badly observed facts, from the false problems investigated by the weak-minded of the realm of science, and from the pseudo-discoveries of charlatans and scientists extolled by the daily press."[71] The eugenicists had assiduously courted public opinion through the popular press, then blamed the press when support for their ideas cooled.

In one respect, the eugenics movement came full circle, and that was with horses. Davenport, of the Cold Springs Harbor laboratory, had initiated a financial windfall for the movement when he approached the heiress of a railroad fortune, Mrs. E. Harriman, for support for the Eugenics Record office. Davenport won the money after the heiress's daughter had spent part of the summer of 1905 working at the laboratory. She arranged a meeting between her mother and Davenport, who knew that Mrs. Harriman's husband had been a horseman. His appeal for her support claimed that the eugenicists' "progressive revolution" would occur only if "human matings could be placed upon the same high plane as that of horse breeding."[72]

About a half-century later, another eugenicist, Leon Whitney, wrote in his autobiography that he applied his training in eugenics to racing pigeons with "exceedingly good results" and profitably used eugenic principles in the horse business. He said that Harry Laughlin had spent some time with a man who contributed more than a half-million dollars to science. Laughlin and this individual started figuring out the value of horses based on eugenic principles. The person did so well at auctions that others took note of his acumen, and he had to send surrogates to bid for him at auctions because prices would go through the ceiling if people saw him bidding.[73]

It was not the search for publicity that set the eugenicists apart so much as it was the way they wedded the science of genetics to social and political issues such as welfare and immigration. Eugenics was even adaptable to American myths of individualism and success. The movement proved useful to those who wanted to attack the decadence of the Old World and promote the idea of an Eden-like New World, all of which fit well with isolationist sympathies and racist impulses. In addition, the eugenicists built a political organization that enlisted laymen and politicians to spread the ideas, collect data, and provide financial support. They promoted eugenic laws at the state level, influenced federal immigration policy, and even made themselves a presence in religious life. In many respects, they were quite successful, but the achievements of the American eugenicists still paled beside what was emerging in Nazi Germany, a state founded upon racism and radical eugenics.

Chapter 7

A Veneer of Science:
The Popular Press and Nazi Science

Let us make a composite picture of a typical Teuton. . . . Let him be as blond
as Hitler, as dolichocephalic [long-headed] as Rosenberg, as tall as Goebbels,
as slender as Goering and as manly as Streicher.
—JULIAN HUXLEY AND A. C. HADDON, *We Europeans*

The era of Nazi Germany, one of civilization's greatest failures in the twentieth
century, is a dismal chapter in the history of science. The Nazis went to an extreme
in incorporating a biological theory into a political system. The National Socialists
used science to reinforce the intellectually rotten foundation of the idea of "Aryan"
superiority. Darwin's "survival of the fittest" was twisted into a Nazi vision of biological apocalypse, in which humanity would become a genetic Sodom and Gomorra
if the laws of nature were perverted further by restraining the Aryan race from
fulfilling its destiny.

For Herbert Spencer, evolution was an engine of progress, and social science,
including social Darwinism, was a means of improving and advancing society. But
ultimately the Nazis, who looked backward toward a mythical people of mythical
accomplishments, turned this vision on its head. Rather than using science to look
forward, as Spencer had, eugenicists in Germany and the United States were at-

tempting to recreate a past that never existed, a past of racial purity. By discarding the role of cooperation and elevating social strife, many eugenicists were Darwinian fundamentalists in their adherence to a radical, narrow interpretation of survival of the fittest. And as fundamentalists are inclined to do, they seized on only a part of the text, and that was conflict. They considered only selected data, which showed their own groups to be the fittest. They ignored other data. If the immigrants of southern and eastern Europe were so demonstrably unfit, for example, why were they breeding so profusely, and sometimes prospering, in Germany and America? For eugenicists in the United States and Germany, it seemed not to be an issue that, in simple Darwinian terms, the success of a "race" in a given environment would be a good measure of its fitness.

The blending of science, politics, and myth raises numerous important historical questions, but the focus of this chapter is the popular response to the development of social Darwinism's dark side. Germans seized upon Hitler's Aryan myth, and he stated:

> I know perfectly well, just as well as these tremendously clever intellectuals, that in the scientific sense there is no such thing as race. But you as a farmer and cattle-breeder cannot get your breeding successfully achieved without the conception of race. And I as a politician need a conception which enables the order which has hitherto existed on a historic basis, to be abolished and an entirely new and anti-historic order endorsed and given an intellectual basis. . . . And for this purpose the conception serves me well. . . . With the conception of race, National Socialism will carry its revolution abroad and recast the world. . . . This revolution of ours is the exact counterpart of the great French Revolution and no Jewish God will save the democracies from it.[1]

Hitler knew that scientific legitimation of his ideas was valuable for both domestic and foreign consumption of Nazism. In November 1941, he stated, "The Third Reich for the first time was using methodical scholarship as a means of combating International Jewry." Universities took on a National Socialist mission, as faculties were purged of "non-Aryans." Various race institutes were established to pursue racial theories and practices, including the Frank Institute, the Goebbels Institute, the Christian-Nazi Institute in Jena, the Frankfort Institute, and the Krakow Institute for Ostarbeit.[2]

The relationship of science and culture was clear: Nazis used science to confer credibility. The Nazis were brutal, sadistic, even contradictory in their so-called thinking about race, but they were not stupid. The veneer of even a little scientific respectability could help stall international decisiveness about the Nazi's actions and intentions. While Hitler exterminated Jews, space in popular media in America often was devoted to serious critiques of Nazi science, analysis of philosophical foundations of Nazism, and a revival of Malthus and

Spencer. Although the American public usually was not being fed information that endorsed Nazism, the debate over Nazi science helped deflect attention from the bizarre reality of National Socialism.

The Volk Philosophy

Discourse on race assumed a Darwinian tone in both the United States and Germany in the late nineteenth century. However, the United States lacked a critical ingredient that moved German eugenics from social idealism into a program of eliminating "undesirables." That ingredient was the "Volk" philosophy, a combination of mysticism, paganism, romanticism, racism, and nationalism. The Volkish ideology helped to transform the struggle for survival into a racial imperative. Before Darwinism, Volk was primarily linguistic and national. But social Darwinism became a catalyst to the racial aspects of the philosophy and provided an apparently scientific foundation for them.

According to the Volkish thinkers, Aryans were the most highly evolved race of humans, and were distinguishable by distinct physical features that reflected noble inner qualities. Likewise, the Aryans' antagonists, it was believed, were betrayed by certain characteristics. When Volkish racism adopted Darwinism, Jews were depicted as an evolutionary dead end, a fossil race lacking strength and the ability to progress. One author even claimed that God created Jews as a buffer between man and apes.

A simplistic, brutal interpretation of social Darwinism complemented Volkish thinking, which was saturated with ideas of force and cruelty, and which glorified strife in German history by holding up as a model for future racial war the long-past wars against degenerate Romans and doctrinaire Christianity. For nineteenth-century Volkish thinkers, their peasant heroes' ferocity became a moral virtue, and so became a trait of the ideal German character.[3]

Racial ideas were so deeply ingrained in the German people that even visual evidence could not deter such thinking. For example, the periodical *Die Sonne* in 1933 assured readers that, despite photographs to the contrary, Hitler was blue-eyed and blond—critical features of the Aryan stereotype.

Evolution presented a problem for Volkish ideologues. How could inherent racial superiority exist if one assumed a common beginning for all races?[4] But mythology reigned where science fell short in meeting ideological dictates. Volk philosophy elevated mysticism as it rejected the rationalism of the Enlightenment, and it embraced the Nietzchean love of action. In creating a mythical past and adopting it as creed and law in the 1920s and 1930s, the Germans attempted to live out the myths of primitivism and pastoralism.

At the same time, they adhered fanatically to an apocalyptic vision that placed the destruction of Germany in the genes of the Jews in particular. The city, which so many seers of destruction have viewed as a breeding ground of apocalypse, conjured up images of rootless people. These wanderers, who lacked history and Germanic roots, were foreigners who were not merely incompatible with the Volk. They were a threat. Volkish thinkers saw in urbanization the spread of internationalism and, worst of all, expansion of the "domain of the Jew." One writer called cities "the tombs of Germanism."[5]

Jews commonly were depicted as people who left the city and came to the countryside to take the peasant's land, an act seen as particularly insidious because land was not mere property. The German peasant's land was his link to *cosmos,* the life-force that, in mystical, quasi-pagan fashion, tied the individual to the power of the land. Internationalism was related to another threat, and that was Communism, which emanated from Russia and cast itself as an international movement. The cities, for the Volkish, not only were centers of these dread elements but also were antithetical to the primitive pastoralism that linked the power of Germans to the land, where they had spiritual roots that linked them to greater cosmic purposes.

In the Volk philosophy, Germans abandoned reality in favor of mysticism and mythology. Even the reality of the German state was subordinated to the Volk. The subjugation of reality to fantasy made racial distinctions even more important, because nation was defined by blood and mythical history rather than by borders and political institutions. The Volk philosophy also solved a problematical contradiction in social Darwinism: how could a race be "inferior" if it was thriving? The Volk, not the state, was the foundation of Germanism and was by definition superior; the intrusion of any other race was a contamination of Volk purity. Nation was a spiritual essence, in which people were bound together by blood and ideals. So a state contaminated by Jews and other inferior races was in no way a reflection of true Germans, but a degenerate political structure to be indicted. The revival of Germanism was to be found in a return to Volkish roots and recognition of the Jew as a pervasive, pernicious foe.

Within the Volk ideology and beyond social Darwinism, race was raised from a scientific concept to a metaphysical one. Physical features and behavioral stereotypes came to represent the essence of a race. Jews were seen as malevolent and extremely powerful, a permanent threat to German society. Volkishness and racism eventually became so entwined that the differences became indistinguishable. The result of anti-Semitism and stereotyping was the idea that Jews were obstacles to fulfillment of the Volk vision. The anti-Semitism became so deeply ingrained that the "common-sense" conclusion of a Jewish threat became one of the central features shaping twentieth-century Germany. Jews were a symbol of anything wrong with Germany and so helped to define Volkishness by becoming its antithesis. The Jews were everything that Volkishness was not.[6]

The Volk glorification of primitivism could be seen in the image of the tree, which was used as a symbol of peasant strength, its roots anchored in German soil and history, limbs reaching heavenward. Like the tree, Germans had deep roots, and the Volk thinkers saw themselves as ancient people on ancient soil. The early Volk movement seized upon Tacitus, the Roman propagandist, for evidence of the ancient purity of Germans. Tacitus, in *Germania,* portrayed Germans as "pure," inasmuch as they had not mixed with other tribes, and he depicted Jews unfavorably. Then it followed, according to Volkish historians, that Jews were racially impure, and the German-Jewish antagonism was sanctioned by history. They went even further, claiming that the racially pure Germans represented all creative accomplishments from the beginning of time. The ancient Greeks were made into Germans, and modern Greeks were detached from their history. It also followed that Rome's illustrious history *must* have been a result of German leadership.[7]

Volk values were manifested in an idyllic past, which could be renewed in order to recreate the social order sanctioned in a mythical history. George Mosse has described the Volk values as being the good and the beautiful, which were "products of man's self identification with the cosmos through the intermediary of the Volk, which as a higher reality established in the ancient and historical past, could not change any more than nature could negate its essence." The peasant, like the tree, was rooted in the earth. The nature of people and the character of the land in which they lived were intimately linked. Jews were desert people, and so were depicted as arid, "dry," and shallow. They lacked spiritual depth or profundity, in diametrical opposition to the German Volk, who were people of the rich, dark forests. The Volk, like the forests, were deep and mysterious.

This thought process reveals the way in which Volk thinkers came to the conclusion that Jews were soulless people. Anti-Semitism's philosophical rationale was found in the Volkish assertion that Jews, being rootless, lacked virtues and ethics, and so were at odds with the natural world around them. By extension, they were in conflict with the natural order of the cosmos. Germans, however, were rooted in their glorious, heroic history, in the rich German soil, and in communion with the cosmos. Jews, lacking roots and spiritual depth, could never become Germans. The Jew also was a Volk, but a rootless one because a Jew was seen as being a restless wanderer. Jews were the snake in the Aryan garden, and the life of the garden meant getting rid of the serpent. The Volkish movement held that exorcising the Jew from Germany was a matter of force and faith. The Volk philosophy and the myths it created were the means by which Germans after World War I could escape reality. As the economic crisis worsened and Communism threatened, the Volk offered slogans, ideas, and rationales for nationalism and racism. Ancient legends, mythology, and symbols, including the rune and the swastika, took on importance as sources of primeval strength.[8]

The Volk philosophy dehumanized Jews, and social Darwinism provided a rationale for the mythology built up around them. Evil was objectified and personified in Jews, who were characterized as corpulent and greedy and who were held up as a contrast to the aesthetic beauty of Germans. The pastor Walter Hochstadter, a hospital chaplain, summed up the matter well: "We live in an age which is raging throughout with mad ideas and demons, no less than the Middle Ages. Our allegedly 'enlightened' age, instead of indulging in an orgy of crazed witch-hunting, feasts itself in an orgy of maniacal Jew-hatred."[9] Mythology, social Darwinism, and Volk racism converged in the Nazi demonizing of Judaism.

Nazi Race-Science

The Reichstag, meeting in Nuremberg in September 1935, adopted two laws that enshrined racism and necessitated a definition of race. One law decreed that only German nationals could be citizens. The other law was aimed at Jews, labeling them undesirable aliens and dangerous to Germany. This law included restrictions on Jewish employment and prohibited marriage between Jews and German nationals. The laws were designed to protect "German blood" from dishonor. The earlier "Aryan Decree," issued in April 1933, had defined as a non-Aryan anyone having non-Aryan, especially Jewish, parents or grandparents.[10] These laws, which wedded the foggy ideas of nation, culture, and "blood," formalized the bond between rabidly nationalistic politics and racial science in Nazi Germany.

Nazi race-science was a radical variation on social policy ideas that had been advocated since the late nineteenth century, sometimes on progressive grounds. Nazism pushed the scientific-utopian ideals to their extremes as they swept a whole population into a racist scheme for purifying the body politic, the soul of the nation. The plan called not only for building up the "race" but also for eradicating the nonconforming elements, the non-Aryan types. The Nazis believed that legitimizing racism was an important mission of science, a mission that was central to the National Socialist program of defining racial ideals and providing social norms to regulate.[11]

Germans, going back to the illustrious Ernst Haeckel (1834–1919), had been leaders in scientific research into evolutionary theory.[12] Haeckel, a friend of Thomas Huxley's, believed that biological laws governed human society, and that different human races were as distinctive as different animal species. He saw Germany as the pinnacle of human evolution; consequently, the purity of Germans became important to the rest of humanity. Haeckel wrote in 1915 that one German "warrior . . . has a higher intellectual and moral life-value than hundreds of the raw primitives whom England and France, Russia and Italy are pitting against them."[13] Some of Haeckel's followers even proposed that votes of more intelligent people count more than the votes of the less intelligent. His widespread influence and scientific authority were important in the popular acceptance of the racial-state idea.[14]

Racism became part of the nationalist ideology, and eventually a non-Aryan was seen as anyone who was anti-Nazi. In the nineteenth century, the Germans already had idealized nationalism, patriotism, and racism; to this formula for a policy of predatory nationalism, Georg Wilhelm Friedrich Hegel (1770–1831) added the divinity of state. In years following World War I and the economic hardship that befell Germany, Hegel's ideas about the state assumed increasing vigor. In the

Philosophy of Right, Hegel conceived the state as a divine idea, through which human will and freedom were manifested.[15]

Hegel's vision of the divine state was followed by the Count Joseph Arthur de Gobineau's philosophy of race. He believed that race predicted mental and physical capacity. Gobineau, a Frenchman, stated that racial intermarriage resulted in the degeneration of the stronger race. He "discovered" that Aryans were the highest race of humanity and that Germans were the highest race among Aryan races.

An Englishman, Houston Stewart Chamberlain, published what became a Bible of German racism, *Foundations of the Nineteenth Century* (1899). This book asserted that the "moral Aryan" produced everything of value to civilization, as contrasted with Jewish disruption of the progress of civilization. Like Gobineau, Chamberlain believed that Germans were the elite of the Teutonic race and were undeniably the master race. Chamberlain went so far as to proclaim it nearly certain that Christ did not have a drop of Jewish blood. He "knew" this because Christ's great accomplishments made it impossible for him to be Jewish. This circular reasoning was convenient for Nazis, who in the 1930s found church sentiment strong enough that they could not simply discard Christianity. Yet they had to contend with its Jewish roots.[16] Chamberlain apparently needed to refer to "moral," and not just physiological, Aryans because he was not German by blood, but only by marriage and "attitude."

Drawing on this hodgepodge of Hegel, Gobineau, Chamberlain, Darwin, and others, the Nazi logic was as follows. Nations struggle for space, just as animals struggle for survival in a jungle; the stronger nations, like the stronger animals, survive, while the weaker ones die. Alien or non-Aryan races, especially Jews, threaten German vitality by making the race weaker; Germans are obligated to eradicate inferior races in order to assure survival of the superior race. These natural laws are also the laws of God. Thus Nazis made the extermination of "inferior" people a moral mission.[17]

In the hands of the Nazis, science helped to build an instrument of terror. Nazi race-science created norms for social behavior, which was the target of regulation. Behavior became part of the definition of one's so-called "racial character," as is shown in an extract published by the Reich's Racial Hygiene Research Centre:

> Although membership of the Gypsies in terms of blood is denied by family X, the racial diagnosis as regards the members of family X is undoubtedly "Gypsy" and/or "Gypsy-Negro-Hybrid."
>
> This verdict is based on
>
> 1. racial and psychological features
>
> 2. anthropological features
>
> 3. genealogical data
>
> 4. the fact that the family is regarded as Magyar by Hungarians. . .
>
> These few data are sufficient on their own for family X to be regarded as presumptively Gypsy. Itinerancy and unsettled journeying as a family unit are characteristic of Gypsies. . . .

Whereas the external appearance of family X is not entirely typical Gypsy. . . the gestures, affectivity and overall behavior are not only alien-type but in fact positively indicate Gypsy descent. The false show of civility of manner, the moulding of emotional impulses (in any case superficial in themselves) to prevailing external circumstance, the lack of discernment and poor judgement on matters of factual evaluation and inference, and the deficiency as regards opinions and instability of personal attitudes indicate, for all the artfulness and cunning, what is essentially a high degree of naiveté and primitivity. This type of slackness is not encountered among settled Europeans with a developed work sense.[18]

The Nazis had made behavior just as important as, if not more important than, any physiological standard for determining race. So one could be an undesirable by virtue of physical characteristics, behavior, or family history, all of which the Nazis claimed to be judging in a systemic or scientific fashion. Ironically, many German racial hygienists considered Hitler an un-Nordic East Slav.[19]

No-Fault Science

A few popular publications in America reflected the nation's reticence about confronting Nazism and the rhetoric of race-science. Scientists, the reasoning went, were not responsible for the applications or abuses of their ideas and could only denounce such practices and attempt to expose them as unscientific. This rationale permitted scientists and their apologists to distance themselves from tough moral issues while maintaining their respectable positions at the center of knowledgeable criticism.

One magazine that supported this view, *Science*, explained in 1939 how science was more compatible with some political systems than with others. The writer, a professor from the Massachusetts Institute of Technology, decided that democracy, not totalitarianism, was the political system most in conformity with Darwin's theory of evolution. Using the "survival of the fittest" analogy, the article argued that regimentation drained a system of vitality by depriving it of diversity and hence tended toward biological stagnation.[20] Although he condemned fascism, the author implicitly endorsed the Nazi concept that society was driven by biological law.

Employing similar logic, a *Scientific American* article asked, "What Can Science Do?":

Wherever men of science gather for discussion today . . . one significant subject usually comes in for debate—the glaring misuse and prostitution of the great gifts that scientists have made to the world. . . .

The most recent by-product of the growth of science, some think, is the totalitarian state. . . .

At root, the cause of war has nothing to do with science; it is as old as mankind. . . .

. . . Some are saying that science "should do something about it." New discoveries should be released only under certain safeguards. . . . Others are saying that men of science themselves should assume direct responsibility in connection with the control of their discoveries. . . . But scientific men as a whole are the last type on earth either to desire to direct or to know how to direct the rest of the human race; *they are a type apart, their minds functioning in so different a manner as seldom to understand the world or be understood by it* [my emphasis]. . . .

Probably in a case such as this there is nothing that science can do, as long as man is chained to his own nature.[21]

The editorial disavowed scientific responsibility for ideas at the root of totalitarianism and then noted, with unintentional irony, that scientists were a "type apart"—exemplifying the very thinking about "types" that Hitler would have applauded.

An editorial in March 1937 even personified science, making it sound like a Greek god who bargains with and cajoles mortals: "Science can plead and urge, but until man can remake his nature, the scientist's hands are practically tied."[22] Scientists, again, were depicted as apart from and above the rest of humanity.

The magazine asked, more directly, in an editorial, "Can Science Save Civilization?" and pointed out that scientific responsibility had come to include the application of theories to society and politics, despite scientists' protests. The ability of science to create a better world was touted, and "social biology" was cited, as being in need of a "regenerative influence . . . to save civilization from disaster."[23] So, yes, science could save civilization, or destroy it; and social biology was not wrong, but merely astray.

Not all popular opinion held science blameless. The *New York Times,* in an editorial reprinted in *Science,* said that German scientists were goose-stepping with the Nazis:

> The controversy which is now being waged in Hitler's personal organ, the *Voelkische Beobachter,* on the superior qualities of "Nordic" research should make scientists everywhere blush for their vaunted objectivity. . . . Germany has sunk low indeed when it can found a new journal, *Deutsche Mathematick,* for no other purpose than that of substituting narrow nationalism for the internationalism that has always ruled mathematics. . . .
>
> . . . Yet not since the time of Galileo has science been in such danger. . . . Physics, mathematics, chemistry stepping out to Nazi music—it is a sad spectacle.[24]

In 1937, scientists themselves organized to promote political and social goals. The American Association of Scientific Workers (AASW) was formed with several goals in mind: to bring scientific workers together to promote an understanding of the relationship between science and social problems; to organize and express their opinions on the steps to be taken toward the solution of these problems; to promote all possible action on these conclusions.

At its inception, the AASW identified four major problems confronting scientists worldwide: (1) economic insecurity, due to low salaries, expensive educations, high unemployment, and sometimes a lack of pensions; (2) the misapplication of science, and "inefficiency" in providing the benefits of science to the public; (3) interference with science by funding cuts and interference with freedom of expression; and (4) using pseudoscience to excuse war and attack democracy. To combat the problems, members intended to become activists and publicists, forming local and national organizations, providing information to the press, drafting legislation and lobbying for its passage, and publishing a journal. The association saw its ambitious goals as a way to unify scientists and to work with other organizations, including labor and medical groups, to promote "a wider application of science . . . for the welfare of society." The members also intended to expose antisocial applications of science and pseudoscience, "particularly where such are used as justification for anti-social, anti-democratic, anti-labor, or pro-war policies."

Recognizing some problems in the press coverage of Nazism, the Boston-Cambridge branch created a public relations committee that, in addition to publicizing itself, concerned itself with improving the quality of science reporting. In a tract that was critical of the press, the organization cited the "flood of pseudo-scientific commercial propaganda in our newspapers." The same branch recommended a boycott of German scientific material, but only of those publications for which substitutes could be found. In late 1938 and early 1939, the AASW began a study of scientific research under different political systems, and the organization determined that the Nazis had nearly destroyed German science. The association effectively died in 1940, when a number of members, especially those in the very activist Boston-Cambridge group, became Communist sympathizers. Although only a small number resigned, the actions halted the organization's momentum and injured its credibility.[25]

Stoddard and Grant: Racism for the Masses

During the 1920s and 1930s, two individuals were particularly prolific in writing about eugenics for popular audiences. Madison Grant (1865–1937) and Theodore Lothrop Stoddard (1883–1950) attracted a number of the most enthusiastic supporters of Nazism in the United States. Both were well-known in Germany, where one anthropologist even credited them with being the "spiritual fathers" of American immigration legislation. This legislation he further credited with providing models for German policies. In fact, the German Law on Preventing Hereditarily Ill Progeny was inspired by California's sterilization law and was based on a Model Eugenic Sterilization Law developed by an American eugenicist in 1922.[26]

Stoddard, founder of the Immigration Restriction League, gained prominence in the 1920s and 1930s for his books about the threats posed by "lesser" races. As a layman's eugenicist, his name was commonly cited in periodicals of the day. He and Grant were well-known writers on the subject of race science and social policy, and both wrote for popular audiences. Stoddard, who had no training in science, held a law degree and a Ph.D. degree in history from Harvard; he spent his life writing popular books and working for newspapers, magazines, and radio. He wrote more than twenty books, many of them on race and society. In addition, he worked for WMAL radio in Washington, D.C., owned by the *Washington Star,* where Stoddard was an editorial writer at the time of his death. Among his more notable books were *The Rising Tide of Color Against White-World Supremacy* (1920), *The Revolt Against Civilization* (1922), *Racial Realities in Europe* (1924), and *Into the Darkness: Nazi Germany Today* (1940). .

Stoddard wrote *Into the Darkness* after returning from four months in Nazi Germany, where he personally met Hitler and Heinrich Himmler, chief of German Secret Police and the Schutzstaffel (S.S.). In recounting his visit, Stoddard pointed out that, when the Nazis came to power, the German people were "biologically in a bad way" as a result of war, depression, and unemployment. The higher social strata had a low birth rate, while the lower strata had a more rapid birth rate. He figured that the "morons, criminals, and other antisocial elements" were breeding nine times as fast as the rest of the population and that it cost more to support these "defectives" than to run the government of the nation. As for his visit with the Führer, he was honor-bound to reveal nothing of the content of remarks by Hitler. He could, however, report on the appearance of the man and the surroundings. Stoddard was awestruck: "I had the feeling that I was being ushered into the presence of a Roman Emperor." During the twenty-minute conversation, Stoddard reported, the discussion dealt not with war and politics, but with the great rebuilding plans that had been postponed by the war in Europe. He contrasted Hitler, whom Stoddard found "matter-of-fact," simple, and undramatic, with Mussolini, with whom he had had an audience several years earlier. With unintended irony, Stoddard wrote, "I came away feeling that, however interested Hitler may be in people collectively, he is not interested in the average individual, as such."[27] Stoddard charged that the truth about Nazi racism had been obscured by "passion and propaganda."

Stoddard considered his visit merely an opportunity to observe the practical applications of biology and eugenics. However, the writer, described as a "persona grata" to the Nazis because of his racial theories, was not in Germany only as an observer. He was there as a correspondent for the North American Newspaper Alliance, a leading specialty news agency founded in 1930 by a group of metropolitan newspapers.

Stoddard called Goebbels a "master psychologist" and reported with enthusiasm on the workings of a Nazi eugenics court, which he concluded was conducted scientifically and humanely. In *Into the Darkness*, Stoddard described the four cases he was permitted to view. The first case, a rather "ape-like" man in his mid-thirties, Stoddard found "an excellent candidate for sterilization." The second case was "obviously unbalanced mentally. . . . There was no doubt that he should be sterilized." Cases three and four were a deaf-mute eighteen-year-old girl and a seventeen-year-old girl who "looked feeble-minded." In three of the cases, the court found that further research was needed, and in the fourth it found that the girl should not be sterilized. Stoddard was impressed by the "painstaking, methodical fashion" of the court, whose judgments, "if anything. . . were almost too conservative."[28] It apparently never occurred to Stoddard that he might be witnessing show trials, conducted for his sake and for the favorable publicity to follow.

He returned to the United States with positive reports of Nazi eugenic policy, and his and other eugenicists' statements formed a counterweight to the negative reports by Jewish and other German scientists who attempted to tell the public about the Nazi program.[29] Stoddard's career as public apologist for racism went into decline after the beginning of World War II. He was, of course, not the only enthusiast for eugenics and Hitler, but he held a sizable audience for popularizing Nazi science. He never wrote for experts, but he cloaked himself in scientific authority.

Madison Grant, amateur zoologist and wealthy New York socialite, was one of the more radical eugenicists. His lifelong interest had been the natural world and animal life, along with the history of people. He was vice president of the Immigration Restriction League from 1922 until his death in 1937. He was educated in private schools in New York City, traveled in Europe, and graduated from Yale, with honors, in 1887. He took a degree in law at Columbia University in 1890. His interest in eugenics was not a sudden infatuation, given his lifelong fascination with the natural world and considering that he was a charter member of the American Eugenics Society. In 1916, he published *The Passing of the Great Race,* a book that became very well known both in the United States and abroad. The work, one of the most influential publications on race, intelligence, and immigration, was Grant's interpretation of the Darwinian selection process in society and the consequences of subverting the course of natural law.

Grant even sent copies of his book to Nazi Germany, where it apparently attracted attention. Grant at one time reportedly produced a letter from Hitler thanking him for his copy of *The Passing of the Great Race* and telling Grant that the "book was his Bible." The chief Nazi in charge of killing mentally handicapped people, Karl Brandt, said in 1946 at his trial at Nuremberg that the Nazi program was inspired in part by eugenics in America, and he offered Grant's *The Passing of the Great Race* in his defense.[30] The book offered nearly 150 pages of "evidence"—notes, maps, tables of data—in the appendices. Its popularity was demonstrated, too, by the fact that it was reprinted at least seven times before World War II, in addition to being translated into German, French, and Norwegian.

The message of the book was that people from southern and eastern Europe were inferior to "Nordics," those from Scandinavia, Germany, Ireland, and England.[31] He called it a "fatuous belief" that environment, education, and opportunity could alter heredity; "it has taken us fifty years to learn that speaking English, wearing good clothes and going to school and to church does not transform a Negro into a white man." Grant railed against interracial marriage, claiming that the children were a "mongrel race." "Whether we like to admit it or not, the result of the mixture of two races, in the long run, gives us a race reverting to the more ancient, generalized and lower type."[32]

In 1933, when Grant published *The Conquest of a Continent,* the *New York Times* said, "Substitute *Aryan* for *Nordic,* and a good deal of Mr. Grant's argument would lend itself without much difficulty to the support of some recent pronouncements in Germany." Grant, whose audience included a substantial number of university faculty members in the United States, had copies sent to German eugenicists, and a translation appeared in 1937, the foreword of which said Grant was "no stranger to German readers."[33] Grant believed that moral and intellectual attributes were passed from generation to generation. He also persisted in promoting the measurement of skulls, the cephalic index, as a way of determining race. Use of the index, he said, identified three subspecies of Europeans: Nordic, or Baltic; Mediterranean, or Iberian; and Alpine. Skull shape, eye color, hair color, and stature were, in Grant's opinion, "sufficient to enable us to differentiate clearly between the three main subspecies of Europe."[34]

Franz Boas: Combating the Myth

Grant had his detractors, and one scientist who was especially prominent in his attacks on Nazi science was Franz Boas (1858–1942), a Columbia University professor of anthropology. Boas was a Jew who had obtained his Ph.D. degree in Germany. Boas's students in 1908 had begun a study of body measurements of nearly eighteen thousand European immigrants and their children. The work showed that differences in offspring were not a result of human "types," but of the effects of environment, and indicated that immigration would not result in America's racial deterioration. As early as 1916, Boas stated, "Eugenics is not a panacea that will cure human ills." His critics insisted on the immutability of certain human types and cited such physiological proof as skull measurements. Proponents of this concept, including Grant, were tenacious, and they ignored or denied Boas's empirical refutation of the idea of human types.[35]

In 1938, Boas said that German science was declining, because young scientists had been trained under the Nazi regime and were hopelessly confused about the difference between characteristics that are racially determined and those formed by social environment. The books on mental characteristics of races, he said, had "not a whit of scientific basis."[36] Boas scoffed at such ideas as those espoused by Grant: "It is easy to show that racism has no scientific standing. It is based fundamentally on two misconceptions: the one, the confusion of heredity in a family and heredity in a population; the other, the unproved assumption that the differences in culture which we observe among peoples of different type are primarily due to biological causes."[37] He said that the idea of an Aryan race had no foundation in fact, but he admitted that it was a "fiction that has taken hold of minds wherever the Teutonic, German, or Anglo-Saxon type—however it may be called—prevails."[38]

Boas, whose name was at the top of a declaration of more than twelve hundred scientists condemning the Nazis,[39] charged that science in Germany clearly had become the domain of crude, fanatic ideologues. In tracing the deterioration of German science, he wrote, "I shall leave aside in this discussion the question of whom they considered aliens and the whole weary discussion of the race nonsense preached by Hitler, Goebbels and the unspeakable Streicher; with Hitler, probably an expression of fanatical ignorance; with the other two, infamous lying."[40]

Boas's strong reaction was related not just to science but to his personal experiences. He emigrated to the United States from Germany late in the nineteenth century, during the rise of anti-Semitism in his homeland. The United States, he felt, was more open to people who differed, and the country's outlook emphasized equality. In *The Mind of Primitive Man* (1911), Boas stated his opposition to the idea that cultural differences were a result of innate capacity. He believed that heredity and race had nothing to do with mental and behavioral characteristics, and he even went so far as to declare that so-called savages did not differ in mental ability from civilized people, an assertion which departed radically from the traditional anthropological view that human groups developed through a series of stages—savagery to barbarism to civilization. The differences, Boas declared, were a result of different histories, not biology.[41]

Boas had shown, nearly two decades before the rise of the Nazis, that little scientific knowledge existed about the human races. He said that it was erroneous to speak of European "types" and especially the existence of a "pure type": "The concern that is felt by many in regard to the continuance of racial purity of our nation is to a great extent imaginary."[42] In this respect, Boas was reflecting the Darwinian idea that species exist along a continuum of differences, rather than as distinct types with inviolable boundaries.

Boas eventually was vindicated. Popular literature began to reflect his distaste, both scientifically and ethically, for race-science. For example, a 1938 review of *The Biological Basis of Human Nature* neatly dissected its eugenic views and faulted the book's lack of evidence and misinterpretation of limited evidence on mixing races and resulting "disharmonies." The author of the *Science* review, a Harvard professor, concluded:

> We like to think of the Negro as an inferior. We like to think of Negro-white crosses as a degradation of the white race. We look for evidence in support of the idea and try to persuade ourselves that we have found it even when the resemblance is very slight. The honestly made records of Davenport and Steggerda tell a very different story about hybrid Jamaicans from that which Davenport and Jennings tell about them in broad sweeping statements. [The latter people were the ones under attack in the review.] The former will never reach the ears of eugenics propagandists and Congressional committees; the latter will be with us as the bogey men of pure-race enthusiasts for the next hundred years.[43]

The Assault on Racism

A wide range of popular reviews specifically addressed German racism. *Living Age,* which promoted a cosmopolitan world view, said that the whole Nazi philosophy of race was grossly illogical and resulted in a number of "absurd situations" as Nazis sorted people by race.[44] *Commonweal* also took Nazi logic, both scientific and legal, to task. The magazine correctly pointed out that provisions in Nazi law for steriliz- ing those who were "feeble-minded" were open to abuse through such practices as identifying those opposed to Nazi policy as being unfit, which the Nazis did. In ad- dition, the article said that sufferers of alcoholism could be subjected to steriliza- tion, on the basis of the hereditary nature of alcoholism, which the article said had not been shown. "Nothing proves so insubstantial at times as some of the suppos- edly scientific conclusions that are suggested for application to human affairs."[45] The *Catholic World* stated that "no scientific justification" existed for the idea of superior and inferior races. Gobineau was eloquent, but not scientific; and the Nazi adapta- tions of his ideas also were declared scientifically invalid. "There is absolutely no such thing as the American Race, the German Race, the British Race, or the Zulu Race." The magazine, however, did not accuse Hitler of being absolutely illogical. To the contrary: "His actions were not and are not the actions of an irresponsible wild man, as the secular press in America would hold; rather, Herr Hitler is ruthlessly and quite logically following out the Nazi theory of race and blood. . . . Hitler is quite rea- sonable and logical in so far as he sticks to his program of racial purification."[46]

Even *Reader's Digest* warned that Nazi Germany was adopting a "world as jungle" view, "in which the individual is nothing and the herd is everything." Eradicating divergent thoughts, people, and democracy, the magazine said, was all part of the scheme.[47]

But condemnations were qualified. In some cases, those who damned Nazi sci- ence ended up considering, or even endorsing, the racial ideas. *Living Age,* in an article on "'Pure' Races," argued that, while sterilization generally was unacceptable, in some cases it was appropriate, such as the few cases where "grave dominant defects," including imbecility or schizophrenia, could be prevented. No explanation was given as to how one could define those conditions so as to avoid committing the same crimes as the Nazis.[48]

The Nazis had been working hard to support racism not only biologically, but also historically. In bolstering the Aryan myth, the Nazis set out to show nothing less than German culture's responsibility for all the major intellectual and technical advances in the history of Western civilization. Hitler even claimed that the ancient Greeks were Germans who wandered southward after a natural catastrophe. It fol- lowed, from this warped view, that the Nazis could relocate or exterminate people who occupied what had once been Germanic lands.[49]

A review of Alfred Rosenberg's *The Myth of the Twentieth Century* did not chal- lenge the "incontrovertible scientific fact" that prehistoric patterns of German mi- gration were linked to the establishment of civilization: "Thus it is the German racial element which always and everywhere has evolved order out of chaos, light out of darkness."[50] In a similar fashion, the *Literary Digest* wrote glowingly of Hitler's "fresh, strong, young Germans"; their strenuous regimen, health, and vigor; their "austere and serious" lives, and simply noted without comment that education was composed of "racial research, history, philosophy, sociology, and economics."[51] The *North American Review* even entertained the idea of Nazism's redemptive potential: "One must not assume, because Hitler and his queer companions make hay of the propositions of liberal democracy, and throw into the pile the very axioms on which those propositions are based, that what they themselves say is out of all touch with reality; or that the way it strikes an intelligent American newspaper man is a sufficient interpretation of it. . . . There is retreat (disguised as racial superiority) from the intolerable complexities of the European situation, and a falling back upon the idea of blood, the Redeemer."[52]

The religious metaphor was unusual, but a willingness to consider the legitimacy of Nazi science was not. Several articles in science magazines also suggested legitimacy for Nazi science. The *Science News Letter* briefly reported on a study of the "tallest blond communities" in Germany, the idea of "pure Nordics," and the opportunities for studying family trees. Inbreeding had not "harmed the stock," and the article whimsically noted that "gentlemen of the community just about have to prefer blonds." The magazine did not speak to the study's essential concept, Aryanism.[53] A *Scientific American* article, which did not directly discuss race-science, was an illustrated exposition on the "truth" that could be discerned from studying skeletons. Generalizations were made about the shape of Negro skulls versus that of Caucasians. "The anthropologist not only identifies each type with ease but, if the subject is not 'pure,' can usually determine the *exact* [my emphasis] degree of intermixture of the two."[54] Only a few years earlier, the magazine had given the German point of view free rein. An article on "The Sterilization Law in Germany," written by a German doctor, defended German racism: "It was only because of a hyper-civilization that hereditary inferior types . . . could, without any responsibility, propagate their kind without limit. . . . National Socialist Germany considers interference with unfit life to be a sound application of true Christian love of one's fellow man."[55] The writer also stated that the "bad outbreed the good" and that a number of American states had enacted laws aimed at limiting reproduction of "inferiors." In fact, by the late 1920s, about two dozen states had passed such laws, which permitted state institutions and prisons to perform vasectomies and tubal ligations on inmates who were "feeble-minded," epileptic, or insane.[56]

Malthusianism

It was possible to reject Nazi fanaticism but still retain the foundations of Nazi social thought. Thus, while not endorsing or even mentioning the National Socialists, one still might find merit in a view of human life and society as "survival of the fittest."

Popular articles offered a bleak view at times, as when *Scientific American* portrayed the "face of nature . . . [as wearing a] deep scowl resulting from murderous impulses." Hearkening back to Tennyson's lament concerning "nature red in tooth and claw," the article characterized nature thus: "Instead of peacefulness and content throughout, it is an arena of injury, torture, and death. . . . Nature advances her interests in the formation of species by purposes not in the least allied to pity or peacefulness."[57] Not only was nature personified, it was even given a will, which the writer saw as uncaring and deadly.

Malthus's presumption that disease, warfare, and starvation are means of controlling human populations by eradicating the weak rang out in the passage, which depicted a savage battle for existence and the extermination of the less fit. *Scientific American* resurrected Malthus in a short article on "Social Service and the Weaklings." The author of the piece worried that the less fit were reproducing more rapidly than the more fit: "Let us beware lest in our desire to be kind to the weaker brethren of today we are not more than unkind to all the brethren of tomorrow. . . . Finally, the inherently unfit should be actively discouraged from reproduction. Good nurture cannot be a makeweight against bad breeding."[58] The Nazi rationale was similar. Reproductive misbehavior in the past was blamed for degeneration of Germany, and the problems of the present and future would be solved, in part, by correcting such misbehavior and eliminating "bad breeding."

The *American Mercury* was plainly Malthusian in "Enemies Are Valuable," which argued that humanity's loss of natural enemies had weakened the species. A "quota of enemies" would help maintain vigor. And humanity would be penalized for "disobeying the law of natural selection" because the species would be promoting its own deterioration.[59] Warfare, however, was criticized as a means of selection, because the fit, not the unfit, were the ones sent off to fight. A university president made the same argument in 1935. He argued that "feeble-mindedness" was an increasingly serious problem and that sterilization would be the "intelligent" solution. He did not mention the Nazis or race-science, but his ideas were not far from theirs:

With an individual or a race, the price of ease is destruction. . . .

. . . [Nature] selects the best to propagate the race in hopes that the race may be still better. She has nothing against the weak individually, but the only way she can be sure that they do not pollute the blood stream is to get rid of them. . . . Nature looks through the experience of a million years; we look through the experience of a few minutes. Personally, I prefer to trust her.

. . . The result [of modern medicine and philanthropy] has been a protected race rather than a resistant race, and some day the protection is going to find itself inadequate and the race will be decimated, if not doomed.

Of course, the injury is not in prolonging the lives of the unfit in itself, for the end of the generation would be the end of the menace, but prolonging the lives of the unfit to become the breeding stock of the nation is suicidal.[60]

He was a thoroughgoing Malthusian, decrying social welfare, fretting about the vigor of the race, espousing sterilization, and asserting that "we must have competition . . . to advance." In such publications, race science was finding a wide and respectable audience in America; although the *Mercury* was declining in the 1930s, it was by 1936 still circulating about thirty thousand copies among an intelligent, upscale readership. Walter Lippman called its first editor, H. L. Mencken, "the most powerful personal influence on this whole generation of educated people." Its heavy dose of satire and attention to American problems and ideas appealed especially to young intellectuals.[61]

In another article, arrogant even by *American Mercury* standards, the author wondered why things were so bad for the human species after so many centuries of natural selection. The article, "Why We Do Not Behave Like Human Beings," was prefaced by an editor's note, which said that the article was being reprinted because it was "one of the most important contributions ever made to an American magazine." And readers were invited to apply the conclusions of the article to "the social and political disintegration now so markedly in progress in America." The problem was not a lack of progress among the upper strata of humanity, but among the lower strata:

> The just line of demarcation should be drawn, not between Neolithic Man and the anthropoid ape, but between the glorified and triumphant human being and the Neolithic mass which was, is now and ever shall be. . . .
>
> Free and compulsory education, democratic government and universal suffrage, and the unlimited opportunities of industrial civilization have clothed him with the deceptive garments of equality, but underneath he is forever the same . . . [W]e see it close at home in the sort of men that we choose to govern us in our cities, our State legislatures, and the Congress; the bluntness of intellect and lack of vision in big business and finance; or when we consider the monkeyshines of popular evangelists, comic strips, dance- and bicycle- and Bible-reading marathons, that we are awakened to a realization of the fact that there is something wrong with our categories.
>
> Those who live in these things that they have made are *not* [emphasis in original] behaving like the human beings we have chosen for ourselves out of history as determinants of that entity, and this for the reason that they are still men of the Neolithic Age that no camouflage of civilization can change. . . .
>
> I suggest that the cause of comprehensive failure and the bar to recovery is the persistence of the everlasting Neolithic Man and his assumption of universal control.[62]

Again, Darwin was dragged, albeit awkwardly, into differentiating among human beings. This perspective, of more advanced and less advanced people, was very close to the Nazi race idea. Although the article in *American Mercury* suggested no remedies and did not hint at approving eugenics or Nazis, it accepted the intellectual foundation of such brutality. The foundation was belief in the existence of inferior and superior types of people.

Newsweek may have encapsulated very well American scientists' and society's dilemma: being appalled by Nazis but not rejecting Nazi science. In a few short paragraphs in 1933, the magazine reported that nearly half a million "unfit" individuals would be sterilized. The article began, "Germany continues to astound the world." It outlined the German law, estimated the number of sterilizations, and supplied the reasons for the sterilizations. The article even reported that, while it would cost more than $5 million for the sterilization program, those people being sterilized cost Germany between $100 million and $300 million annually. The Pope, the magazine said, condemned the practice.[63] *Newsweek* did not.

The press presented Nazi science in a eugenicist-science framework, not in the context of the Volk philosophy or the demonic-Jew mythology that thrived in German culture. The popular press in American culture favored a perspective of rational science over irrational mythology. The press tended to view the social Darwinism of Nazism apart from the Volk and the demonology, making social Darwinism a scientific issue rather than a cultural one. What the American press presented to the public was a playing out of the eugenic ideal, not the mythology that was the real core of Nazi ideology.

Between the Idea and the Reality

Popular publications, with such notable exceptions as the writings of Stoddard and Grant, rarely espoused Nazism. But there were endorsements of ideas that constituted the foundation of Nazism, a distinct line of thinking that connected race, science, and society. The distinction in America, though, was that no one took the final step that Hitler and his followers did—and that was the ruthless application of supposed laws of nature. The eugenics movement and the Immigration Act of 1924 have been compared to Nazism,[64] but the comparison is an unfair one, because of the vast difference between the two cultures. One took that fateful, radical final step in promoting "the fittest," while the other stopped far short of a program of extermination.

The radical eugenics of the Nazis and their sympathizers was an extreme case of culture redefining science for social and political purposes. Nazis and a few Americans, such as Grant and Stoddard, used science to prop up the circular logic of their claims for racial supremacy. The "science" of Nazi racism begins and ends with the same idea: the utopian myth of racial purity. The desire to confirm the unworthiness of different groups of people motivated the initiation of race-science. As the data were assembled to prove racial inferiority, scientific legitimacy was bestowed upon racism, and the scientific process gave racially motivated legislation the appearance of having a foundation in reason rather than emotion. Then the assembled data predictably supported the racist myths that initially had provoked the research. In this fashion, Hitler latched onto the idea of a pure Aryan race, defined variously by geography, cultural accomplishments, language, physical characteristics, and even behavior. Nazi medicine and science spent a great deal of energy showing the validity of the myth, creating behavioral and physical standards for conformity, and explaining the reasons for penalizing those who failed to meet the standards. Those who did not measure up were ostensibly outside those "scientifically" established norms. But the real offense was their absence from both the beginnings of the mythical Aryan nation and the Nazi vision of utopia.

The greater myth embedded in Nazism was utopianism, along with medieval superstitions about demonic Jews. The Nazis were going to recreate a "pure" race and build their racially pure Garden on German soil. Eugenics, legitimated by the Darwinian tradition and by recent advances in genetics, was available and convenient as a tool for cleansing and regenerating the race.

Conclusion

Myths and Misuses of Darwinism

Since its introduction in 1859, Darwin's theory of natural selection sometimes has reinforced old myths of race and change and served sinister purposes. Cultural myths, in effect, absorbed science. Darwin's materialism, with its lack of interest in moral, political, and theological implications, evolved into a philosophy of racial supremacy that assimilated myths of human origins, destiny, and perfectibility. Darwinism's incorporation into popular culture, along with changes in the ideas and myths associated with it, was accomplished through magazines, newspapers, books, political and social movements, and wars. Even churches became part of the process, as shown in the willingness of some ministers to adapt the gospel to the eugenic message.

Darwin proposed an ever-evolving world in which organisms varied randomly and retained those variations that gave them an advantage in the struggle to survive. *The Origin* hewed closely to Darwin's data on variability within species, shunning implications beyond his immediate problem of speciation. Darwin was so fully focused on his data and the scientific issues that his work was nonmythic, meaning simply that it was detached from theology or other myth-driven or myth-generating forms of knowledge. In this respect, *The Origin* might be viewed as a masterpiece of logic, and Darwin himself referred to it as "one long argument."[1]

Darwin's accomplishment was the theory of natural selection; Spencer's accomplishment was a philosophy that synthesized all knowledge under the umbrella of a single idea, which was evolution. Spencer, like Darwin, embraced the idea of a constantly evolving world. But he pushed the idea further, applying it to everything, not just the development of species. Spencer's theory of the evolution of human society stressed goal-directed improvement. Society improved as it absorbed greater understanding of the laws of nature.

Spencer believed that the evolution of society, or the struggle for existence in society, should be unimpeded. "Poor laws," government regulation of factory and housing conditions, the establishment of state education systems, and even state banking or postal systems—all these misguided reforms ran counter to the force of natural law. Accordingly, he was a proponent of free trade, of laissez-faire economics. People, he argued in *The Study of Sociology* (1873), eventually would adapt to circumstances if left alone to wage the struggle for existence. Interfering with natural social evolution, on the other hand, meant that people no longer would adapt to change, and social dissolution would follow.[2] He stressed the legal, social, economic, and political conditions that would facilitate progress to a better society. And people could help to shape these conditions, at the very least by not interfering with the natural evolution of society. This was the critical intermediate step between Darwin and eugenicists.

Spencer was intermediate because he bridged the inductive-objective approach of Darwin, and the inductive-normative science of the eugenicists. Spencer was a deductive philosopher and so had minimal use for natural selection, but he dealt with the same grand idea as Darwin, and that was evolution. Darwin explained how evolution worked. He did not create a model of how human beings, or any other species, came to be. His is not a theory with a goal. Spencer, on the other hand, explained *why* society worked as it did, and predicted where evolution would lead. Darwin's objectivity is revealed in the fact that generally he eschewed social values in his work, although they did arise upon occasion, as in his aside in *Descent of Man* about the superiority of civilized people.[3] But Spencer built much of his philosophy upon two political-social values, liberty and individualism. The eugenicists were in the tradition of Darwin because they compiled massive amounts of data to support their conclusions. They were Spencerian in the prescription of values and solutions.

Like Darwin, the eugenicists were good publicists, but they had more knowledge of heredity than either Darwin or Spencer. Eugenicists believed that individuals could be improved and consequently all of society uplifted. Their intellectual energy was focused not on the environment, which Spencer stressed, nor on variability among organisms, on which Darwin dwelled, but on *behavior*, especially sexual behavior. A utopian vision was implicit in the push to eradicate unfit individuals and replace them with more fit people, who would create a better world. The vision was more explicit in Nazi eugenics than in American eugenics. The Nazis intended to recreate the mythical Aryan nation, which had been contaminated by less fit races, whom the Nazis saw as the snakes in the Aryan Garden. For the Nazis, myth and reality were inseparable.

Myth also became reality in Huxley's alleged defeat of Wilberforce, which at one level is merely a good story. The evidence is biased, long removed from the event, inconclusive, and in a few cases even in favor of Wilberforce. It is far from clear that Huxley won an outright victory. However, the truth of the story is not in re- counting the event and its outcome. The truth is the larger reality it symbolizes, a myth showing that science (Huxley) did in fact confront theology (Wilberforce) and declare its independence from religion. The myth survives as a symbol of numer- ous values, including truth and individualism. It also shows the heroism of confront- ing tyranny (intellectual, in this case), and the superiority of individual independence to institutional conformity. Huxley is the seeker after truth, fearless about where it might lead him; Wilberforce is the agent of an intellectually conservative institu- tion of tradition that shunned new insights. Huxley spoke for himself that day, when he said he would rather be descended from an ape than have for a grandfather a man of great talents who used his ability to introduce ridicule into grave scientific dis- cussion. Huxley challenged the whole institution of organized religion and was as unlikely to prevail against the bishop as Jacob was against the angel, whom Jacob refused to release until he was blessed.

Like the Huxley myth, the story of Darwin's recantation is a story in which the facts are ignored. It is a myth, however, for the subculture that persists in rejecting the theory of evolution. That subculture finds useful and comforting a myth which celebrates the revival of revealed knowledge in the person who is the very symbol of its rejection. This is how canards become myths and are used to organize and understand the world.

Scientists, the religious, the larger culture—all were involved in the dynamic process of creating and promoting myths. But myths also were used to promote science, as in Huxley's statement that "extinguished theologians lie about the cradle of every science as the strangled snakes beside that of Hercules."[4] Like the infant Hercules, science grew in power. Huxley's symbolic inversion in casting theologians as serpents could not have been lost on his audience. Lady Hope's countermyth at- tempted to restore knowledge and truth to the theological tradition.

The two myths illustrate, too, the role of a popular press in creating and main- taining myths. A number of science histories, including both Darwin's and Huxley's "life and letters" volumes, promoted the myth of Huxley's victory over Wilberforce. The victory remains standard fare, in spite of recent scholarship that has raised doubts about such an outcome. In contrast, Darwin's recantation never entered the larger culture and has been confined to the newspapers, pamphlets, and books of the cre- ationist subculture. Mainstream publishers largely have ignored the myth, except occasionally to challenge it.

The myth of Huxley's victory reveals something of human nature—a love of drama, sympathy for the underdog, dislike of arrogance and tyranny. But, more important, the myth teaches a lesson. At one level, meddling theologians are put in their place; by extension, the triumph applies to all meddlers. At another level, the tale teaches the moral superiority of pursuing truth in the face of adversity.

Universal Myths

Any number of myths weave in and out of the Darwinian phenomena: utopia, Eden, change or rebirth, doomsday or the apocalypse. In the biblical myth, rebirth represents triumph over evil. In social Darwinism, rebirth means the renewal of the "most fit." The triumph is over "less fit" people, over that which would drag down humanity. To promote the existence of the "less fit" would be a violation of natural, rather than biblical, law. The idea of rebirth, which is related to both the Garden myth and the concept of cosmic cycles, found a place for science. Leo Marx, considering the impact of the machine age on the pastoral ideal, stated, "The machine's sudden entrance into the garden presents a problem that ultimately belongs not to art but to politics."[5] That is just where social Darwinism and eugenics put science. The threat to the Garden was answered with the political solution, such as legalizing the sterilization of feeble-minded people and restricting immigration of certain groups. The purpose was to control the less fit. In order to recreate lost Eden, the eugenicists based their social and political goals on science.

The concept of cosmic cycles was a potent one in the early twentieth century, even among scientists.[6] It is an idea well suited to evolutionary theory, one expressing what Wyn Wachhorst calls the "root duality that all myths must finally resolve."[7] Wachhorst explains the duality in terms of Sisyphus, who angered Zeus with his disrespect and was sentenced for eternity to roll a boulder up one side of a mountain, only to see it roll down after reaching the top, and to roll it back up again: "He chooses, in essence, a faith—a faith that the rock placed on the hilltop belongs there and will remain there. Yet it has always been man's ultimate, if unconscious, perception that the rock must roll down and the struggle must be eternally renewed—that the reality of the individual is lesser and linear, while that of the collective is greater and cyclical. It is this root duality which all myths must finally resolve."[8]

In the initial battle over the acceptance of Darwin, Huxley struggled against orthodoxy. It was a self-righteous struggle in which Huxley grew, intellectually and morally. As the sons of Huxley and Darwin went about creating the myth of Wilberforce's defeat, they undertook a Sisyphean effort. At the peak of the mountain, they witnessed the triumph of Darwinian theory in particular, and of empirical, professional science in general. For those individuals, the path was linear one, and the destiny distinct and finite. But the myth was built in the greater context of the search for truth, unlike the Darwinian island, which was a discrete landmark in an endless sea of human ignorance. Truth was the greater struggle, and once any single truth was discovered—the boulder had reached the mountain top—the cycle began again with new questions that demanded a resumption of the struggle.

Myth also is a device for both exploiting and containing the tension of duality. Myths exist at two levels—the story and the truth within the story. The myth of the Huxley victory exploits the duality of the lesser, linear reality of individualism, and the greater, cyclical reality of the collective. It is the individual, Huxley, who begins as the underdog and prevails. The narrative, in its linear form, ends. But the greater reality is the ongoing struggle for truth, inevitably against established standards of knowledge. The tension of the duality makes Huxley's heroism even greater, more than prevailing in a brief debate. The debate myth limits the tension by reducing it to a single, discrete event and making it comprehensible within a fairly simple story, thereby rendering the tension less threatening. The myth offers momentary relief in the eternal struggle for truth, at both individual and collective levels.

When Lady Hope turned the Huxley myth on its head, she did more than just trumpet religion over science. The recantation myth attempted to shatter Sisyphus's boulder, or at least to have Darwin achieve the peak, see the scientific boulder roll down the opposite side, and admit that he had been pushing the wrong rock all the time. But it was not just a different rock that Lady Hope pushed. An individual could achieve the summit by witnessing Christ, but he or she then had to endure the boulder in bringing the word to the rest of humanity. Her story is false because it is contrary to the evidence. It is a myth because the fable, in and of itself, is not nearly so important as the greater truth it attempts to teach—the power and beauty of God. Like the Huxley-Wilberforce myth, Lady Hope's is a myth of struggle, triumph, and truth.

In its most radical form, the myth of change or rebirth becomes the apocalypse, which is the ultimate change in order to prepare for the regeneration of humanity. Social Darwinism warned of such an apocalypse—the breakdown of society—if natural law was ignored and society's less fit were given, via misguided social policy, special advantages in the competition for survival with their biological superiors. The idea of a future social breakdown is not peculiar to social Darwinism and has been linked to science in other contexts, including nuclear energy.[9] In Nazi Germany, scientific progress was heralded as an aid in averting social breakdown but instead helped the country achieve its degeneration into barbarism.

The Garden in America

There are two kinds of pastoralism, according to Leo Marx, the first an expression of feelings (versus thought), and hard to define. An example is the flight from the city, the longing for "natural" environments, and the search for outdoor recreation. In this type of pastoralism, the tendency is to idealize rural ways, and an element of primitivism resides in its sentimentality. The second kind of pastoralism is imaginative and complex, and contrasts two worlds: rural peace and simplicity versus urban power and sophistication. Complex pastoralism recognizes a larger, more complicated order of experience, such as the dispossessed herdsman or the sound of the locomotive in the woods.[10] It was the more complex pastoralism, with the use of modern science to promote social progress, which encompassed a society governed by "natural law."

In theory, social Darwinism was a natural law, and the society it produced inevitably would be good because it was "natural." On the one hand, social Darwinism suggested a simple pastoralism by citing cities as breeding grounds of the unfit and as case studies in social degeneration. This thinking was not restricted to social Darwinists or to a few points in time. Population theorists, from Malthus to the eugenicists to recent concerns about a population bomb, have concentrated their warnings on the city, not the countryside.[11] Even recent political debates about the deterioration of American society have focused on urban communities, not rural or small-town settings. On the other hand, social Darwinism suggested a more complex pastoralism by virtue of finding values in the individual strength of the frontiersman, taking his ability to survive under adverse conditions as prima facie evidence of fitness, and transferring those ideals to social policy that included urban America. However, woodlands were not the centers of social progress, which depended upon many factors, including economics, politics, social cohesion, and the development of knowledge. For these things, cities were the center of power. As the empirical age encroached on the simple pastoral myth of rural longings, social Darwinism was an idea that could bridge the two kinds of pastoralism by elevating individual fitness as part of the solution for problems in a complex, increasingly urban society.

Social Darwinists, as they made individualism scientifically respectable, spread the myth of science in America, which James Robertson called a "modern variant of a much older myth of Western rationalism, the myth of finding law."[12] In the latter part of the nineteenth century, Darwinism brought together the ideas of science and progress. As Robertson stated:

> The promise of the myth of science underlay the growth and spread of progressivism. That promise is that science would bring ultimate truth into everyday, secular, natural life—a promise religion had fulfilled in the dark past, but did no longer, for many Americans. Science would be "liberal and exact," humanitarian as well as utilitarian. It would and could, using only present, visible, palpable materials and observations, be able to describe the present, and tell the truth about both past and future, and solve our problems. . . .
>
> For Americans, evolution provided scientific proof, taken from the evidence of the physical universe, of the purpose, mission, and meaning of America. Evolution was proof of progress—unceasing, inevitable progress. And America is, as all Americans believe, the living, national embodiment of progress.[13]

Eugenicists adopted the pastoral myth when they espoused a cleansing of human races, the implications being, first, the prior existence of a race unspoiled by crossbreeding with other races; and, second, the promise that the original race could be recovered by genetically sifting out the less fit. The Garden in which the original race existed was, of course, scientifically irrelevant for American eugenicists. But America was the place in which the regeneration was to occur. The Garden just needed weeding. For the Germans, it was an Aryan Garden, in German soil of centuries past, identifiable both geographically and racially.

American Myths

Social Darwinism was supported widely in nineteenth-century America, where Spencer's ideas about social and political issues were well known. The willingness of Americans to hear and accept Spencer, who at the time was as influential as Darwin, grew out of values traced back to the beginning of the nation. The U.S. Constitution was motivated, to a significant degree, by belief in the inalienable right of the individual to personal freedom, which also meant freedom from interference by government. Government was supposed to protect individual freedoms, and this idea made Spencer's thought congenial to Americans.

A related school of thought in America was based on political economists who, writing in eighteenth-century England and France, believed that natural laws governed economic processes and that interfering with the laws was perilous. Adam Smith (1723–1790), for example, said it was a natural law that an individual seeks his own economic interest, and that this seeking in turn is in the general economic interest of the community. The positive response to Spencer and Darwin naturally followed the general acceptance of laissez-faire economics in the United States in the nineteenth century.[14]

Two archetypal figures emerged in the mythology of an individualistic, opportunistic culture: the Puritan and the frontiersman. Survival is their common trait. In the frontier of the New World, both adapt and survive.[15] Social Darwinism complemented the archetypes because it was built on the twin imperatives of adaptability and survival. It also blended the archetypes by providing a common philosophy to support the Puritan idea that success was a sign of God's Grace, and that individual survival in the face of adversity was proof of fitness. Thus, Horatio Alger succeeded by grace and by individual fitness.

With the rise of technology and empirical science in the late nineteenth century, Americans increasingly turned to scientific explanations. There was a drive for efficiency in the rapidly industrializing nation, and Spencer's philosophy was appealing because it identified conditions that facilitated social and economic progress, as well as those which hindered social evolution. With the rise of the city, the emergence of reform politics, and the closing of the frontier, eugenics became a progressive idea, part of the inevitable change but endowed with the power of science, which could explain change. If change were understood, then perhaps it could be controlled. And if it could be controlled, it was no longer a threat, and actually could become a means of promoting social progress.

Evolution, the grandest scheme of change, was explained by natural selection. So, the argument ran, the power of Darwin's scientific explanation could be harnessed for positive social change. In the early twentieth century, the mobilization that began in World War I promoted cooperation among business, government, and labor; and science continued to be a force for progress.[16] The spirit of building and growth worked with the myth of individualism to create an atmosphere amenable to eugenics, which elevated individual fitness for the sake of the social good and so accommodated both the spirit of cooperation and the myth of the individual. For eugenicists, individuals were the unit of analysis, but it was their place in the larger organization—society—and their impact upon it that really mattered.

Spencer Weart points out that the images of science and technology are used to manipulate others and can be used to promote undesirable ends. But imagery, tested against reality and human feelings, can be the beginning of a solution. Images are effective when they include a particular set of traditions, social tensions, and personal impulses, "joining them in an alliance to work upon minds."[17] For social Darwinism, the traditions were individualism, nationalism, tribalism, and change/rebirth. The same was true of eugenics, which held out the lure of recreating the Garden while playing on fears that new immigrants would rend the familiar social fabric. In particular, the impulse to breed was preserved for those smart enough or sufficiently well positioned in society. These people already had shown themselves fit by virtue of economic success. So science was used to defend their most fundamental personal impulse—to reproduce.

The Purpose of Myths

Robertson argues that American myths arrange themselves around four questions: What is the purpose of America? What is the place of the individual? What is the nature of the community? What is power for?[18] Although social Darwinism did not answer such questions directly, it was sufficiently malleable for people of many different, and even competing, perspectives to mold its concepts to support their own purposes.

During the Spanish-American War, for example, both isolationists and expansionists found Spencer's philosophy supportive of their arguments; in doing so, they offered answers to questions about the purpose of America. For isolationists, Spencer showed the folly of interfering with the natural evolution of any society; imperialism would hinder American progress by diverting energy and resources away from the development of American society. For expansionists, the imperialist impulse was the natural expression of a vital, strong society. Like other biological organisms, a strong society would seek to dominate others in a natural struggle to ensure its place in the competition for survival.

Social Darwinism further complemented American mythology by providing yet another gospel for the missionaries of national destiny, which could be measured politically, economically, geographically, or in any number of other ways. But however national destiny was measured, social Darwinism could manufacture the yardstick. Social Darwinism also accommodated both the frontiersman and the Puritan. The mythical frontiersman was an individualistic conqueror who possessed an unusual degree of fitness. The Pilgrim, too, had a special fitness, which was applied to building a community rather than being dissipated in lone forays into the wilderness. In either case, community builder or lone woodsman, social Darwinism bestowed significance on American myth.

The purpose of the community could be explained in Darwinian terms as the Spencerian idea of the "social organism." If society were an organism, in the same sense of a biological organism, then the community's purpose was to survive, and competition or cooperation with other communities was for the sake of increasing the chances of survival.

So power, the fourth of Robertson's questions that myths need to answer, was for social Darwinists a means of social progress. The Darwinian model was not a matter solely of power (the Nazi interpretation) but also was a matter of cooperation. Dominant "social organisms," such as American society, could use power in a number of ways, according to social Darwinists, and thereby further national, individual, and community interests. One such social Darwinian interpretation might run this way: The hegemonic extension of American society through imperialism was a working out of the natural law that would further strengthen the nation and spread democracy and capitalism—values which were themselves expressions of natural law. The subsequent environment in the newly acquired territories would create conditions that strengthened individuals. Meanwhile, communities uplifted less fit people, by *private* philanthropy, and thereby promoted the health of both society and individuals. So power was an instrument of progress because it promoted natural law, which in turn invigorated society.

To achieve utopia was one of the reasons for wrestling with the forces of nature—an image not unique to social Darwinists. Others who sought to bring about utopia also were portrayed as wrestling with natural forces. This was the case with both Thomas Edison and Charles Steinmetz, a prominent mathematician and engineer known for his work with General Electric. Edison and Steinmetz, along with Henry Ford, were cultural heroes of the 1920s. Many saw Edison and Steinmetz as men who would help the nation achieve an electrical utopia.[19] A similar image was at work with the eugenicists, men trying to direct another "electrical" force, the urge to procreate, in order to create a utopia founded upon good breeding. Like electricity, procreation was dangerous if uncontrolled but beneficial if reserved for the fit, at least in the eyes of eugenicists. With the help of the popular press, Edison had promoted technology as wizardry, and the public had accepted it. The case for eugenics was similar—science would solve problems and make society better. Newspapers, magazines, and popular books helped to promote eugenics, both as a science and as a solution to social problems. If science could work wonders to produce material comforts, why could it not do so with human progeny? Science could modify the environment, improving the "nurture" side of the equation; so it also could fix the "nature" side. Wachhorst said that Edison saw the present as the beginning of the future rather than as the end of the past.[20] This also was true of the American eugenicists, who were part of a stream of progressive thinking inasmuch as their political activity was promoting the welfare of society. They saw their science as a means to create a better future.

In spite of the fact that science has been, and continues to be, a singular and highly successful method of generating knowledge about the world, it does not transcend human cultures. Cultures bend science to their own purposes, which is understandable if sometimes not morally defensible. It seems inevitable that, in the process of making scientific work public and sharing accumulated knowledge with other scientists in order to promote the creation of new knowledge, Darwin's ideas would be adapted to unforeseen, even irrational, concepts. Scientific ideas eventually are put to work in the service of social and political goals, and are incorporated or made into myths. Thus, the concepts are removed from the control of the scientists but yet retain the authority of science.

Ideas have consequences. A theory that began with observations of Galapagos finches and turtles in the 1830s did not long remain limited to explaining the creation of new species. Darwin changed the course of Western thought, and his ideas even were perverted to justify murdering millions of people. Darwinism's strength was as a scientific theory that had the ability to explain a great deal. Its foible was its adaptability to almost any purpose. And so the theory will continue to be a beacon of knowledge and a rationalized foundation for irrational impulses.

Notes

Abbreviations

AESP   American Eugenics Society Papers, American Philosophical Society, Philadelphia, Pennsylvania

APS   American Philosophical Society, Philadelphia, Pennsylvania

CBDP   Charles B. Davenport Papers, American Philosophical Society, Philadelphia, Pennsylvania

CDP   Charles Darwin Papers, Univ. Library, Cambridge Univ., England

JDHP   Joseph Dalton Hooker Papers, Royal Botanical Gardens, Kew, England

THP   Thomas Huxley Papers, Imperial College, London

Introduction

1. Newspaper clipping in CDP, vols. 106–7, item 52–53. The name of the source newspaper is not given.

2. The word anomalies is used in the sense discussed by Thomas Kuhn, *The Structure of Scientific Revolutions*, 2d ed. (Chicago: Univ. of Chicago Press, 1972).

3. An extremely good source for such material is Tom McIver, *Anti-Evolution: An Annotated Bibliography* (Jefferson, N.C.: McFarland & Co., 1988).

4. On the press as a record for historical public opinion, see Alvar Ellegard, "Public Opinion and the Press: Reactions to Darwinism," *Journal of the History of Ideas* 19 (June 1958): 379–87. See also Lucy Brown, *Victorian News and Newspapers* (New York: Oxford Univ. Press, 1985), 48–50, 273–74.

5. Richard Hofstadter, *Social Darwinism in American Thought* (Boston: Beacon Press, 1955), 188.

6. Quoted in George Brown Tindall, *America: A Narrative History* (New York: Norton, 1984), 825.

7. Ibid., 864–67.

8. The "vogue" is from "Vogue of Spencer," title of chapter 2 of Hofstadter, *Social Darwinism.*

9. Thomas J. Curran, *The Immigrant Experience in America* (Boston: Twayne Publishers, 1976), chs. 6–8.

10. Daniel J. Kevles, "Controlling the Genetic Arsenal," *Wilson Quarterly* 16 (2) (Spring 1992): 70–71.

11. A good example of such concerns is the backlash generated by Richard J. Herrnstein and Charles Murray, *The Bell Curve: Intelligence and Class Structure in American Life* (New York: Free Press, 1994). Their sins have been described variously as tackling a subject that many feel should not be discussed, having substantial methodological flaws, and simply coming to the wrong conclusions.

12. On the politics of the genome project, see Robert Cook-Deegan, *The Gene Wars: Science, Politics and the Human Genome Project* (New York: Norton, 1994). See also U.S. Dept. of Energy, *Human Genome 1993 Program Report* (Washington, D.C., 1994), for the budget for fiscal year 1993. The expenditures to which I allude are allocated to "Ethical, Legal and Social Issues" in the budget line.

13. Gertrude Himmelfarb, *Darwin and the Darwinian Revolution* (Gloucester, Mass.: Peter Smith, 1967), 22–27; Francis Darwin, ed., *The Life and Letters of Charles Darwin* (1888; reprint, New York: Basic Books, 1959), 2:301.

14. F. Darwin, *Life and Letters of Charles Darwin,* 2:371.

Part I. Myths of Darwinism

1. Adrian Desmond and James Moore, *Darwin: The Life of a Tormented Evolutionist* (New York: Warner, 1991), 284.

Chapter 1. The Bishop Eaters

Primary sources for this chapter are three archives: CDP, JDHP, and THP.

1. Thomas Huxley to Joseph Dalton Hooker, Oct. 6, 1864, JDHP.

2. Michael Ruse, *The Darwinian Revolution: Science Red in Tooth and Claw* (Chicago: Univ. of Chicago Press, 1979), 137.

3. William Irvine, *Apes, Angels, and Victorians: The Story of Darwin, Huxley, and Evolution* (Lanham, Md.: Univ. Press of America, 1983), 1–5.

4. For a more skeptical view of the illness, see Irvine, *Apes, Angels,* 63–65. See also Douglas Hubble, "The Life of the Shawl," *Lancet* 265 (Dec. 26, 1953): 1351–54. A recent, and very good, analysis of Darwin's ailment is Fabienne Smith, "Charles Darwin's Health Problems: The Allergy Hypothesis," *Journal of the History of Biology* 25, no. 2 (summer 1992): 285–306.

5. Some especially good recent Darwin biographies are: Peter J. Bowler, *Charles Darwin: The Man and His Influence* (Oxford: Blackwell, 1990); John Bowlby, *Charles Darwin: A New Life* (New York: Norton, 1990); Desmond and Moore, *Darwin: The Life.* Not as recent, but very insightful about the relationship between Thomas Huxley and Charles Darwin, is Irvine, *Apes, Angels.*

6. Ruse, *Darwinian Revolution,* 23, 33–34, 138.

7. Desmond and Moore, *Darwin: The Life,* 313, 318; W. B. Turrill, *Joseph Dalton Hooker: Botanist, Explorer, and Administrator* (London: Thomas Nelson and Sons, 1963), chap. 5.

8. Peter J. Bowler, *Evolution: The History of an Idea* (Los Angeles: Univ. of California Press, 1984), 173–75.

9. Turrill, *Joseph Dalton Hooker,* 90.

10. Desmond and Moore, *Darwin: The Life,* xiii.

11. Ibid., xv.

12. T. Huxley to C. Darwin, Nov. 23, 1859, THP.

13. Ruse, *Darwinian Revolution,* 138–40; J. Vernon Jensen, *Thomas Henry Huxley: Communicating for Science* (Newark, Del.: Univ. of Delaware Press, 1991), 16.

14. Ruse, *Darwinian Revolution,* 204.

15. Desmond and Moore, *Darwin: The Life,* 404. The authors are quite convincing in their thesis that Huxley, Hooker, and other young allies of Darwin were motivated not only by the substance of Darwin's ideas, but also by professional ambition. They were working their way into the scientific establishment, and natural selection served them well as a device to dislodge Owen and his ilk.

16. T. Huxley to Hooker, Sept. 5, 1858, JDHP.

17. Roy M. MacLeod, "Evolutionism and Richard Owen, 1830–1868: An Episode in Darwin's Century," *Isis* 56 (Fall 1965): 259–80; see also Ruse, *Darwinian Revolution,* 26–27, 141–44.

18. Bowler, *Evolution,* 123–26.

19. Richard Owen [grandson], *The Life of Richard Owen* (1894; reprint, New York: AMS Press, 1975), 2:166–67.

20. Adrian Desmond, *Huxley: The Devil's Disciple* (London: Michael Joseph, 1994), 333.

21. MacLeod, "Evolutionism and Owen," 260–64.

22. Desmond, *Huxley,* 230.

23. Ruse, *Darwinian Revolution,* 141–44.

24. MacLeod, "Evolutionism and Owen," 264; Ruse, *Darwinian Revolution,* 144.

25. MacLeod, "Evolutionism and Owen," 274, 278.

26. C. Darwin to Hooker, Dec. 14, 1859, JDHP.

27. C. Darwin to Hooker, May 15, 1860, JDHP.

28. C. Darwin to Hooker, Nov. 1859, JDHP.

29. C. Darwin to T. Huxley, July 3, 1860, THP.

30. C. Darwin to T. Huxley, Dec. 28, 1859, THP.

31. Desmond and Moore, *Darwin: The Life,* 373, 408–9.

32. C. Darwin to T. Huxley, Mar. 4, 1860, THP.

33. C. Darwin to T. Huxley, Dec. 2, 1860, THP.

34. T. Huxley to Hooker, Dec. 19, 1860, JDHP.

35. C. Darwin to T. Huxley, May 7, 1860, THP.

36. C. Darwin to Hooker, Sept. 6, 1860, JDHP.

37. T. Huxley to Hooker, Dec. 31, 1859, JDHP.

38. C. Darwin to Hooker, Mar. 3, 1860, JDHP.

39. Desmond, *Huxley,* 272.

40. Hooker to C. Darwin, Apr. 20, 1860, CDP.

41. Hooker to C. Darwin, Apr. 15, 1863, CDP.

42. Ruse, *Darwinian Revolution*, 66.

43. Francis Darwin, ed., *The Autobiography of Charles Darwin* (1892; reprint, New York: Dover Books, 1958), 38–39.

44. Hooker to C. Darwin, Dec. 16, 1862, CDP.

45. Leonard Huxley, ed., *Life and Letters of Thomas Henry Huxley* (New York: D. Appleton and Co., 1901), 1:189–90.

46. T. Huxley to Hooker, Dec. 31, 1859, JDHP.

47. The "general agent" reference is in C. Darwin to T. Huxley, Mar. 4, 1860, THP. The other comment is in C. Darwin to T. Huxley, Mar. 27, 1861, THP.

48. T. Huxley to Hooker, Sept. 8, 1858, JDHP.

49. T. Huxley to Hooker, Dec. 2, 1859, JDHP.

50. Desmond, *Huxley*, 284, 289–90; Alvar Ellegard, *The Readership of the Periodical Press in Mid-Victorian Britain* (Göteborg, Sweden: Göteborgs Universitets Arsskrift, 1957), 28–29.

51. Ellegard, *Readership of the Periodical Press,* 24–28.

52. T. Huxley to Hooker, Apr. 20, 1858, THP.

53. T. Huxley to Hooker, Aug. 6, 1860, JDHP.

54. C. Darwin to Hooker, June 5, 1860, JDHP.

55. C. Darwin to Hooker, July 2, 1860, JDHP.

56. C. Darwin to Hooker, Mar. 23, 1861(?), JDHP.

57. C. Darwin to Hooker, undated letter, 1860(?), JDHP.

58. C. Darwin to T. Huxley, Feb. 17, 1862, THP; C. Darwin to T. Huxley, Sept. 10, 1860, THP. The publication was *Magazine of Natural History.*

59. C. Darwin to Hooker, Feb. 20, 1861, JDHP.

60. C. Darwin to Hooker, May 30, 1860, JDHP.

61. Hooker to C. Darwin, Nov. 7, 1862, CDP.

62. Hooker to C. Darwin, Nov. 11, 1859, CDP.

63. C. Darwin to Hooker, Jan. 25, 1862, JDHP.

64. Hooker to C. Darwin, Sept. 4, 1866, CDP.

65. Hooker to C. Darwin, July 1, 1865, CDP.

66. Ellegard, *Readership of the Periodical Press,* 24.

67. T. Huxley to C. Darwin, Oct. 9, 1862, CDP.

68. See Ernst Haeckel to C. Darwin, July 12, 1864, CDP; C. Darwin to Hooker, Nov. 26, 1864, CDP.

69. C. Darwin to T. Huxley, May 27, 1865, THP.

70. C. Darwin to T. Huxley, Nov. 5, 1864, THP.

71. Hooker to C. Darwin, July 1, 1865, CDP.

72. T. Huxley to Hooker, Apr. 24, 1863, JDHP.

73. C. Darwin to Hooker, Mar. 13, 1863, JDHP; C. Darwin to Hooker, Apr. 23, 1863, JDHP.

74. C. Darwin to Hooker, Mar. 17, 1863, JDHP.

75. C. Darwin to Hooker, Apr. 17, 1863, JDHP.

76. C. Darwin to Hooker, Dec. 28, 1866, JDHP.

77. C. Darwin to Hooker, May 11, 1863, JDHP.

78. Alvar Ellegard, *Darwin and the General Reader* (1958; reprint, Chicago: Univ. of Chicago Press, 1990), chap. 15.

79. Ruse, *Darwinian Revolution*, 272; Desmond and Moore, *Darwin: The Life*, 508.

80. Desmond, *Huxley*, 252–53, 361.

81. Hooker to T. Huxley, Nov. 16, 1872, JDHP. See also Hooker to T. Huxley, Nov. 11, 1872, JDHP; Hooker to T. Huxley, Nov. 15, 1872, JDHP.

82. Hooker to T. Huxley, Dec. 2, 1869, JDHP.

83. Hooker to C. Darwin, Feb. 26, 1869, CDP.

84. Hooker to C. Darwin, July 25, 1868, CDP; C. Darwin to Hooker, July 28, 1868, CDP.

85. Lucy Brown, *Victorian News*, 45, 109–10; Ellegard, *Readership of the Periodical Press*, 18–19, 22–24, 27–28; Alvin Sullivan, ed., *British Literary Magazines: The Victorian and Edwardian Age, 1837–1913* (Westport, Conn.: Greenwood Press, 1983), 185–89; Alvin Sullivan, ed., *British Literary Magazines: The Romantic Age, 1789–1836* (Westport, Conn.: Greenwood Press, 1983), 21–24. The *Athenaeum* endorsed Darwin's theories up to 1871, when a change in editors led to a change in editorial policy toward Darwinism.

86. C. Darwin to Hooker, Sept. 8, 1868, CDP; see P. G. Tait, "Geological Time," *North British Quarterly* 50 (1869): 406–39; C. Darwin to Hooker, July 24, 1869, CDP.

87. C. Darwin to Hooker, Aug. 23, 1868, CDP.

88. C. Darwin to Hooker, Feb. 23, 1868, CDP.

89. T. Huxley to John Tyndall, Nov. 12, 1867, THP.

90. T. Huxley to Rev. Francis Morris, Sept. 30, 1869, THP; Morris to T. Huxley, Sept. 16 and Oct. 8, 1869, THP.

91. Hooker to C. Darwin, Aug. 30, 1868, CDP.

92. Desmond and Moore, *Darwin: The Life*, 472–78.

93. Hooker to C. Darwin, Sept. 5, 1868, CDP.

94. Hooker to C. Darwin, Aug. 30, 1868, CDP.

95. Cyril Bibby, *T. H. Huxley: Scientist, Humanist, Educator* (London: Watts, 1959), 20, 95–96.

96. C. Darwin to Hooker, July 14, Feb. 10, and Sept. 1, 1868, CDP.

97. On Mendel and heredity, see Peter J. Bowler, *The Mendelian Revolution* (Baltimore, Md.: Johns Hopkins Univ. Press, 1989).

98. Daniel J. Kevles, *In the Name of Eugenics: Genetics and the Uses of Human Heredity* (Berkeley: Univ. of California Press, 1985), 41–42.

Chapter 2. Huxley and Wilberforce

1. Stephen J. Gould, "Knight Takes Bishop? The Facts about the Great Wilberforce-Huxley Debate Don't Always Fit the Legend," *Natural History* 95 (May 1986): 31–32.

2. Desmond, *Huxley*, 278.

3. Standish Meacham, *Lord Bishop: The Life of Samuel Wilberforce, 1805–1873* (Cambridge, Mass.: Harvard Univ. Press, 1970), 12, 26, 36, 209, 212, 309–12.

4. Richard Wrangham, "Bishop Wilberforce: Natural Selection and the Descent of Man," *Nature* 287 (Sept. 18, 1980): 192.

5. Wilberforce to Huxley, Jan. 30, 1871, THP. Their work together is discussed in Desmond, *Huxley*, 302.

6. The number of sources available for this episode is very lengthy. I had to stop somewhere, so I included sources that have been cited with some consistency by others. The histories reviewed for this study are: Bibby, *T. H. Huxley*; Peter J. Bowler, *The Non-Darwinian Revolution: Reinterpreting a Historical Myth* (Baltimore, Md.: Johns Hopkins Univ. Press, 1988); Bowler, *Evolution*; J. W. Burrow, "Introduction," in Charles Darwin, *On the Origin of Species* (1859; reprint, New York: Penguin Books, 1982); Ronald W. Clark, *The Huxleys* (New York: McGraw-Hill, 1968); Ronald W. Clark, *The Survival of Charles Darwin* (New York: Random House, 1984); I. B. Cohen, "Three Notes on the Reception of Darwin's Ideas on Natural Selection: (Henry Baker Tristam, Alfred Newton, Samuel Wilberforce,)" in *Darwinian Heritage,* ed. David Kohn (Princeton, N.J.: Princeton Univ. Press, 1985), 589–607; F. Darwin, *Life and Letters of Charles Darwin*; Gavin de Beer, *Charles Darwin: Evolution by Natural Selection* (Garden City, N.Y.: Doubleday, 1964); A. Hunter Dupree, *Asa Gray* (Cambridge, Mass.: Belknap Press of Harvard Univ. Press, 1959); Leonard Huxley, *Life and Letters of Thomas Huxley*; Loren Eiseley, *Darwin's Century* (Garden City, N.Y.: Anchor Books ed., Doubleday, 1961); Ellegard, *Darwin and the General Reader*; Stephen J. Gould, *Ever Since Darwin: Reflections in Natural History* (New York: Norton, 1977); Himmelfarb, *Darwin and the Darwinian Revolution*; Hofstadter, *Social Darwinism*; Irvine, *Apes, Angels*; Meacham, *Lord Bishop*; D. R. Oldroyd, *Darwinian Impacts* (Atlantic Highlands, N.J.: Humanities Press, 1983); Ruse, *Darwinian Revolution*; Turrill, *Joseph Dalton Hooker*.

7. *Jackson's Oxford Journal,* July 7, 1860, p. 4.

8. J. Vernon Jensen, "Return to the Huxley-Wilberforce Debate," *British Journal for the History of Science* 21, pt. 2, no. 69 (June 1988): 164.

9. Leonard Huxley, *Life and Letters of Thomas Huxley,* 1:196–97.

10. Ibid., 1:202.

11. Jensen, "Return to the Huxley-Wilberforce Debate," 169–70.

12. Leonard Huxley, *Life and Letters of Thomas Huxley,* 1:204.

13. Even the revisionists agree on the general outline of events. The revisionists to whom I allude are Jensen; Gould; and Joseph L. Altholz, "The Huxley-Wilberforce Debate Revisited," *Journal of the History of Medicine and the Allied Sciences* 35 (1980): 313–16. J. R. Lucas, "Wilberforce and Huxley: A Legendary Encounter," *Historical Journal* 22, no. 2 (1979): 313–30, is not as revisionist as the others cited in this note. However, he does offer an alternative interpretation that varies somewhat from the traditional histories. Lucas believes that Hooker was the real winner, and he notes the problem of confirming contemporary accounts that depict an event involving important words or effects. Lucas also points out that the debate was unimportant in itself, as it was simply one of several skirmishes; rather, it suggests more about the currents of thought in the late 19th century, when science increasingly was perceived as a specialty, and it no longer was deemed permissible for a bishop to venture into scientific questions about which he had no real knowledge.

14. Altholz, "Huxley-Wilberforce Debate Revisited"; Jensen, "Return to the Huxley-Wilberforce Debate"; Lucas, "Wilberforce and Huxley: A Legendary Encounter."

15. Of the works cited in chapter 2, note 6, above, only six said that the facts of the debate might be at issue.

16. T. Huxley to F. Dyster, Sept. 9, 1860, THP. The letter is reprinted in Cyril Bibby, *The Essence of T. H. Huxley* (New York: St. Martin's Press, 1969), 12.

17. A letter written by Wilberforce three days after the event is cited in Altholz, "Huxley-Wilberforce Debate Revisited," 315. In the letter, Wilberforce says, "I think I thoroughly beat him [Huxley]." See also Reginald Wilberforce, *Life of the Right Rev. Samuel Wilberforce, D.D.* (London: Murray, 1881), 2:450.

18. C. Darwin to Hooker, July 20, 1860, JDHP.

19. Leslie Stephens, ed., *Letters of John Richard Green* (London, Macmillan, 1901).

20. Hooker to C. Darwin, July 2, 1860, CDP; C. Darwin to T. Huxley, July 3, 1860, THP. The Hooker letter is reprinted in Leonard Huxley, *Life and Letters of Sir Joseph Dalton Hooker* (1918; reprint, New York: Arno Press, 1978), 525–27. Leonard Huxley attempted to lessen the confusion with a footnote on 524–25, in which he tried to sort out what words his father actually said in his retort to Wilberforce. But the younger Huxley admits to being left with only an "impression."

21. W. Tuckwell, *Reminiscences of Oxford* (London: Smith, Elder, 1907), 53–57.

22. [Isabella Sidgwick?], "A Grandmother's Tales," *Macmillan's Magazine* 78, no. 468 (Oct. 1898), 433–44. The author was not identified in the magazine, but, according to Lucas, "Wilberforce and Huxley," n. 3, p. 313, it was written by Isabella Sidgwick.

23. "Science: British Association," *Athenaeum,* July 7, 1860, 18–19; "Section D—Zoology and Botany, Including Physiology," July 14, 1860, 64–65.

24. Ellegard, *Darwin and the General Reader,* 370; Sullivan, *British Literary Magazines: 1789–1836,* 21–24.

25. Janet Browne, "The Charles Darwin–Joseph Hooker Correspondence: An Analysis of Manuscript Resources and Their Use in Biography," *Journal of the Society for the Bibliography of Natural History* 8, no. 4 (1978): 351–66.

26. Lucy Brown, *Victorian News,* 100–111.

27. Jensen, "Return to the Huxley-Wilberforce Debate," 170–71, citing *Jackson's Oxford Journal.* The *Journal* does allude to the lack of accommodations for the press, although there is no direct reference to poor relations.

28. Ellegard, *Darwin and the General Reader,* 65–69; on the lack of accommodations, he cites the *London Daily News,* June 30, 1860, 3.

29. Gould, "Knight Takes Bishop?" 31–32.

30. Leonard Huxley, *Life and Letters of Thomas Huxley,* 1:193.

31. C. Darwin to T. Huxley, July 3, 1860, THP.

32. T. Huxley to Dyster, Sept. 9, 1860, THP.

33. T. Huxley to Hooker, Aug. 6, 1860, THP.

34. C. Darwin to T. Huxley, July 3, 1860, THP.

35. C. Darwin to T. Huxley, July 5, 1860, THP.

36. C. Darwin to T. Huxley, July 20, 1860, THP.

37. George J. Allman to T. Huxley, July 9, 1860, THP.

38. C. Darwin to Hooker, Jan. 21, 1866, JDHP.

39. George Rolleston to T. Huxley, Dec. 1860, CDP.

40. Hooker to C. Darwin, July 2, 1860, CDP.

41. Francis Darwin to Leonard Huxley, Dec. 3, 1890, THP. Leonard Huxley used the Freemantle account in his *Life and Letters of Thomas Huxley,* 1:201.

42. F. Darwin to T. Huxley, 1886, THP.

43. G. Johnstone Storey to F. Darwin, May 18, 1895, CDP.

44. Hooker to F. Darwin, Jan. 3, 1897, JDHP.

45. F. Darwin to Hooker, Jan. 7, 1897, JDHP.

46. Hooker to F. Darwin, Jan. 1897, JDHP.

47. F. Darwin to Hooker, June 1899, JDHP.

48. A. G. V. Harcourt to Leonard Huxley, July 9, 1899, THP.

49. Adam S. Farrar to Leonard Huxley, July 12, 1899, THP.

50. J. Mark Baldwin, "Psychology" (a lecture to Philosophical Club of Bryn Mawr College), *American Naturalist* 31 (June 1897): 553.

51. "Science: British Association," *Athenaeum,* July 7, 1860, 19.

52. Ellegard, *Readership of the Periodical Press,* 22; Sullivan, *British Literary Magazines: 1789–1837,* 21–24.

53. "Section D—Zoology and Botany, Including Physiology," *Athenaeum,* July 14, 1860, 65.

54. "University Intelligence," *Times of London,* July 5, 1860, 10.

55. *Times of London,* Nov. 29, 1887, 10.

56. *Times of London,* Dec. 1, 1887, 8.

57. Sullivan, *British Literary Magazines: 1837–1913,* 215–19.

58. *Macmillan's Magazine* 78 (Oct. 1898): 433–34.

59. *Macmillan's Magazine* 3 (Dec. 1860): 83.

60. Ibid., 88.

61. *Chamber's Journal,* pt. 2, no. 343 (July 28, 1860): 54.

62. *Manchester Guardian,* July 3, 1860, pp. 2–3.

63. Lucy Brown, *Victorian News,* 32, 44, 53, 69; Ellegard, *Readership of the Periodical Press,* 17.

64. *Manchester Guardian,* July 5, 1860, 4.

65. *John Bull,* July 7, 1860, 422.

66. *The Press* (London), July 7, 1860, 656.

67. *Manchester Guardian,* July 11, 1860, 612–13.

68. *Manchester Guardian,* July 4, 1860, 593.

69. *Jackson's Oxford Journal,* July 7, 1860, 2.

70. *Evening Star* (London), July 2, 1860, 3.

71. It should be noted that Leonard Huxley also wrote and edited *The Life and Letters of Joseph Dalton Hooker,* which treats the debate, 1:520–27, exactly as one would expect: Hooker and Huxley won.

Chapter 3. Darwin's Recantation of Evolution

1. *Boston Watchman-Examiner,* Aug. 19, 1915. See also *Bombay Guardian,* Mar. 25, 1916.

2. *Boston Watchman-Examiner,* Aug. 19, 1915.

3. Desmond and Moore, *Darwin: The Life,* 6.

4. Charles J. Deduchson to T. Huxley, Jan. 24, 1887; F. Darwin to T. Huxley, Feb. 8, 1887; T. Huxley to Deduchson, Feb. 12, 1887, THP.

5. Ian Taylor, *In the Minds of Men: Darwin and the New World Order* (Toronto, Canada: TFE Publishing, 1984), 136–37. On Charles and Emma Darwin and the subject of religion, see also Desmond and Moore, *Darwin: The Life,* 270, 280–81, 361–62, 507, 623. Still, no evidence exists for Emma as the source of the story, and she remained devoted to Charles despite his religious views, or lack of them.

6. Harry Levin, "Some Meanings of Myth," in *Myth and Mythmakers,* ed. Henry A. Murray (New York: George Braziller, 1960), 114.

7. Ronald L. Numbers, *The Creationists* (New York: Alfred A. Knopf, 1992), x–xi.

8. Several works among those McIver cites, in addition to the ones discussed in chapter 3, are: (1) "Collapse of Evolution," by Luther T. Townsend (Reading, Penn.: Frank Boyer, 1922). The pamphlet is available in Special Collections, Library, Univ. of Tennessee, Knoxville. This pamphlet reprinted the story and cited the *Boston Watchman-Examiner.* (2) Randall Hedtke, *The Secret of the Sixth Edition* (New York: Vantage Press, 1983). Hedtke quotes selectively from the Lady Hope story, which he accepts, and cites a pamphlet, "Darwin and Christianity: Evolution Protest Movement," published by A. E. Norris and Sons, Ltd. (3) H. Enoch, *Evolution or Creation* (London: Evangelical Press, 1967, reprinted 1968 and 1972). Enoch reprints the Lady Hope story from the *Bombay Guardian* in his 1967 edition, but omits it in the 1972 edition. (4) Bolton Davidheiser, *Evolution and Christian Faith* (Grand Rapids, Mich.: Baker Book House, 1969). Davidheiser cautions that the Lady Hope story probably is not true. (5) Layman's Home Missionary Movement, "The Evolutionary Theory Examined" (Chester Springs, Pa.: Layman's Home Missionary Movement, n.d.). This pamphlet quotes and accepts the Lady Hope story. (6) John McAlister, *The Scientific Proofs of Origins by Creation* (Midland, Texas: Privately published, n.d.). This booklet is distributed by the "Servants for the Coming New Order," which McIver says may be composed only of McAlister, who quotes and accepts the Lady Hope story.

9. M. Bowden, *The Rise of Evolution Fraud (An Exposure of Its Roots)* (San Diego, Calif.: Creation-Life Publishers, 1982).

10. Alexander Hardie, *Evolution: Is It Philosophical, Scientific, or Scriptural?* (Los Angeles, Calif.: Times-Mirror Press, 1924).

11. John Raymond Hand, *Why I Accept the Genesis Record: Am I Rational?* (Wheaton, Ill.: Van Kampen Press, 1953).

12. James Moore, *The Darwin Legend* (Grand Rapids, Mich.: Baker Books, 1994). Moore provides an exhaustive bibliography on the subject of Lady Hope and the Darwin recantation tale. For the background for Lady Hope, see 24, 84–90. Her obituary appears in the *Times of London,* Mar. 14, 1922, p. 15b.

13. Sir Hedley Atkins, *Down: The House of the Darwins* (London: Royal College of Surgeons of En-

gland, 1976), 52. My own journey to Down provided no satisfactory physical evidence. The alleged summer house at the end of the sandwalk no longer existed, although the curator of the property was fairly sure it once was there. Access to the upstairs bedrooms was unavailable, so I could not investigate whether Darwin could have pointed in the proper direction from his bedroom window, assuming the placement of the summer house. Indeed, it was not even known which bedroom belonged to Charles Darwin. So, as in much of history, the evidence was inconclusive.

14. James F. Findlay, *Dwight L. Moody: American Evangelist, 1837–1899* (Chicago: Univ. of Chicago Press, 1969), 192–93, 400, 409–10; Richard K. Curtis, *They Called Him Mr. Moody* (Grand Rapids, Mich.: Eerdmans Publishing Co., 1967), 1, 20, 235.

15. *Boston Watchman-Examiner,* Aug. 19, 1915.

16. Pat Sloan, "Demythologizing Darwin," *Humanist* (London) 80 (Apr. 1965): 106–10.

17. Pat Sloan, "The Myth of Darwin's Conversion," *Humanist* (London) 75 (Mar. 1960): 70–72.

18. *A Supplement to Allibone's Dictionary of English Literature and British and American Authors* (Philadelphia: Lippincott, 1891), 2:847.

19. Elizabeth R. Hope [Elizabeth R. Cotton], *Our Coffee-Room* (London: James Nisbet Co., 1876).

20. *New York Times,* Jan. 21, 1923, 14.

21. For a fuller discussion, see J. Durant, *Darwinism and Divinity: Essays on Evolution and Religious Belief* (Norwich, England: Page Bros., 1985); Ruse, *Darwinian Revolution;* Oldroyd, *Darwinian Impacts;* Bowler, *Non-Darwinian Revolution;* D. C. Lindbergh and Ronald L. Numbers, eds., *God and Nature: Historical Essays on the Encounter Between Christianity and Science* (Los Angeles: Univ. of California Press, 1986).

22. Irvine, *Apes, Angels,* 277–78.

23. Atkins, *Down: The House,* recounts Henrietta's denial, 51–52.

24. F. Darwin, *Autobiography,* 61.

25. Ibid., 62–66.

26. Desmond and Moore, *Darwin: The Life,* 636.

27. F. Darwin, *Autobiography,* 66.

28. Moore, *Darwin Legend,* 60–65.

29. Ibid., 63–65.

30. F. Burch Brown, *The Evolution of Darwin's Religious Views* (Macon, Ga.: Mercer Univ. Press, 1986), 27.

31. Ibid., 45–46.

32. F. Darwin, *Autobiography,* 45.

33. C. Darwin to F. E. Abbott, Cambridge, Mass., Sept. 6, 1871, in F. Darwin, *Autobiography,* 59–60.

34. Arnold J. Toynbee, *A Study of History,* abridgment of vols. 1–6 (New York: Oxford Univ. Press, 1946), 44.

35. Bowler, *Non-Darwinian Revolution,* 185.

36. Philip Rieff, "A Modern Mythmaker," in Henry A. Murray, *Myth and Mythmaking,* 252.

37. Mark Schorer, "The Necessity of Myth," in Henry A. Murray, *Myth and Mythmaking,* 355.

38. *The Oxford Annotated Bible with the Apocrypha* (New York: Oxford Univ. Press, 1965), 1453.

39. Durant, *Darwinism and Divinity,* 27–28.

40. Lindberg and Numbers, *God and Nature,* 394; Durant, *Darwinism and Divinity,* 23; Sydney E. Ahlstrom, *A Religious History of the American People* (New Haven, Conn.: Yale Univ. Press, 1972), 910.

41. Ahlstrom, *Religious History,* 815–16, 910.

42. Lindberg and Numbers, *God and Nature,* 393.

43. Ibid., 407–10. See also Edward Caudill, "The Roots of Bias: An Empiricist Press and Coverage of the Scopes Trial," *Journalism Monographs,* no. 114 (Columbia, S.C.: Association for Education in Journalism and Mass Communication, July 1989).

44. Max Lerner, *America as a Civilization* (New York: Henry Holt, 1987), 803.

45. Edward Caudill, *Darwinism in the Press: The Evolution of an Idea* (Hillsdale, N.J.: Erlbaum, 1989). Chapter 7 discusses the creationist controversy.

46. Henry Nash Smith, *Virgin Land: The American West as Symbol and Myth* (Cambridge, Mass.: Harvard Univ. Press, 1950); Wilbur F. Cash, *The Mind of the South* (New York: Knopf, 1941).

Chapter 4. Social Darwinism

1. Books on American history and ideas in American history often refer to the social Darwinism of the late 19th century. The best volume on the subject is Robert Bannister, *Social Darwinism: Science and Myth in Anglo-American Social Thought* (Philadelphia: Temple Univ. Press, 1979). The "traditional" concept of a dog-eat-dog social movement is exemplified in a number of volumes, of which these are a sampling: Hofstadter, *Social Darwinism;* Donald Fleming, "Social Darwinism," in *Paths of American Thought,* ed. Arthur M. Schlesinger, Jr., and Morton White (Boston: Houghton Mifflin Co., 1973), 123–46; Merle Curti, *The Growth of American Thought* (New York: Harper & Brothers, 1943); Henry Steele Commager, *The American Mind* (New Haven, Conn.: Yale Univ. Press, 1952); and Tindall, *America: A Narrative History.* The revisionists, who either downplay the impact of the movement or modify its viciousness, include: C. E. Russett, *Darwinism in America: The Intellectual Response, 1865–1912* (San Francisco: W. H. Freeman, 1976); I. G. Wyllie, "Social Darwinism and the Businessman," *Proceedings of the American Philosophical Society* 103 (Oct. 1959): 629–35; Bowler, "Social Darwinism," chap. 7 of *Non-Darwinian Revolution;* and Bannister, *Social Darwinism.*

2. Bannister and Bowler, *Non-Darwinian Revolution,* give excellent overviews of the variety of meanings attached to the idea. See also Gertrude Himmelfarb, "Varieties of Social Darwinism," chap. 12 of her *Victorian Minds* (New York: Alfred A. Knopf, 1968).

3. Charles Darwin, *Descent of Man and Selection in Relation to Sex,* 2d ed. (London: John Murray, 1874), 160–61.

4. Ibid., 151; 207–8.

5. C. Darwin to Hooker, Apr. 9, 1866, JDHP.

6. C. Darwin to Hooker, Oct. 2, 1866, JDHP.

7. C. Darwin to Hooker, Nov. 3, 1864, JDHP.

8. Himmelfarb, *Victorian Minds,* 316–17.

9. For a discussion of the problem of studying the press and public opinion, see Alvar Ellegard, "Pub-

lic Opinion and the Press: Reactions to Darwinism," *Journal of the History of Ideas* 19 (June 1959): 379–87. A number of very good studies of the two men exist, including: James G. Kennedy, *Herbert Spencer* (Boston: Twayne Publishers, 1978); Hugh Elliot, *Herbert Spencer* (1917; reprint, Westport, Conn.: Greenwood, 1970); Jay Rumney, *Herbert Spencer's Sociology* (New York: Atherton Press, 1966); Bruce Curtis, *William Graham Sumner* (Boston: Twayne Publishers, 1981); Maurice R. Davie, *William Graham Sumner* (New York: Crowell, 1963); see also the works cited in chap. 4, n. 1, above, for sections dealing with Sumner and Spencer.

10. Hofstadter, *Social Darwinism,* often cites *Popular Science Monthly, Atlantic Monthly, North American Review, Scribner's, Nation, Forum,* and other popular journals.

11. "Sketch of Herbert Spencer," *Popular Science Monthly* 8 (Mar. 1876): 625.

12. E. L. Youmans, "Herbert Spencer and the Doctrine of Evolution," *Popular Science Monthly* 6 (Nov. 1874): 20–48; reprint of a lecture.

13. "Herbert Spencer at Seventy-nine," *Popular Science Monthly* 55 (Aug. 1889): 543.

14. A especially good overview of the Nazis and race science is George J. Stein, "Biological Science and the Roots of Nazism," *American Scientist* 76 (Jan.–Feb. 1988): 50–58. See also Joseph Tenenbaum, *Race and Reich: The Story of an Epoch* (New York: Twayne Publishers, 1956).

15. Jacques Barzun, *Darwin, Marx, Wagner: Critique of a Heritage* (Boston: Little, Brown, 1941), 98.

16. Curti, *Growth of American Thought,* 576–77; others are cited in chap. 4, n. 1, above.

17. Antonello LaVergata, "Images of Darwin: An Historiographic Overview," in *Darwinian Heritage,* ed. Kohn, 958.

18. Bannister, *Social Darwinism,* 8. Part 1 of the introduction briefly explores the contours of the idea.

19. Irvine, *Apes, Angels,* 34.

20. Hofstadter, *Social Darwinism,* 33. On the history of sociology, see Jerzy Szacki, *History of Sociological Thought* (Westport, Conn.: Greenwood Press, 1979); and L. L. Bernard and J. Bernard, *Origins of American Sociology: The Social Science Movement in the United States* (New York: Russell and Russell, 1965).

21. Davie, *William Graham Sumner,* vii–ix, 3–4.

22. Bannister, in chapter 5 of *Social Darwinism,* reevaluates Sumner's intellectual debt to Spencer, concluding that Sumner was not a Spencerian in any important sense. He makes a very good case, but I cannot fully accept it because the public writings link the two in American social Darwinism.

23. Davie, *William Graham Sumner,* 7.

24. James Allen Rogers, "Darwinism and Social Darwinism," *Journal of the History of Ideas* 33, no. 2 (Apr.–June 1972): 266.

25. Oldroyd, *Darwinian Impacts,* 67–68.

26. See Gavin de Beer, *Charles Darwin: A Scientific Biography* (Garden City, N.Y.: Anchor Books, 1965), 14–15. Caudill, *Darwinism in the Press,* 11, points out that, for Darwin, Malthus perhaps was more inspirational than informational.

27. For a discussion of this idea, see Ruse, *Darwinian Revolution,* 12–14.

28. Oldroyd, *Darwinian Impacts,* 43–44.

29. Herbert Spencer, "The Study of Sociology," *Popular Science Monthly* 1 (May 1872): 1–17.

30. "Editor's Table," *Popular Science Monthly* 1 (Oct. 1872): 754–55.

31. See "Editor's Table" throughout the first six volumes of *Popular Science Monthly*, May 1872–Apr. 1875.

32. "Editor's Table," *Popular Science Monthly* 39 (Oct. 1891): 843.

33. "Editor's Table," *Popular Science Monthly* 4 (Dec. 1873): 242–44.

34. Charles M. Haar, "E. L. Youmans: A Chapter in the Diffusion of Science in America," *Journal of the History of Ideas* 9, no. 2 (Apr. 1948): 193–213.

35. "Editor's Table," *Popular Science Monthly* 1 (May 1872): 113.

36. Harr, "E. L. Youmans," n. 25, p. 200.

37. John Fiske, *Edward Livingston Youmans* (New York: D. Appleton and Co., 1894), 199–200, quoted in Hofstadter, *Social Darwinism,* 33.

38. See *Popular Science Monthly,* vols. 4, 5, 17, 18, 21, 26, for exchanges between Spencer and his critics.

39. Haar, "E. L. Youmans," n. 57, p. 211. While Spencer was in the U.S., Youmans was the only journalist to interview him, and Spencer did a bit of press bashing for inaccuracies about "important truths."

40. "Editor's Table," *Popular Science Monthly* 1 (May 1872): 113–15.

41. "Editor's Table," *Popular Science Monthly* 30 (Mar. 1887): 698–99. His obituary is "Sketch of Edward L. Youmans," *Popular Science Monthly* 30 (Mar. 1887): 689–97.

42. Frank Luther Mott, *A History of American Magazines,* vol. 3: *1865–1885* (Cambridge, Mass.: Harvard Univ. Press, 1938), 498.

43. Frank Luther Mott, *A History of American Magazines,* vol. 4: *1885–1905* (Cambridge, Mass.: Harvard Univ. Press, 1957), 306.

44. John Fiske, "Edward Livingston Youmans: The Man and His Work," *Popular Science Monthly* 37 (May 1890): 4.

45. Alan Nourie and Barbara Nourie, *American Mass-Market Magazines* (Westport, Conn.: Greenwood Press, 1990), 149–52; Frank Luther Mott, *A History of American Magazines,* vol. 2: *1850–1865* (Cambridge, Mass.: Harvard Univ. Press, 1938), 383–405. In addition to fiction and science, *Harper's* published travel (exploration being a favorite), news, and humor. This phenomenally successful magazine started in 1850 with an edition of 7,500 and was up to 200,000 by the beginning of the Civil War.

46. Alan Nourie and Barbara Nourie, *American Mass-Market,* 458–59.

47. Sullivan, *British Literary Magazines: 1837–1913,* 185–90.

48. Ibid., 275–80.

49. For a discussion of the ideas presented to the public about Darwinism, see Caudill, *Darwinism in the Press.*

50. See, e.g., E. L. Youmans, "Herbert Spencer and the Doctrine of Evolution," *Popular Science Monthly* 6 (Nov. 1874): 20–48; Grant Allen, "Spencer and Darwin," *Popular Science Monthly* 50 (Apr. 1897): 815–27; William H. Hudson, "Herbert Spencer and the Synthetic Philosophy," *Popular Science Monthly* 41 (May 1892): 5–16; "Editor's Table," *Popular Science Monthly* 27 (June 1885): 271; Herbert Spencer, "The Study of Sociology," pt. 14, *Popular Science Monthly* 3 (Sept. 1873): n. 8, p. 608; "Editor's Table," *Popular Science Monthly* 8 (Dec. 1875): 239; Herbert Spencer, "The Factors of Organic Evolution," pt. 1, *Popular Science Monthly* 28 (Apr. 1886): 754–59.

51. Herbert Spencer, "The Inadequacy of Natural Selection," *Popular Science Monthly* 42 (Apr. 1893): 799–812.

52. Herbert Spencer, "The Limits of State Duties," *Popular Science Monthly* 39 (Oct. 1891): 639–45.

53. There are numerous references to Spencer as a philosopher. See, e.g., E. L. Youmans, "Herbert Spencer and the Doctrine of Evolution," 20–48.

54. Herbert Spencer, "Predatory and Industrial Society," *Popular Science Monthly* 9 (Oct. 1876): 726, 732.

55. Herbert Spencer, "Private Relief of the Poor," *Popular Science Monthly* 43 (July 1893): 315–16.

56. Herbert Spencer, "The Study of Sociology," pt. 10, *Popular Science Monthly* 3 (May 1873): 46, 57.

57. Herbert Spencer, "A Rejoinder to M. De Laveleye," *Popular Science Monthly* 27 (June 1885): 193.

58. "Editor's Table," *Popular Science Monthly* 53 (June 1898): 269.

59. *New York Times,* Nov. 11, 1882, p. 5.

60. See the bibliography in Albert G. Keller and Maurice R. Davie, eds., *Essays of William Graham Sumner,* vol. 2 (New Haven, Conn.: Yale Univ. Press, 1934).

61. Alan Nourie and Barbara Nourie, *American Mass-Market,* 53–54; Mott, *History of American Magazines,* 4:453–57.

62. Mott, *History of American Magazines,* 4:480–84.

63. "Sketch of William Graham Sumner," *Popular Science Monthly* 35 (June 1889): 261–68.

64. Davie, *William Graham Sumner,* vii, 6–8, 23, 99; Bannister, *Social Darwinism,* 100. From a different perspective, Bannister argued that Sumner was not a Spencerian in any important way, except in recognition of the significance of the individual and advocacy of laissez-faire. Sumner's *Folkways,* Bannister said, reflected the fact that its author gradually came to accept the idea of solidarity and social control. Bannister is disdainful of "culling scattered references to the survival of the fittest" in assessing Sumner, but in fact the references are consistent in Sumner's life, and much of Sumner's writing was rather disorganized and scattered. Of course, Darwin himself also pointed out that "survival of the fittest" often entailed cooperation, as between insects and plants, and not just antagonism. Sumner's conception of laissez-faire was quite Darwinian, because eventually he recognized the utility of both individual vitality and social cooperation in the propagation of the species.

65. William Graham Sumner, *What Social Classes Owe Each Other* (1883; reprint, Caldwell, Idaho: Caxton Printer, 1966), 88.

66. William Graham Sumner, "Memorial Day Address" (1872), in William Graham Sumner, *The Challenge of Facts and Other Essays,* ed. Albert G. Keller (New Haven, Conn.: Yale Univ. Press, 1914), 353.

67. William Graham Sumner, "Some Points in the New Social Creed," in William Graham Sumner, *Earth-Hunger and Other Essays,* ed. Albert G. Keller (New Haven, Conn.: Yale Univ. Press, 1913), 208; orig. published in *The Independent,* Apr. 21, 1887.

68. Ibid., 216.

69. William Graham Sumner, "Federal Legislation on Railroads," in Sumner, *Challenge of Facts,* 182; orig. published in *The Independent,* Jan. 20, 1887.

70. See, e.g., William Graham Sumner, "Democracy and Plutocracy," in Sumner, *Earth-Hunger,* 283; orig. published in *The Independent,* June 15, 1888.

71. William Graham Sumner, "Earth-Hunger, or the Philosophy of Land Grabbing," in Sumner, *Earth-Hunger,* 45; article written in 1896, according to the bibliography in Keller and Davie, *Essays of William Graham Sumner,* vol. 2.

72. William Graham Sumner, "The Significance of the Demand for Men," in Sumner, *Challenge of Facts,* 119; orig. published in *The Independent,* Oct. 16, 1890.

73. See also these essays: William Graham Sumner, "Some Natural Rights," in *Earth-Hunger,* 222–27; orig. published in *The Independent,* July 28, 1887. William Graham Sumner, "Democracy and Responsible Government," in Sumner, *Challenge of Facts,* 243–67. William Graham Sumner, "The Challenge of Facts," in Sumner, *Challenge of Facts,* 15–52; the piece was written sometime in the 1880s, according to the bibliography in Keller and Davie, *Essays of William Graham Sumner,* vol. 2.

74. Sumner, "Some Natural Rights," 226.

75. Sumner, "Earth-Hunger, or the Philosophy of Land Grabbing," 35.

76. Ibid., 45.

77. William Graham Sumner, "What Makes the Rich Richer and the Poor Poorer," in Sumner, *Challenge of Facts,* 67; orig. published in *Popular Science Monthly* 30 (Jan. 1887): 289–96.

78. William Graham Sumner, "The Concentration of Wealth: Its Economic Justification," in Sumner, *Challenge of Facts,* 87, 90.

79. Sumner, "Challenge of Facts," 25.

80. Ibid.

81. Ibid., 37, 52.

82. William Graham Sumner, "Reply to a Socialist," in Sumner, *Challenge of Facts,* 29; orig. published in *Collier's Weekly,* Oct. 29, 1904.

83. William Graham Sumner, "What is Civil Liberty?" in Sumner, *Earth-Hunger,* 127; orig. published in *Popular Science Monthly* 35 (July 1889): 289–313.

84. William Graham Sumner, "Equality," in Sumner *Earth-Hunger,* 88; the piece was written between 1900 and 1906, according to the bibliography in Keller and Davie, *Essays of William Graham Sumner,* vol. 2.

85. William Graham Sumner, "The State and Monopoly," in Sumner, *Earth-Hunger,* 271; orig. published in *The Independent,* Sept. 13 and Oct. 11, 1888.

86. William Graham Sumner, "What Emancipates," in Sumner, *Challenge of Facts,* 137; orig. published in *The Independent,* Aug. 14, 1890.

87. William Graham Sumner, "The Demand for Men," in Sumner, *Challenge of Facts,* 112; orig. published in *The Independent,* Sept. 11, 1890.

88. Hofstadter, *Social Darwinism,* 201–2.

89. Andrew Carnegie, "Wealth," *North American Review* 148 (June 1889): 655–57.

Chapter 5. The Spanish-American War

1. Hofstadter, in *Social Darwinism,* also gave Spencer the substantial credit he is owed as the central thinker of the 19th-century movement.

2. On the press and public opinion, see Charles H. Brown, *The Correspondents' War: Journalists in the Spanish-American War* (New York: Charles H. Scribner's Sons, 1967).

3. Ibid., 172.

4. Richard E. Welch, *Response to Imperialism: The United States and the Philippine-American War, 1899–1902* (Chapel Hill: Univ. of North Carolina Press, 1979), 11–16, 104–6, 115–16.

5. Walter LaFeber, *The New Empire: An Interpretation of American Expansion, 1860–1898* (Ithaca, N.Y.: Cornell Univ. Press, 1963), 98–99.

6. David Healy, *U.S. Expansionism: The Imperialist Urge in the 1890s* (Madison: Univ. of Wisconsin Press, 1970).

7. Gould, *Ever Since Darwin,* 218–19.

8. Bannister, *Social Darwinism,* 226–35.

9. Thomas F. Gossett, *Race: The History of an Idea in America* (New York: Schocken Books, 1965), 311.

10. White, "Prologue: Coherence and Correspondence in American Thought," in Schlesinger and White, *Paths of American Thought,* 5; Donald Fleming, "Social Darwinism," 126–27.

11. Paul F. Boller, Jr., *American Thought in Transition: The Impact of Evolutionary Naturalism, 1865–1900* (Chicago: Rand McNally, 1970), 199–218.

12. Curti, *Growth of American Thought,* 670–73.

13. David F. Trask, *The War with Spain in 1898* (New York: Macmillan, 1981), 475.

14. Marcus M. Wilkerson, *Public Opinion and the Spanish-American War* (New York: Russell and Russell, 1967). See also: Stuart Creighton Miller, *Benevolent Assimilation* (New Haven, Conn.: Yale Univ. Press, 1982); Ernest R. May, *American Imperialism: A Speculative Essay* (New York: Athenaeum, 1968); Richard H. Miller, ed., *American Imperialism in 1898: The Quest for National Fulfillment* (New York: John Wiley & Sons, 1970).

15. Herbert Pelham, "The Outlook in Cuba," *Atlantic Monthly* 83 (May 1899): 826–36.

16. Hofstadter, *Social Darwinism,* 99–101.

17. Benjamin Kidd, "The United States and Control of the Tropics," *Atlantic Monthly* 82 (Dec. 1898): 721–27.

18. Ibid., 725.

19. For more detail on racial attitudes and their relationship to science, see Michael Banton, *Racial Theories* (Cambridge, England: Cambridge Univ. Press, 1987); John S. Haller, Jr., *Outcasts from Evolution: Scientific Attitudes of Racial Inferiority* (Urbana: Univ. of Illinois Press, 1971); and Caudill, *Darwinism in the Press.*

20. Kidd, "United States and Control," 721–27.

21. Ibid., 726.

22. Mott, *History of American Magazines,* 4:511–23.

23. John B. Proctor, "Isolation of Imperialism?" *Forum* 26 (Sept. 1898): 15–26.

24. Ibid., 25–26.

25. Carl Evans Boyd, "Our Government of Newly Acquired Territory," *Atlantic Monthly* 82 (Dec. 1898): 732.

26. Charles Conant, "Can New Openings Be Found for Capital?" *Atlantic Monthly* 84 (Nov. 1899): 600–608.

27. Charles Conant, "The Economic Basis of Imperialism," *North American Review* 167 (Sept. 1898): 327.

28. Charles W. Dilke, John Barrett, and Hugh H. Lusk, "The Problem of the Philippines," *North American Review* 167 (Sept. 1898): 257–77.

29. Hofstadter, *Social Darwinism*, 29–30, 106; Boller, *American Thought in Transition*, 33–35, 47. Abbott was among the guests at a banquet in honor of Herbert Spencer during Spencer's 1882 visit to the U.S.

30. Lyman Abbott, "The Basis of Anglo-American Understanding," *North American Review* 166 (May 1898): 513–21.

31. Ibid.

32. William Cunningham, "Prospects of Universal Peace," *Atlantic Monthly* 84 (Aug. 1899): 236–41.

33. George Burton Adams, "A Century of Anglo-Saxon Expansion," *Atlantic Monthly* 79 (Apr. 1897): 528–38.

34. Lawrence Lowell, "The Colonial Expansion of the United States," *Atlantic Monthly* 83 (Feb. 1899): 145–54.

35. James Bryce, "Some Thoughts on the Policy of the United States," *Harper's* 97 (Sept. 1898): 609–18.

36. Albert Bushnell Hart, "A Century of Cuban Diplomacy," *Harper's* 97 (June 1898): 127–34.

37. Albert Bushnell Hart, "U.S. as World Power," *Harper's* 98 (Mar. 1899): 493–94.

38. Kidd, "United States and Control," 722.

39. W. Alleyne Ireland, "European Experience with Tropical Colonies," *Atlantic Monthly* 82 (Dec. 1898): 729–35.

40. Hart, "Century of Cuban Diplomacy," 127–34.

41. A. V. Dicey, "England and America," *Atlantic Monthly* 82 (Oct. 1898): 441–45. See also Arthur May Knapp, "Japan and the Philippines," *Atlantic Monthly* 83 (June 1899): 737–42.

42. Archibald R. Colquhoun, "Eastward Expansion of the United States," *Harper's* 97 (Nov. 1898): 932–38.

43. See, e.g., Herbert Pelham Williams, "The Outlook in Cuba," *Atlantic Monthly* 83 (May 1899): 827–36.

44. James K. Hosmer, "The American Evolution: Dependence, Independence, Interdependence," *Atlantic Monthly* 82 (July 1898): 29–36.

45. Francis Newton Thorpe, "The Civil Service and Colonization," *Harper's* 98 (May 1899): 858–62.

46. Dilke, Barrett, and Lusk, "Problem of the Philippines," 257–77.

47. See also: James Bryce, "The Essential Unity of Britain and America," *Atlantic Monthly* 82 (July 1898): 22–29; William V. Pettit, "Porto Rico," *Atlantic Monthly* 83 (May 1899): 634–44; J. G. Carlisle, "Our Future Policy," *Harper's* 97 (Oct. 1898): 720–28; James Bryce, "Some Thoughts on the Policy of the United States," 609–18.

48. Darwin outlined his method of studying species as a unit in "Variation Under Domestication" and "Variation Under Nature," chs. 1 and 2 of his *On the Origin of Species*.

49. J. L. M. Curry, "The Negro Question," *Popular Science Monthly* 55 (June 1899): 177–85. The issue of distinguishing among races also was posed as "polygenetics" versus "monogenetics." Adherents of the latter stance believed that races had arisen separately in different places on the earth, while the adherents of the former believed that the different races had arisen from a common

stock. However, monogeneticists were no more sympathetic to non-Caucasians, deeming them inferior as a result of centuries of poor breeding. See Haller, *Outcasts from Evolution.*

50. Colquhoun, "Eastward Expansion," 932–38.

51. Worthington T. Ford, "Trade Policy with the Colonies," *Harper's* 97 (July 1899): 293–303.

52. Henry Cabot Lodge, "The Spanish American War," pt. 1: "The Unsettled Question," *Harper's* 98 (Mar. 1899): 449–64. Lodge was a close adviser to Theodore Roosevelt, served on the Senate Foreign Relations Committee (he helped draft the resolutions that led to war with Spain), and later in his career was a leading figure among those who wanted to keep the U.S. out of the League of Nations.

53. Stephen B. Luce, "The Benefits of War," *North American Review* 153 (Dec. 1891): 672–83.

54. Dumas Malone, ed., *Dictionary of American Biography* (New York: Charles Scribner's Sons, 1933), 11:488–89.

55. Charles Morris, "War as a Factor in Civilization," *Popular Science Monthly* 47 (Oct. 1895): 823–35.

56. John Proctor, "Isolation of Imperialism?" 14–26.

57. On Shaler, see Caudill, *Darwinism in the Press,* 82–86.

58. J. G. Carlisle, "Our Future Policy," *Harper's* 97 (Oct. 1898): 720–29. The quotation is from 724.

59. "The Hell of War," *Popular Science Monthly* 54 (Mar. 1899): 718–19.

60. Herbert Spencer, "Evolutionary Ethics," *Popular Science Monthly* 52 (Feb. 1898): 497–502.

61. Trask, *War with Spain,* 475–76. Another interesting and well executed perspective on anti-imperialism is Donald Pickens, "William Graham Sumner as a Critic of the Spanish American War," *Continuity,* no. 11 (1987): 75–92. Pickens argues that Sumner was not even a social Darwinist, a conclusion that I do not accept, but Pickens points to Sumner's reliance on the Republican legacy as yet another foundation for anti-imperialism.

Chapter 6. Eugenics

The research for this chapter was conducted at the American Philosophical Society (APS), Philadelphia, Pa. The letters and papers cited here are in the genetics archives at the APS. One important group of papers is the Charles B. Davenport Papers (CBDP). The APS genetics collection is detailed in Bentley Glass, *A Guide to the Genetics Collections of the American Philosophical Society* (Philadelphia, Pa.: American Philosophical Society, 1988).

1. "Leon Whitney autobiography" manuscript, 202–3, CBDP.

2. Two very good books on the history of eugenics are: Kevles, *In the Name of Eugenics;* Allan Chase, *The Legacy of Malthus: The Social Costs of the New Scientific Racism* (New York: Knopf, 1977).

3. James Oliver Robertson, *American Myth, American Reality* (New York: Hall and Wang, 1980), 12–13.

4. Leonard Darwin, *The Need for Eugenic Reform* (London: John Murray, 1926).

5. Chase, *Legacy of Malthus,* 289–91.

6. Robertson, *American Myth,* 33.

7. Spencer R. Weart, *Nuclear Fear: A History of Images* (Cambridge, Mass.: Harvard Univ. Press, 1988), 38–40.

8. Bowler, *Mendelian Revolution,* 163–64.

9. Kevles, *In the Name of Eugenics,* ix, 7–9.

10. Darwin realized that his theory lacked an explanation of how traits were passed from one generation to another, but the best he could do was the "pangenesis" hypothesis, which held that "gemmules" existed in body fluids, and that these units which contained the codes for physical characteristics were passed on in reproduction, with the parents' gemmules being blended in the process. Mendel's research had been completed in the mid-1860s but made no impact, perhaps a result of his being outside the network of mainstream science, or perhaps because scientists didn't understand what he was doing and simply were not ready for his research. Mendel was not "discovered" until 1900.

11. Kevles, *In the Name of Eugenics,* 23, 30–33.

12. Ibid., 37–40.

13. Daniel J. Boorstin, *The Americans: The National Experience* (New York: Vintage Books, 1965), 281.

14. Glass, *Guide to the Genetics Collections,* 89.

15. Kevles, *In the Name of Eugenics,* 59–60.

16. Pat Shipman, *The Evolution of Racism: Human Differences and the Use and Abuse of Science* (New York: Simon and Schuster, 1994), 132.

17. "Eugenics Committee of the United States of America," item on "Origin" and "Organization," AESP, Whitney Papers.

18. "History of the American Eugenics Society," in Frederick Osborn Papers, APS.

19. "Eugenics Committee of the United States of America," in AESP, Whitney Papers.

20. Whitney autobiography, 186.

21. "Report and Recommendations, Popular Education Committee, American Eugenics Society, Inc.," Sept. 9, 1930, in AESP.

22. Kevles, *In the Name of Eugenics,* 61.

23. Whitney autobiography, 195.

24. "Fitter Families Examination" form for Kansas Free Fair, Topeka; Charles B. Davenport to Dr. Florence Sherbon, Oct. 6, 1924, CBDP.

25. Kevles, *In the Name of Eugenics,* 62.

26. Ibid.

27. See Chase, *Legacy of Malthus,* chapter 6, for a discussion of the sterilization laws in the U.S.

28. Kevles, *In the Name of Eugenics,* 170.

29. Frederick Osborn, "Eugenics: An Elementary Text," outline for book, in Osborn Papers, APS.

30. "State Legislative Program," American Eugenics Society file, in Whitney Papers.

31. "A Constructive Program for Eugenics Work in Nassau County," in CBDP; Raymond Pearl to President Calvin Coolidge, Oct. 21, 1925, in Pearl Papers, APS.

32. Mary H. Rumsey, "Nassau County Association," Mar. 15, 1913, in CBDP.

33. C. Davenport, "Application of Mendel's Law to Human Heredity," in CBDP.

34. Kevles, *In the Name of Eugenics,* 47; Glass, *Guide to the Genetics Collections,* 13–18.

35. Pearl to Coolidge, Oct. 21, 1925, in Pearl Papers, APS.

36. Pearl to President Herbert Hoover, May 5, 1922, in Pearl Papers, APS.

37. Pearl to George Akerson, secretary to the president, Aug. 14, 1929; and Akerson to Pearl, Aug.

15, 1929; both in Pearl Papers, APS. There was more than mere politics between them. Writing to Pearl's wife in 1940, upon the death of Pearl, Hoover said, "He was one of my most devoted friends over all these years." Hoover to Mrs. Pearl, telegram, Nov. 18, 1940, in Pearl Papers, APS. The White House response to *Cosmopolitan* is from Kevles, *In the Name of Eugenics,* 114.

38. Whitney autobiography, 198.

39. "Second form to student workers," American Eugenics Society file, Whitney Papers.

40. Whitney autobiography, 195.

41. "Eugenics Sermon Contest, 1928," letter from Committee on Cooperation with Clergymen, of the American Eugenics Society, CBDP.

42. "Your body is a temple of the Holy Spirit," in American Eugenics Society File, Whitney Papers.

43. "Whose son art thou, young man?" in American Eugenics Society File, Whitney Papers.

44. "Do men gather grapes of thorns, or figs of thistles?" in American Eugenics Society File, Whitney Papers.

45. "Offer of Prize for Best Study on Causes of Fall in Birth-Rate" and "Announcement of Prizes" in CBDP.

46. Shipman, *Evolution of Racism,* 125.

47. Clipping from *Eugenics Magazine,* Sept. 1929, 33, CBDP.

48. On Huxley as a public advocate of science in general and Darwinism in particular, see Jensen, *Thomas Henry Huxley.*

49. Eugenics Committee of USA, American Eugenics Society file, CBDP; Whitney autobiography, 186–87.

50. Herbert Spencer Jennings Papers, file 73, APS.

51. Managing editor of *Survey* magazine to Jennings, Oct. 25, 1923, in Jennings Papers, APS.

52. *Survey* to Jennings, June 12, 1923, in Jennings Papers, APS.

53. Mott, *History of American Magazines,* 4:741–50. Some of the topics the *Survey* covered are "Family Life in America" (Dec. 1927) and "Blacks in America" (Mar. 1925). The Jan. 1933 issue was devoted to the U.S. President's Committee on Social Trends.

54. On Mencken's Saturday Night Club, see Louis Cheslock, "Mencken, Music, and the Saturday Night Club," *Menckeniana: A Quarterly Review,* no. 83 (Fall 1982): 13–16.

55. Pearl Papers, APS, contain exchanges of letters with these publications.

56. Pearl to Hamilton Owens, Nov. 12, 1925, in Pearl Papers, APS.

57. Pearl to Mencken, Sept. 8, 1924, in Pearl Papers, APS.

58. Mencken to Pearl, July 1925, from Dayton, Tenn.; see also Mencken to Pearl, July 1928, from Kansas City, Mo., in which Mencken satirizes the sexual mores of Kansas City; both in Pearl Papers, APS.

59. Joseph Wood Krutch to Jennings, Sept. 16, 1935; Krutch to Jennings, Oct. 14, 1935; Henry Hazlitt, acting managing editor of *Nation,* to Jennings, Sept. 15, 1931; all in Jennings Papers, APS.

60. Radio script for "The Parents' Forum, A radio feature prepared for your station by the editors of The Parents' Magazine"; Mrs. G. V. Buchanan, managing editor of *Parents' Magazine,* to Jennings, Apr. 15, 1931; George J. Hecht, president, *Parents' Magazine,* to Jennings, Feb. 14, 1931; all in Jennings Papers, APS.

61. "Adventures in Science," script of radio program, CBS, Nov. 14, 1940, in Osborn Papers, APS.

62. "Conference on Education and Eugenics," summary of the discussion, Mar. 20, 1937, American Eugenics Society file, Whitney Papers.

63. "Summary of the Conference of Publicists of the AES," New York City, Dec. 11, 1937, American Eugenics Society file, Whitney Papers.

64. "Report of Conference on Eugenics and Education," undated, American Eugenics Society file, Whitney Papers.

65. "Preliminary Notes on the Conference on Eugenic Education," New York City, Mar. 20, 1937, American Eugenics Society file, Whitney Papers.

66. "A Eugenics Program for the United States," American Eugenics Society file, Frederick Osborn Papers I, Whitney Papers. The document is undated, but it is from 1934–38, because the president named on the document is E. Huntington.

67. Whitney autobiography, 219.

68. Pearl to Ira J. Williams, Mar. 10, 1939, in Pearl Papers, APS.

69. See also Williams to Pearl, Feb. 1939; Pearl to Williams, Apr. 28, 1939; Williams to Pearl, Nov. 1939; Pearl to Williams, Nov. 7, 1939; and Pearl to Williams, Jan. 4, 1940; all in Pearl Papers, APS.

70. Kevles, *In the Name of Eugenics,* 182.

71. H. S. Jennings, "Biological Recommendations for the Ills of Mankind," talk delivered at Oxford Univ., June 3, 1936, in Jennings Papers, APS.

72. Shipman, *Evolution of Racism,* 126.

73. Whitney autobiography, 177–78.

Chapter 7. A Veneer of Science

1. Hermann Rauschning, *Hitler Speaks* (New York: Putnam, 1940), 229–30. Rauschning, however, points out quotations showing the deep racial convictions of Hitler; n. 10, p. 429.

2. Tenenbaum, *Race and Reich,* 17–28, provides a detailed description of the various race institutes.

3. George L. Mosse, *The Crisis of German Ideology* (New York: Schocken Books, 1981), 25, 136, 143.

4. Ibid., 103, 106.

5. Ibid., 314, 23.

6. Ibid., 88, 132; Daniel J. Goldhagen, *Hitler's Willing Executioners: Ordinary Germans and the Holocaust* (New York: Alfred A. Knopf, 1996), 68, 74–78, 444.

7. Mosse, *Crisis of German Ideology,* 67–69.

8. Ibid., 4–5, 22–29, 50, 71, 129.

9. Ibid., 140; Goldhagen, *Hitler's Willing Executioners,* 431.

10. Tenenbaum, *Race and Reich,* 3–4.

11. Detlev J. K. Peukert, *Inside Nazi Germany: Conformity, Opposition and Racism in Everyday Life,* trans. Richard Deveson (London: B. T. Batsford, 1987), 248, and chap. 12.

12. For a synopsis of German thought in this area, see Stein, "Biological Science and the Roots of Nazism." For a more detailed analysis of the growth of evolutionary thought in general, including Germany and Haeckel's contribution, see Bowler, *Evolution.*

13. Peukert, *Inside Nazi Germany,* 222.

14. Shipman, *Evolution of Racism,* 102–3.

15. Tenenbaum, *Race and Reich,* 6–7.

16. Ibid., 9–11, 20. *Aryan* actually is a designation for Indo-European languages, not an ethnic group. The group, of course, was rather difficult to identify.

17. Tenenbaum, *Race and Reich,* 211–12.

18. Peukert, *Inside Nazi Germany,* 215–16.

19. Kevles, "Controlling the Genetic Arsenal." The comment on Hitler is on 73.

20. H. W. Shimer, "Expanding Consciousness and Democracy," *Science* 89 (Apr. 14, 1939): 325–29. See also Anne Freemantle, "The Pedigree of Aryanism," *Nineteenth Century* 115 (May 1934): 573–86. The article provides a good explanation of Hitler's ideas about race and state, and in particular how those ideas are related to Gobineau.

21. "What Can Science Do?" *Scientific American* 156 (Jan. 1937): 11.

22. A. G. Ingalls, "Whose Fault Is It?" *Scientific American* 162 (Mar. 1937): 137.

23. "Can Science Save Civilization?" *Scientific American* 155 (Dec. 1936): 366–67. See also "Wrong to Use Darwin to Justify Aggression," *Science News Letter* 34 (Dec. 17, 1938): 391, in which the same editorialist again was critical of the interpretation of Darwinism as being only competitive, to the exclusion of cooperation.

24. "German Science Goose-steps," *Science* 83 (Mar. 30, 1936): 285.

25. Peter Kuznick, *Beyond the Laboratory: Scientists as Political Activists in 1930s America* (Chicago: Univ. of Chicago Press, 1987). See chapter 8 on the history of the American Association of Scientific Workers (AASW).

26. Stefan Kuhl, *The Nazi Connection: Eugenics, American Racism, and German National Socialism* (New York: Oxford Univ. Press, 1994), 38–39.

27. Lothrop Stoddard, *Into the Darkness: Nazi Germany Today* (New York: Duell, Sloan and Pearce, 1940), 190–91, 207–8.

28. Ibid., 192–96. On Goebbels as a "master psychologist," see "Foreign News: Toothache," *Time* 35 (Jan. 22, 1940): 33.

29. Kuhl, *Nazi Connection,* 61–63.

30. Ibid., 85, 101.

31. Madison Grant, *The Passing of the Great Race* (New York: Charles Scribner's Sons, 1918).

32. Ibid., 16, 18.

33. Kuhl, *Nazi Connection,* 74. Review in *New York Times,* Nov. 5, 1933, is quoted in Kuhl, 74.

34. Grant, *Passing of the Great Race,* 19–20, 30. Phrenology was, in fact, invented by a German, Franz Joseph Gall (1758–1828), who believed that physical differences were inherent and that moral and intellectual predispositions could be discovered through studying the configurations and protuberances of an individual's head. See Mosse, *Crisis of German Ideology,* 89.

35. Chase, *Legacy of Malthus,* 183–89, discusses Boas's fight with eugenicists.

36. "Decay of German Science Foreseen by Anthropologist," *Science News Letter* 33 (Feb. 5, 1938): 86.

37. Franz Boas, *Race and Democratic Society* (1945; reprint, New York: Biblo and Tannen, 1969), 30.

38. Ibid., 106.

39. "Scientists Against Nazis," *New Republic,* Dec. 12, 1938, 188–89.

40. Franz Boas, "Science in Nazi Germany," *Survey Graphic* 26 (Aug. 1937): 415.

41. Carl N. Degler, *In Search of Human Nature* (New York: Oxford Univ. Press, 1991), 62.

42. Franz Boas, "Race Problems in America," *Science* 29 n.s. (May 28, 1909): 842, 845–48.

43. W. E. Castle, "Race Mixture and Physical Disharmonies," *Science* 71 (June 13, 1930): 603–6.

44. Georges Oudard, "The Unwanted Jew," *Living Age* 355 (Nov. 1938): 248–57, translated from *Revue de Paris*. *Living Age* was an interesting American magazine of the period. In the 1920s, during which its circulation rose to 1.5 million, the publication included translations from a number of European periodicals. However, despite its success with its generally highbrow appeal and cosmopolitan outlook, it ceased publication in 1941, after its owner pleaded guilty to being a propaganda agent for Japan, which had provided money for the purchase of the magazine in 1938, underwriting losses in exchange for articles. The owner and his associates were given an estimated $125,000 by the Japanese government in order to buy or establish publications. The same people bought the *North American Review* in 1938. On the magazines' histories, see Alan Nourie and Barbara Nourie, *American Mass-Market*, 222–25, 333–39; see also Theodore Peterson, *Magazines in the Twentieth Century* (Urbana: Univ. of Illinois Press, 1956), 145–50.

45. James T. Walsh, "Race Betterment," *Commonweal* 19 (Feb. 2, 1934): 371–72.

46. Richard L-G. Ceverall, "Racism," *Catholic World* 148 (Jan. 1939): 398–404.

47. Otto D. Tolischus, "The German Book of Destiny," *Reader's Digest* 29 (Dec. 1936): 37–40.

48. Otto L. Mohr, "Heredity and Human Affairs: Some Considerations on Modern Problems in Genetics," *Living Age* 92 (Aug. 1934): 118–21.

49. Bettina Arnold, "The Past as Propaganda," *Archeology* 45 (July–Aug. 1992): 1, 30–37.

50. Charles Sarolea, "The Religion of the Blood," *Contemporary Review* 148 (Oct. 1935): 424–30. The magazine focused on politics and world affairs. It had no political affiliation, though it had a tradition of liberalism, and appealed largely to the intellectual-cultural establishment. It was published in London. On the magazine, see Alvin Sullivan, ed., *British Literary Magazines: The Modern Age, 1914–1984* (Westport, Conn.: Greenwood Press, 1983), 91–103.

51. "Tyro Fuehrers," *Literary Digest* 121 (May 9, 1936): 25–26.

52. William Orton, "Understanding the Nazis," *North American Review* 239 (Mar. 1935): 226–33. The *North American Review* suffered the same fate as *Living Age*, treated in chap. 7, n. 44, above, because it was found to have been purchased with money from the Japanese government. It was shut down in 1942 and reestablished in 1964. The *Review* was an eclectic journal during the 1920s and 1930s. Though circulating to only about 13,000 in the mid-1920s, it built its respectable reputation on high-quality literature and symposia. The politically moderate magazine, in addition to politics, covered social problems, economics, literature, and art, and it had departments devoted to book reviews and essays. On the magazines' histories, see Alan Nourie and Barbara Nourie, *American Mass-Market*, 222–25, 333–39.

53. "Tallest Blond Communities Studied in North Germany," *Science News Letter* 32 (July 7, 1937): 42.

54. Wilton Marion Krogman, "The Skeleton Talks," *Scientific American* 159 (Aug. 1938): 61–64.

55. C. Thomalla, "The Sterilization Law in Germany," *Scientific American* 151 (Sept. 1934): 126–27.

56. Kevles, "Controlling the Genetic Arsenal," 71. But he also points out on p. 73 that states often did not enforce the sterilization laws.

57. S. F. Aaron, "Is Nature Kind?" *Scientific American* 157 (July 1937): 30–31.

58. "Social Service and the Weaklings," *Scientific American* 156 (May 1937): 345, reprinted from the *Journal of the American Medical Association*.

59. John Hodgdon Bradley, "Enemies are Valuable," *American Mercury* 44 (July 1936): 302–6.

60. George Barton Cutten, "The Perils of Preserving the Unfit," *Vital Speeches of the Day* 2 (Oct. 21, 1935): 34–36. Cutten was the speaker, and he was president of Colgate Univ.

61. Frank Luther Mott, *A History of American Magazines,* vol. 5: *1905–1930* (Cambridge, Mass.: Harvard Univ. Press, 1968), 3–26.

62. Ralph Adams Cram, "Why We Do Not Behave Like Human Beings," *American Mercury* 44 (Aug. 1938): 418–28. Two letters appeared in response to the article, one supporting Cram and the other criticizing him; see "Mr. Cram's Human Beings," *American Mercury* 45 (Oct. 1938): 252–53.

63. "Germany: Nearly Half Million 'Unfit' Will Be Sterilized," *Newsweek* 2 (Dec. 30, 1933): 11–12.

64. Chase, *Legacy of Malthus,* 133–35.

Conclusion

1. F. Darwin, *Autobiography,* 55.

2. Oldroyd, *Darwinian Impacts,* 208–9.

3. C. Darwin, *Descent of Man,* 151.

4. Desmond and Moore, *Darwin: The Life,* xv.

5. Leo Marx, *The Machine in the Garden* (New York: Oxford Univ. Press, 1964), 365.

6. Weart, *Nuclear Fear,* 19.

7. Wyn Wachhorst, *Thomas Alva Edison: An American Myth* (Cambridge, Mass.: MIT Press, 1981), 223.

8. Ibid.

9. Weart, *Nuclear Fear,* 20.

10. Marx, *Machine in the Garden,* 5, 19, 228.

11. E.g., see Paul Ehrlich, *The Population Bomb* (Rivercity, Mass.: Rivercity Press, 1975). The foreword alludes to the Sierra Club, and chapter 1 opens with a scene of wretchedness in New Delhi, India. The book, which was wrong in virtually all its predictions and scenarios, illustrates the point about cities being foci of concern about social degeneration.

12. Robertson, *American Myth,* 280–81.

13. Ibid., 288.

14. Oldroyd, *Darwinian Impacts,* 210, 213.

15. Robertson, *American Myth,* 136.

16. Ronald R. Kline, *Steinmetz: Engineer and Socialist* (Baltimore, Md.: Johns Hopkins Univ. Press, 1992), 237.

17. Weart, *Nuclear Fear,* 425–26. He is talking about nuclear energy, not biology.

18. Robertson, *American Myth,* 21.

19. Kline, *Steinmetz,* 192.

20. Wachhorst, *Thomas Alva Edison,* 115.

Bibliography

Archives

Darwin, Charles. Papers. Univ. Library, Cambridge Univ., Cambridge, England. The library's extensive archive of Darwin papers is described in *Handlist of Darwin Papers at the University Library, Cambridge* (1960).

Genetics Collection. American Philosophical Society, Philadelphia, Pennsylvania. The society holds the papers of the American Eugenics Society and major figures in the movement. The holdings are catalogued in Bentley Glass, *A Guide to the Genetics Collections of the American Philosophical Society* (Ann Arbor, Univ. of Michigan Press, 1988).

Hooker, Joseph Dalton. Papers. Royal Botanic Gardens, Kew, England. The holdings of Dalton's letters and papers are indexed at the Library.

Huxley, Thomas. Papers. Imperial College, London. The collection is catalogued and described in Warren Dawson, *The Huxley Papers: A Descriptive Catalogue of the Correspondence, Manuscripts and Miscellaneous Papers of the Rt. Hon. Thomas Henry Huxley* (London: Macmillan and Company, 1946).

Periodicals

American Mercury, 1936, 1938.

The Arena, 1893–1904.

Athenaeum (London), 1860.

Atlantic Monthly, 1897–1901, 1913.

Bombay Guardian (India), 1916.

Boston Watchman-Examiner, 1915.

Catholic World, 1939.

Commonweal, 1934.

Contemporary Review (London), 1935.

Chamber's Journal (London), 1860.

Evening Star (London), 1860.

Forum, 1898, 1934.

Guardian (London), 1860.

Harper's, 1898–99.

Jackson's Oxford Journal (Oxford, England), 1860.

John Bull (London), 1860.

Literary Digest, 1936.

Living Age, 1934, 1938.

Macmillan's Magazine (London), 1860, 1898.

Manchester Guardian (Manchester, England), 1860.

Nation, 1897–98, 1914, 1939.

New Republic, 1934–38.

Newsweek, 1933.

New York Times, 1882, 1898, 1923.

Nineteenth Century, 1934.

North American Review, 1889–98, 1935.

North British Quarterly, 1869.

Popular Science Monthly, 1872–1900.

The Press (London), 1860.

Reader's Digest, 1936.

Saturday Review (London), 1936.

Science, 1909, 1930–39.

Science News Letter, 1937–39.

Scientific American, 1934–41.

Survey Graphic, 1937.

Time, 1940.

Times of London, 1860, 1887, 1922.

Vital Speeches of the Day, 1935.

Books and Monographs

Ahlstrom, Sydney E. *A Religious History of the American People*. New Haven, Conn.: Yale Univ. Press, 1972.

Atkins, Sir Hedley. *Down: The House of the Darwins*. London: Royal College of Surgeons of England, 1974.

Bannister, Robert. *Social Darwinism: Science and Myth in Anglo-American Social Thought*. Philadelphia: Temple Univ. Press, 1979.

Banton, Michael. *Racial Theories*. Cambridge, England: Cambridge Univ. Press, 1987.

Barzun, Jacques. *Darwin, Marx, Wagner: Critique of a Heritage*. Boston: Little, Brown, 1941.

Bernard, Luther L., and Jessie Bernard. *Origins of American Sociology: The Social Science Movement in the United States.* New York: Russell and Russell, 1965.

Bibby, Cyril. *T. H. Huxley: Scientist, Humanist and Educator.* London: Watts, 1959.

———. *The Essence of T. H. Huxley,* New York: St. Martin's Press, 1969.

Boas, Franz. *Race and Democratic Society.* 1945. Reprint, New York: Biblo and Tannen, 1969.

Boller, Paul F., Jr. *American Thought in Transition: The Impact of Evolutionary Naturalism, 1865–1900.* Chicago: Rand McNally, 1970.

Boorstin, Daniel J. *The Americans: The National Experience.* New York: Vintage Books, 1965.

Bowden, M. *The Rise of Evolution Fraud (An Exposure of Its Roots).* San Diego, Calif.: Creation-Life Publishers, 1982.

Bowlby, John. *Charles Darwin: A New Life.* New York: W. W. Norton, 1990.

Bowler, Peter J. *Charles Darwin: The Man and His Influence.* Oxford, England: Blackwell, 1990.

———. *Evolution: The History of an Idea.* Los Angeles: Univ. of California Press, 1984.

———. *The Mendelian Revolution.* Baltimore, Md.: Johns Hopkins Univ. Press, 1989.

———. *The Non-Darwinian Revolution: Reinterpreting a Historical Myth.* Baltimore, Md.: Johns Hopkins Univ. Press, 1988.

Brown, Charles H. *The Correspondent's War: Journalists in the Spanish-American War.* New York: Charles H. Scribner's Sons, 1967.

Brown, F. Burch. *The Evolution of Darwin's Religious Views.* Macon, Ga.: Mercer Univ. Press, 1986.

Brown, Lucy. *Victorian News and Newspapers.* New York: Oxford Univ. Press, 1985.

Burleigh, Michael, and Wolfgang Wipperman. *The Racial State: Germany, 1933–1945.* Cambridge, England: Cambridge Univ. Press, 1991.

Caudill, Edward. *Darwinism in the Press: The Evolution of an Idea.* Hillsdale, N.J.: Erlbaum, 1989.

Caudill, Edward. "The Roots of Bias: An Empiricist Press and Coverage of the Scopes Trial." *Journalism Monographs,* no. 114. Columbia, S.C.: Association for Education in Journalism and Mass Communication, July 1989.

Chase, Allan. *The Legacy of Malthus: The Social Costs of the New Scientific Racism.* New York: Knopf, 1977.

Clark, Ronald W. *The Huxleys.* New York: McGraw-Hill, 1968.

———. *The Survival of Charles Darwin.* New York: Random House, 1984.

Commager, Henry Steele. *The American Mind.* New Haven, Conn.: Yale Univ. Press, 1952.

Cook-Deegan, Robert. *The Gene Wars: Science, Politics and the Human Genome Project.* New York: W. W. Norton, 1994.

Curran, Thomas J. *The Immigrant Experience in America.* Boston: Twayne Publishers, 1976.

Curti, Merle. *The Growth of American Thought.* New York: Harper and Brothers, 1943.

Curtis, Bruce. *William Graham Sumner.* Boston: Twayne Publishers, 1981.

Curtis, Richard K. *They Called Him Mr. Moody.* Grand Rapids, Mich.: Eerdmans Publishing Company, 1967.

Darwin, Charles. *Descent of Man and Selection in Relation to Sex.* 2d ed. London: John Murray, 1874.

———. *On the Origin of Species.* 1859. Reprint, New York: Penguin Books, 1982.

Darwin, Erasmus. *Zoonomia.* 2 vols. 1794–96. Reprint, New York: AMS Press, 1974.

Darwin, Francis, ed. *The Autobiography of Charles Darwin.* 1892. Reprint, New York: Dover Publications, 1958.

————. *The Life and Letters of Charles Darwin.* 2 vols. 1888. Reprint, New York: Basic Books, 1959.

Darwin, Leonard. *The Need for Eugenic Reform.* London: John Murray, 1926.

Davie, Maurice R. *William Graham Sumner.* New York: Crowell, 1963.

Davidheiser, Bolton. *Evolution and Christian Faith.* Grand Rapids, Mich.: Baker Book House, 1969.

de Beer, Gavin. *Charles Darwin: Evolution by Natural Selection.* Garden City, N.Y.: Doubleday, 1964.

————. *Charles Darwin: A Scientific Biography.* Garden City, N.Y.: Anchor Books, 1965.

Degler, Carl N. *In Search of Human Nature.* New York: Oxford Univ. Press, 1991.

Desmond, Adrian. *Huxley: The Devil's Disciple.* London: Michael Joseph, 1994.

Desmond, Adrian, and James Moore. *Darwin: The Life of a Tormented Evolutionist.* New York: Warner, 1991.

Dupree, A. Hunter *Asa Gray.* Cambridge, Mass.: Belknap Press of Harvard Univ. Press, 1959.

Durant, John. *Darwinism and Divinity: Essays on Evolution and Religious Belief.* Norwich, England: Page Brothers, Ltd., 1985.

Eiseley, Loren. *Darwin's Century.* Garden City, N.Y.: Doubleday, 1961.

Ellegard, Alvar. *Darwin and the General Reader.* 1958. Reprint, Chicago: Univ. of Chicago Press, 1990.

————. *The Readership of the Periodical Press in Mid-Victorian Britain.* Göteborg, Sweden: Göteborgs Universitets Arsskrift, 1957.

Elliot, Hugh. *Herbert Spencer.* Westport, Conn.: Greenwood, 1970, reprint of 1917 edition.

Enoch, H. *Evolution or Creation.* London: Evangelical Press, 1967, reprinted 1968, 1972.

Fine, Sidney. *Laissez-Faire and the General-Welfare State: A Study of Conflict in American Thought.* Ann Arbor: Univ. of Michigan Press, 1956.

Findlay, James F., Jr. *Dwight L. Moody: American Evangelist, 1837–1899.* Chicago: Univ. of Chicago Press, 1969.

Glick, Thomas F., ed. *The Comparative Reception of Darwinism.* Austin: Univ. of Texas Press, 1972.

Goldhagen, Daniel J. *Hitler's Willing Executioners: Ordinary Germans and the Holocaust.* New York: Alfred A. Knopf, 1996.

Gould, Stephen J. *Ever Since Darwin: Reflections in Natural History.* New York: W. W. Norton, 1977.

Gossett, Thomas F. *Race: The History of an Idea in America.* New York: Schocken Books, 1965.

Grant, Madison. *The Passing of the Great Race.* New York: Charles Scribner's Sons, 1918.

Grant, Madison, and Charles Stewart Davidson, eds. *The Alien in Our Midst, or, "Selling Our Birthright for a Mess of Pottage."* New York: Galton Publishing Co., 1930.

Hand, John Raymond. *Why I Accept the Genesis Record: Am I Rational?* Wheaton, Ill.: Van Kampen Press, 1953.

Haller, John S., Jr. *Outcasts from Evolution: Scientific Attitudes of Racial Inferiority.* Urbana: Univ. of Illinois Press, 1971.

Hardie, Alexander. *Evolution: Is It Philosophical, Scientific, or Scriptural?* Los Angeles, Calif.: Times-Mirror Press, 1924.

Healy, David. *U.S. Expansionism: The Imperialist Urge in the 1890s.* Madison: Univ. of Wisconsin Press, 1970.

Herrnstein, Richard J., and Charles Murray. *The Bell Curve: Intelligence and Class Structure in American Life.* New York: Free Press, 1994.

Hedtke, Randall. *The Secret of the Sixth Edition.* New York: Vantage Press, 1983.

Himmelfarb, Gertrude. *Darwin and the Darwinian Revolution.* Gloucester, Mass.: Peter Smith, 1967.

———. *Victorian Minds.* New York: Alfred A. Knopf, 1968.

Hofstadter, Richard. *Social Darwinism in American Thought.* Boston: Beacon Press, 1955.

Hope, Elizabeth R. [Elizabeth R. Cotton]. *Our Coffee-Room.* London: James Nisbet and Company, 1876.

Huxley, Leonard, ed. *Life and Letters of Sir Joseph Dalton Hooker.* 2 vols. 1918. Reprint, New York: Arno Press, 1978.

———, ed. *Life and Letters of Thomas Henry Huxley.* 2 vols. New York: D. Appleton and Company, 1901.

Huxley, Julian, and A. C. Haddon. *We Europeans: A Survey of "Racial" Problems.* New York: Harper and Brothers, 1936.

Irvine, William. *Apes, Angels, and Victorians: The Story of Darwin, Huxley, and Evolution.* Lanham, Md.: Univ. Press of America, 1983.

Jensen, J. Vernon. *Thomas Henry Huxley: Communicating for Science.* Newark, Del.: Univ. of Delaware Press, 1991.

Keller, Albert G., and Maurice R. Davie, eds. *Essays of William Graham Sumner.* New Haven, Conn.: Yale Univ. Press, 1934.

Kelley, Alfred. *The Descent of Darwin: The Popularization of Darwin in Germany, 1860–1914.* Chapel Hill: Univ. of North Carolina Press, 1981.

Kennedy, James G. *Herbert Spencer.* Boston: Twayne Publishers, 1978.

Kershaw, Ian. *The "Hitler Myth": Image and Reality in the Third Reich.* Oxford: Clarendon Press, 1987.

Kevles, Daniel J. *In the Name of Eugenics: Genetics and the Uses of Human Heredity.* Berkeley: Univ. of California Press, 1985.

Kline, Ronald R. *Steinmetz: Engineer and Socialist.* Baltimore, Md.: Johns Hopkins Univ. Press, 1992.

Kohn, David, ed. *Darwinian Heritage.* Princeton, N.J.: Princeton Univ. Press, 1985.

Kuhl, Stefan. *The Nazi Connection: Eugenics, American Racism, and German National Socialism.* New York: Oxford Univ. Press, 1994.

Kuznick, Peter. *Beyond the Laboratory: Scientists as Political Activists in 1930s America,* Chicago: Univ. of Chicago Press, 1987.

LaFeber, Walter. *The New Empire: An Interpretation of American Expansion, 1860–1898.* Ithaca, N.Y.: Cornell Univ. Press, 1963.

Lerner, Max. *America as a Civilization.* New York: Henry Holt, 1987.

Lindbergh, David C., and Ronald L. Numbers, eds. *God and Nature: Historical Essays on the Encounter Between Christianity and Science.* Los Angeles: Univ. of California Press, 1986.

Marx, Leo. *The Machine in the Garden.* New York: Oxford Univ. Press, 1964.

May, Ernest R. *American Imperialism: A Speculative Essay.* New York: Athenaeum, 1968.

———. *Imperial Democracy: The Emergence of America as a Great Power.* New York: Harcourt, Brace and World, 1961.

McAlister, John. *The Scientific Proofs of Origins by Creation.* Midland, Tex.: Privately published, n.d.

McIver, Tom. *Anti-Evolution: An Annotated Bibliography.* Jefferson, N.C.: McFarland and Company, 1988.

Meacham, Standish. *Lord Bishop: The Life of Samuel Wilberforce, 1805–1873.* Cambridge, Mass.: Harvard Univ. Press, 1970.

Miller, Richard H., ed. *American Imperialism in 1898: The Quest for National Fulfillment.* New York: John Wiley and Sons, 1970.

Miller, Stuart Creighton. *Benevolent Assimilation.* New Haven, Conn.: Yale Univ. Press, 1982.

Moore, James. *The Darwin Legend.* Grand Rapids, Mich.: Baker Books, 1994.

Mosse, George L. *The Crisis of German Ideology: Intellectual Origins of the Third Reich.* New York: Schocken Books, 1981.

Mott, Frank Luther. *A History of American Magazines.* Vol. 1: *1841–1850.* Cambridge, Mass.: Harvard Univ. Press, 1938.

———. *A History of American Magazines.* Vol. 2: *1850–1865.* Cambridge, Mass.: Harvard Univ. Press, 1938.

———. *A History of American Magazines.* Vol. 3: *1865–1885.* Cambridge, Mass.: Harvard Univ. Press, 1938.

———. *A History of American Magazines.* Vol. 4: *1885–1905.* Cambridge, Mass.: Harvard Univ. Press, 1957.

———. *A History of American Magazines.* Vol. 5: *1905–1930.* Cambridge, Mass.: Harvard Univ. Press, 1968.

Murray, Henry A., ed. *Myth and Mythmaking.* New York: George Braziller, 1960.

Nourie, Alan, and Barbara Nourie. *American Mass Market Magazines.* Westport, Conn.: Greenwood Press, 1990.

Numbers, Ronald L. *The Creationists.* New York, Alfred A. Knopf, 1992.

Oldroyd, D. R. *Darwinian Impacts.* Atlantic Highlands, N.J.: Humanities Press, 1983.

O'Toole, G. J. A. *The Spanish War: An American Epic, 1898.* New York: W. W. Norton, 1984.

Owen, Richard [grandson]. *The Life of Richard Owen.* 2 vols. 1894. Reprint, New York: AMS Press, 1975.

Parrington, Vernon L. *Main Currents in American Thought.* New York: Harcourt Brace, 1958.

Persons, Stow, ed. *Evolutionary Thought in America.* Boston: Archon Books, 1968.

Peterson, Theodore. *Magazines in the Twentieth Century.* Urbana: Univ. of Illinois Press, 1956.

Peukert, Detlev J. K. *Inside Nazi Germany: Conformity, Opposition and Racism in Everyday Life.* Translated by Richard Deveson. London: B. T. Batsford, 1987.

Pickens, Donald K. *Eugenics and the Progressives.* Nashville, Tenn.: Vanderbilt Univ. Press, 1968.

Rauschning, Hermann. *Hitler Speaks.* New York: Putnam, 1940.

Robertson, James Oliver. *American Myth, American Reality.* New York: Hill and Wang, 1980.

Rogers, Everett M. *A History of Communication Study.* New York: Free Press, 1994.

Rumney, Jay. *Herbert Spencer's Sociology.* New York: Atherton Press, 1966.

Ruse, Michael. *The Darwinian Revolution: Science Red in Tooth and Claw.* Chicago: Univ. of Chicago Press, 1979.

Russett, Cynthia E. *Darwinism in America: The Intellectual Response, 1865–1912.* San Francisco: W. H. Freeman, 1976.

Schlesinger, Arthur M., Jr., and Morton White, eds. *Paths of American Thought.* Boston: Houghton Mifflin Company, 1973.

Shipman, Pat. *The Evolution of Racism: Human Differences and the Use and Abuse of Science.* New York: Simon and Schuster, 1994.

Smith, Henry Nash. *Virgin Land: The American West as Symbol and Myth.* Cambridge, Mass.: Harvard Univ. Press, 1950.

Starr, Harris. *William Graham Sumner.* New York: Henry Holt, 1925.

Stephens, Leslie, ed. *Letters of John Richard Green.* London, Macmillan, 1901.

Stoddard, Lothrop. *Into the Darkness: Nazi Germany Today.* New York: Duell, Sloan and Pearce, 1940.

Sullivan, Alvin, ed. *British Literary Magazines: The Modern Age, 1914–1984.* New York: Greenwood Press, 1986.

———. *British Literary Magazines: The Romantic Age, 1789–1836.* Westport, Conn.: Greenwood Press, 1983.

———. *British Literary Magazines: The Victorian and Edwardian Age, 1837–1913.* Westport, Conn.: Greenwood Press, 1984.

Sumner, William Graham. *The Challenge of Facts and Other Essays.* Edited by Albert G. Keller. New Haven, Conn.: Yale Univ. Press, 1914.

———. *Earth-Hunger and Other Essays.* Edited by Albert G. Keller. New Haven, Conn.: Yale Univ. Press, 1913.

———. *What Social Classes Owe Each Other.* 1883. Reprint, Caldwell, Idaho: Caxton Printer, 1966.

Szacki, Jerzy. *History of Sociological Thought.* Westport, Conn.: Greenwood Press, 1979.

Taylor, Ian. *In the Minds of Men: Darwin and the New World Order.* Toronto, Canada: TFE Publishing, 1984.

Tenenbaum, Joseph. *Race and Reich: The Story of an Epoch.* New York: Twayne Publishers, 1956.

Tindall, George Brown. *America: A Narrative History.* New York: W. W. Norton, 1984.

Trask, David F. *The War with Spain in 1898.* New York: Macmillan, 1981.

Tuckwell, W. *Reminiscences of Oxford.* London: Smith, Elder, 1907.

Turrill, W. B. *Joseph Dalton Hooker: Botanist, Explorer, and Administrator.* London: Thomas Nelson and Sons, 1963.

Wachhorst, Wyn. *Thomas Alva Edison: An American Myth.* Cambridge, Mass.: MIT Press, 1981.

Weart, Spencer R., *Nuclear Fear: A History of Images,* Cambridge, Mass.: Harvard Univ. Press, 1988.

Welch, Richard E. *Response to Imperialism: The United States and the Philippine-American War, 1899–1902.* Chapel Hill: Univ. of North Carolina Press, 1979.

Wilberforce, Reginald. *Life of the Right Rev. Samuel Wilberforce, D.D.* 3 vols. London: Murray, 1881.

Wilkerson, Marcus M. *Public Opinion and the Spanish-American War.* New York: Russell and Russell, 1967.

Articles

Altholz, Joseph L. "The Huxley-Wilberforce Debate Revisited." *Journal of the History of Medicine and the Allied Sciences* 35 (1980): 313–16.

Arnold, Bettina. "The Past as Propaganda." *Archeology* 45, no. 1 (July–Aug. 1992): 30–37.

Baldwin, J. Mark. "Psychology." *American Naturalist* 31 (June 1897): 553.

Bowler, Peter J. "The Changing Meaning of Evolution." *Journal of the History of Ideas* 36 (Jan.–Mar. 1957): 95–114.

Browne, Janet. "The Charles Darwin-Joseph Hooker Correspondence: An Analysis of Manuscript

Resources and Their Use in Biography." *Journal of the Society for the Bibliography of Natural History* 8, no. 4 (1978): 351–66.

Burton, David H. "Theodore Roosevelt's Social Darwinism and Views on Imperialism." *Journal of the History of Ideas* 26 (Jan.–Mar. 1965): 103–18.

Cheslock, Louis. "Mencken, Music, and the Saturday Night Club." *Menckeniana: A Quarterly Review* 83 (Fall 1982): 13–16.

Dealy, J. Q. "The Evolution of Society." *Southwest Review* 14 (Oct. 1928–July 1929): 462–73.

Ellegard, Alvar. "Darwinian Theory and Nineteenth-Century Philosophies of Science." *Journal of the History of Ideas* 18 (June 1957): 362–92.

———. "Public Opinion and the Press: Reactions to Darwinism." *Journal of the History of Ideas* 19 (June 1958): 379–87.

Freeman, Derek. "The Evolutionary Theories of Charles Darwin and Herbert Spencer." *Current Anthropology* 15 (Sept. 1974): 211–37.

Garson, Robert, and Richard Maidment. "Social Darwinism and the Liberal Tradition: The Case of William Graham Sumner." *South Atlantic Quarterly* 1 (1981): 61–76.

Glass, Bentley. "Geneticists Embattled: Their Stand Against Rampant Eugenics and Racism in America during the 1920s and 1930s." *Proceedings of the American Philosophical Society* 130 (Mar. 1986): 130–54.

Gould, Stephen J. "Knight Takes Bishop? The Facts about the Great Wilberforce-Huxley Debate Don't Always Fit the Legend." *Natural History* 95 (May 1986): 18–33.

Haar, Charles M. "E. L. Youmans: A Chapter in the Diffusion of Science in America." *Journal of the History of Ideas* 9 (Apr. 1948): 193–213.

Haller, John S. "The Species Problem: Nineteenth-Century Concepts of Racial Inferiority in the Origin of Man Controversy." *American Anthropologist* 72 (Dec. 1970): 1319–29.

Hubble, Douglas. "The Life of the Shawl." *Lancet* 265 (Dec. 26, 1953): 1351–54.

Jensen, J. Vernon. "Return to the Huxley-Wilberforce Debate." *British Journal for the History of Science* 21, pt. 2, no. 69 (June 1988): 164.

Kevles, Daniel J. "Controlling the Genetic Arsenal." *Wilson Quarterly* 16 (2) (Spring 1990): 68–76.

Lasch, Christopher. "The Anti-Imperialists, the Philippines, and the Inequality of Man." *Journal of Southern History* 24 (1958): 319–31.

Lucas, J. R. "Wilberforce and Huxley: A Legendary Encounter." *Historical Journal* 22, no. 2 (1979): 313–30.

MacLeod, R. M. "Evolutionism and Richard Owen, 1830–1868: An Episode in Darwin's Century." *Isis* 56 (Fall 1965): 259–80.

———. "The X Club: A Social Network of Science in Late-Victorian England." *Notes and Records of the Royal Society of London* 24 (1970): 305–22.

Mandelbaum, Maurice. "Darwin's Religious Values." *Journal of the History of Ideas* 19 (June 1958): 363–78.

Marchant, P. D. "Social Darwinism." *Australian Journal of Politics and History* 3 (Nov. 1957): 46–59.

Pickens, Donald. "William Graham Sumner as a Critic of the Spanish American War." *Continuity*, no. 11 (1987): 75–92.

Rogers, James A. "Darwinism and Social Darwinism." *Journal of the History of Ideas* 33 (Apr.–June 1972): 265–80.

Sarton, George. "Herbert Spencer: 1820–1903." *Isis* 3 (1921): 375–90.

Sloan, Pat. "Demythologizing Darwin." *Humanist* (London) 80 (Apr. 1965): 106–10.

———. "The Myth of Darwin's Conversion." *Humanist* (London) 75 (Mar. 1960): 70–72.

Stein, George J. "Biological Science and the Roots of Nazism." *American Scientist* 76 (Jan.–Feb. 1988): 50–58.

Smith, Fabienne "Charles Darwin's Health Problems: The Allergy Hypothesis." *Journal of the History of Biology* 25, no. 2 (Summer 1992): 285–306.

Weindling, Paul. "The 'Sonderweg' of German Eugenics: Nationalism and Scientific Internationalism." *British Journal of the History of Science* 22 (Sept. 1989): 321–33.

Wrangham, Richard. "Bishop Wilberforce: Natural Selection and the Descent of Man." *Nature* 287 (Sept. 18, 1980): 192.

Wyllie, Irvin G. "Social Darwinism and the Businessman." *Proceedings of the American Philosophical Society* 103 (Oct. 1959): 629–35.

Index

Darwinian Myths: The Legends and Misuses of a Theory was designed and typeset on a Macintosh computer system using PageMaker software. The text is set in Perpetua, designed in 1930 by Eric Gill. Chapter numbers are set in Lorrenne. This book was designed by Todd Duren and Valerie Hembree, composed by Kimberly Scarbrough, and printed and bound by Thomson-Shore, Inc. The recycled paper used in this book is designed for an effective life of at least three hundred years.